Growing Up Online

Growing Up Online

Young People and Digital Technologies

Edited by

Sandra Weber and Shanly Dixon

GROWING UP ONLINE

Copyright © Sandra Weber and Shanly Dixon, 2007.

First published in hardcover in 2007 by
PALGRAVE MACMILLAN®
in the United States—a division of St. Martin's Press LLC,
175 Fifth Avenue, New York, NY 10010.

Where this book is distributed in the UK, Europe and the rest of the world,
this is by Palgrave Macmillan, a division of Macmillan Publishers Limited,
registered in England, company number 785998, of Houndmills,
Basingstoke, Hampshire RG21 6XS.

Palgrave Macmillan is the global academic imprint of the above companies
and has companies and representatives throughout the world.

Palgrave® and Macmillan® are registered trademarks in the United States,
the United Kingdom, Europe and other countries.

ISBN: 978–0–230–62001–8

Library of Congress Cataloging-in-Publication Data is available from the
Library of Congress.

A catalogue record of the book is available from the British Library.

Design by Newgen Imaging Systems (P) Ltd., Chennai, India.

First PALGRAVE MACMILLAN paperback edition: May 2010

10 9 8 7 6 5 4 3 2 1

Transferred to Digital Printing in 2010

For my brother Lawrence,
never forgotten, always loved.

For my father Kenneth Dixon,
my first and best teacher.

Contents

List of Illustrations

Table

Figures

Acknowledgments

First and foremost, we wish to thank the talented and collaborative authors who made editing this book such a pleasure. We learned so much from them. Next, to all the young people—girls and boys, tweens and youth, children, nieces and nephews—who participated in the various research projects, we offer a heartfelt cheer for their generosity, their lively spirits, and the many insights they gave us. Without them, this book would not be possible. The impetus and suggestions provided by members of the Digital Girls research project (many of whom are also this book's authors) were invaluable at the crucial proposal writing stage of this book project. The financial support of the Social Sciences and Humanities Research Council of Canada was also essential and much appreciated. We are also grateful to Amanda Moon, and Katie Fahey at Palgrave Press for their support and guidance.

If this book is clearly written, much of the credit should be given to the talented scholar and doctoral candidate Maija Harju who worked long hours with us to improve and clarify portions of the text. We know that all the authors join us in thanking her profusely for her insightful suggestions and comments. Working way beyond the call of duty, Research Assistant Lysanne Rivard gave us just the kind of calm and efficient support we needed to get the manuscript ready for submission. Merci beaucoup, Lysanne.

To all the Concordia MA Child Study graduate students enrolled in our course on Children and technology, we send a sincere thank you for helping us test out some of the book's ideas and for challenging our thinking. A special thank you, as well, to Poppy Baktis, Lara Nasser Shuraida, and Kelly Boudreau for all the many ways, large and small, in which they contributed to our work. We also wish to acknowledge the influence and inspiration we derive from other scholars in the field, some of whom we have the privilege of studying or working with closely. The references in our chapters reflect their impact.

And finally, our deepest appreciation, as always, to our wonderful families and close friends for their support and understanding. Their patience during the long hours we spent holed up away from them to work on this book is duly noted, with gratitude.

About the Contributors

Brandi L. Bell has a PhD in Communication Studies from Concordia University. Her academic and research interests are broadly encompassed within youth, citizenship, and technology studies and her doctoral work focused on how media representations of Canadian youth situate them within particular citizenship positions. She is currently conducting youth health research at the University of Prince Edward Island, with an interest in finding ways to involve youth in research pertaining to their health and well-being.
brbell@upei.ca

Kelly Boudreau is a doctoral student in Film Studies at Université de Montréal. Her research focuses on understanding the player character relationship in video game play and forms of mediated sociality ranging from the dynamics of social identification in online computer games and virtual worlds to the fusion of internet activity and everyday life.

Diane Carr is Lecturer in Media and Cultural Studies at the Institute Of Education, University of London. Diane has published work on meaning, learning, play, identity and representation in various computer games and virtual worlds, and she is co-author of *Computer Games: Text, Narrative and Play* (Polity, 2006). There is more information at her blog: http://playhouse. wordpress.com/.

Shanly Dixon is a doctoral candidate in Concordia University's Humanities Interdisciplinary Studies in Society and Culture Program. Her disciplines include Sociology, Communications and Education to examine the ways in which new media and technology can transform the spaces and experiences of contemporary childhood. Her ethnographic work explores digital culture, transformations in childhood and play, sociality, notions of public and private spaces and cross-generational divides. She teaches the Sociology of Cyberspace at Concordia University and is co-editor of the book *Growing Up Online: Young People and Digital Technologies*.

Seth Giddings is Program Leader for Media and Cultural Studies at the University of the West of England. He is a co-author (Lister et al.) of *New Media: A Critical Introduction* (Routlege, 2nd ed: 2008). He teaches new media theory and practice, and researches popular new media and everyday technoculture.
seth.giddings@uwe.ac.uk

Claudia Mitchell is a James McGill Professor in the Faculty of Education, McGill University and an Honorary Professor in the School of Language, Literacies and Media Education, University of KwaZulu-Natal. Her research areas include work on visual and other participatory approaches to research, girlhood, HIV&AIDS, and media culture. She has authored, co-authored, and edited almost a dozen books; she is also the co-editor of *Girlhood Studies: An Interdisciplinary Journal.*
claudia.mitchell@mcgill.ca

Caroline Pelletier is a researcher at the Institute of Education, University of London. She is based in the school of Culture, Language and Communication. Her work is concerned with how new media technologies shape conceptions of knowledge, learning and teaching.
c.pelletier@ioe.ac.uk

Michele Polak is Assistant Professor in Writing and Rhetoric at Hobart and William Smith Colleges. She been writing about girl-related issues and online discourse for almost a full decade. With a cadre of nieces aged twenty-three years down to three years, she expects that she will always have a source of inspiration. Speak loudly, girls.

Leslie R. Shade is Associate Professor at Concordia University in the Department of Communication Studies. Her research focus since the mid-1990's has been on the social, policy, and ethical aspects of information and communication technologies (ICTs), with particular concerns toward issues of gender, globalization, and political economy.
lshade@alcor.concordia.ca

Jacqueline Reid-Walsh, a specialist in children's historical literature, girls' popular culture, and old and new media teaching is Associate Professor in the Faculty of Education at Penn State University. She has published on topics ranging from girls reading in the eighteenth century to early moveable books to children's websites and computer games. She is co-author of *Researching Children's Popular Culture: The Cultural Spaces of Childhood* (Routledge: 2002) and co-editor of *Seven Going on Seventeen: Tween Studies in the Culture* *of Girlhood* (Lang: 2005): both with Claudia Mitchell. Her emails are jxr67@psu.edu and jacqueline.reid-walsh@mail.mcgill.ca

Grace Sokoya is Associate Professor and Program Leader for the Gender Issues and Youth Development (GIYD) program in the Agricultural Media Resources and Extension Centre (AMREC), University of Agriculture, Abeokuta, Nigeria. She is the Project Coordinator for USG/PEPFAR-UNAAB HIV/AIDS project and AAU/UNAAB HIV/AIDS Policy Development project in the University.
gracesokoya@yahoo.com

Susannah Stern is Associate Professor in the Department of Communication Studies at the University of San Diego. Her research is situated at the intersection of electronic media and youth culture. She focuses on how young people experience the mediated world, how they use media to navigate through adolescence, and how they construct media messages to meet their own needs and fantasies. Her work has appeared in a variety of peer-reviewed journals and edited collections.
susannahstern@sandiego.edu

Julia Weber is a bilingual (English-French) Montreal senior high school student who has been collaborating in research since early childhood. She has presented papers on being a "digital tween" at two major conferences: *Digital Generations, Children, Young People, and New Media*, University of London, England (2004) and *Transforming Spaces: Girlhood, Agency and Power*, Concordia University, Montreal (2003). Julia also stars in a video documentary, *Digital Girls Part I*. Julia's interests include creative writing, nature studies, and art. Active in leadership training programs, she is often called upon to represent her school at board and national levels. Julia has a passion for life and loves to learn. She cares very much about the global environment and issues of social justice.

Sandra Weber is Professor of Education at Concordia University in Montreal where she teaches courses about children's toys and popular culture, media literacy, gender, and digital technologies. Co-founder and director of the *Image and Identity Research Collective* (www.iirc.mcgill.ca), she is concerned with developing participatory visual research methodologies and ways to involve young people more actively in research that is about them. Her current projects research focuses on art-based media education for pregnant teenagers, ethical issues related to the use of photography in research, and the significance of clothing to communication and identity processes. Among her many publications are five books.

Rebekah Willett is Lecturer and a researcher the Institute of Education, University of London. Published widely, she has conducted various research projects on children's media cultures. Her research interests include gender, digital technologies, literacy, and learning. r.willett@ioe.ac.uk

INTRODUCTION

Perspectives on Young People and Technologies

Sandra Weber and Shanly Dixon

Why This Book?

What does it mean to grow up surrounded by digital technologies and media, right from birth? In a growing list of countries, the use of various technologies has permeated almost every aspect of contemporary social life, changing the ways in which we work and play, influencing culture, media, and social rituals, and maybe even changing who we are. How do children and young people in different contexts experience and use new technologies? What does being "online" mean to them or enable them to do? In what ways and under what circumstances do they take up, adapt, and integrate digital technologies into their daily activities?

It is impossible for any one book to adequately cover the topic of children and technology thoroughly, addressing experiences from every perspective, or in every part of the world. This volume closely examines *technologies-in-use*—studying them where they occur, embedded in daily experience, and documenting how various digital technologies are incorporated into young peoples' lives in a variety of ways and situations. Looking at technologies-in-use requires a holistic view, one that examines not only the hardware, software, interface, and user, but also the physical, cultural, social, and personal contexts in which the technologies are situated. Furthermore, the challenge is to examine technologies through multiple perspectives. Many current collections examine one aspect of digital culture—looking at video games or social networking spaces or cell phone use—while this collection brings together a range of digital engagements in order to highlight the varied ways in which digital culture is increasingly embedded in young people's everyday lives. Many of the researchers in this book draw on case studies, ethnographies, or critical "close readings" to investigate the day-to-day ways in which children and youth of different ages use, combine, experience, and view various digital media. In focusing mainly on young peoples' experiences, the authors lead us not only to reconsider notions of childhood and play, but also to re-examine technologies-in-use, interrogating cyberspace as an extension of material space, pondering the role of digital technologies as social and personal modes of becoming, and speculating on how *both* girls and boys change and shape technology as it influences them.

In addition to conceptual and theoretical arguments, the chapters present a series of "behind the scenes"cases from Canada, Britain, the United States, Nigeria, and South Africa that offer new insights into digital childhoods. The researchers describe and analyze a wide range of young peoples' experiences in cyberspace, highlighting the often imaginative and multimodal ways in which digital technologies are being incorporated into contemporary childhood. Collectively, the chapters cross geographical space, race, and social class, moving from a group of French-speaking girls at an alternative Montreal school who created their own webspace in which to hang out (see Boudreau; chapter four), to a group of working-class girls in London who research, discuss, and design websites aimed at "tweens" (see Willett; chapter seven), to a group of girls in Nigeria visiting a cyber café for the first time (see Mitchell and Sokoya; chapter thirteen). The ages of the young people we meet in the chapters range from two to twenty, with a special focus on the so-called tween years where identity and worldviews are in flux (Brown & Gilligan, 1992; Driscoll, 2002; Mitchell & Reid-Walsh, 2005).

Some of the work reported here occurred under the research umbrella of the Digital Girls Research Project (http://www.digitalgirls.org), a program funded by the Social Sciences and Humanities Research Council of Canada, which brought together an international team of researchers. This book synthesizes and reflects on some of that work, offering key insights not only into girls' voices and experiences but also into more general questions of how to research and conceptualize childhood, play, and young people's relationships to technologies.

Positions As Researchers: Generation Matters

Although many researchers have themselves adopted digital technologies in a variety of ways, these technologies have not *always* been a part of their lives. In other words, scholars who write about new technologies and their impact on young people are not writing about an experience they themselves had as children. Researchers, for the most part, grew up "off-line," raised in childhoods without internet or the vast array of digital technologies that are currently inherent to so much of young people's play, communication, and cultural production. This age-related position allows for a unique vantage point; that of having witnessed both the introduction of new technologies to a previous generation, as well as observing how these technologies are now adapted and incorporated into young peoples' everyday lives from birth. The authors of this book thus write from the perspective of a cross-over generation, bridging the gap between analog and digital childhoods. We watch with interest as children of the Net generation, the so-called digital natives,[1] become socialized into the evolving mediascape, and we wonder how these digital experiences might change the ways in which they negotiate, act in, and understand their world. How do online activities, for example, affect such important aspects of childhood and adolescence as socialization, communication, relationships, learning, identity, friendship, gender, and embodiment? These questions echo throughout many of the chapters.

There are some significant changes and updates in this paperback edition of *Growing Up Online*. Most of the chapters, however, have been left unchanged from the original hardcover edition because they serve as valuable digital snapshots, capturing particular moments in time, describing developmental milestones in the social lives of young people, and signposting the rapid evolution of technologies. Although they may address phenomena that occurred five or more years ago, these chapters offer theoretical models and pose important questions that are in some cases even more relevant today than when they were first written. Other chapters such as the one by Leslie R. Shade, have been significantly updated in order to illustrate the ways in which policies surrounding girls and internet safety are evolving. Authors such as Weber have provided the reader with the unique opportunity to continue following the digital lives of the girls portrayed in their original chapters. In chapter Three, Weber looks back over the ways in which one girl adopts and integrates multiple technologies into her everyday life over a period of several years. Similarly, in chapter One, Dixon and Weber re-contextualize their ethnography as they revisit the girls playing video games, looking at the ways in which this particular generation of girls continues to game together, incorporating video game play as a taken-for-granted aspect of their everyday play practices.

Young People's Perspectives, Young People's Access

The authors often use the term "young people" to refer to people from early childhood through to late adolescence, in order to highlight how vague the period of transition from childhood to adulthood is. We use the term as a reminder that children are people, that childhood and indeed children are social constructs, and that the traditional boundaries between childhood and adulthood are blurry and open to debate. Our use of the term thus differs in some respects from the use made by certain scholars (e.g., Bragg & Buckingham, 2003) who apply it to a more specific age group, using it as an alternative to the term "youth" to ensure that females as well as males are included ("youth" is too often construed as referring to boys only). Because this book features chapters that focus on a wide age spectrum, it seems appropriate to use the term "young people".

The authors of this book share the goal of putting the focus directly on young people themselves, incorporating their perspectives and voices where possible. Several of the chapters were written closely with girls: for example, *Playing at and with popular teen culture on "girl" websites: The case of Alice* by Jacqueline Reid-Walsh and *The girls' room: Negotiating schoolyard friendships online* by Kelly Boudreau. *Technology in the everyday lives of "tweens"* by Sandra Weber was actually coauthored by the young girl at the heart of the study. Other chapters incorporate boys' words and experiences, for example, Seth Giddings chapter, *"I'm the one who makes the Lego racers go"*: *Studying virtual and actual play*; Shanly Dixon and Sandra Weber's *Playspaces, childhood, and video games*; Claudia Mitchell and Grace Sokoya's *New girl (and new boy) at the internet café: Digital divides/digital futures*; and Caroline Pelletier's *Producing gender in digital interactions: What young people set out to achieve through computer game design.*

As Dixon and Weber, and Mitchell and Sokoya point out in their chapters, it is important to remember that many young people have limited, if any, access to the internet. Not all children are "born into new technologies" to the same extent. Even in North America there are still homes without computers or internet; not every adolescent has a cell phone, an MP3 player, and a video game console (although it certainly is beginning to seem that way). As research by the Kaiser Family Foundation (2003), Roberts and Foehr (2004), and Seiter (2005) amongst other surveys confirm, there is a class-based digital divide that is overlooked and possibly growing. Moreover, it is naïve to assume that even amongst the most "wired" of young people, all life is digital. Sports, arts, books, camping, bicycles, hobbies, off-line games, and hanging out with friends off-line are still a part of childhood for many middle-class children and youth.

Positioning Childhood and Children: Moral Panics and Utopian Discourses

Over the past two decades, theorists have paid a great deal of attention to the changing nature of childhood and to the ways in which new media technologies have figured in these changes: from utopian perspectives suggesting that new media have empowered children by offering possibilities for creativity and unprecedented access to information (Katz, 1997; Tapscott, 1998), to moral panics suggesting that cyberspace is an inappropriate and unsafe space for children (see chapter fourteen by Leslie Regan Shade). However, as policy makers, educators, child advocates, and parents continue to debate these issues, the voices and experiences of young people remain largely absent. That context makes this collection all the more important because, in varying ways and degrees, all of the chapters bring children's perspectives into the ever-changing debate. In varying ways and degrees, all of the chapters in this book bring children's perspectives into the debate.

As digital culture becomes increasingly pervasive and embedded in young people's everyday experiences, the concerns and panics that previously defined the debates around young people and digital culture are dissipating somewhat, or at least changing. We agree with Mosco (2004) who suggests that it is when new technologies have become banal, an accepted aspect of everyday culture, that they are the most powerful and transformative, developing the potential to shape social norms. As a result of young people's engagement in digital culture, the ways in which they communicate, access information, and understand what constitutes privacy, has shifted. Many adults are uncomfortable with these changing social norms, a reality that increases the potential for inter-generational conflicts and misunderstandings. This makes continued research into young people's experiences and perceptions of digital culture increasingly relevant.

It is often assumed that technologies have changed young peoples' roles or the position they occupy within society. Postman (1994), and in a more critical way Giroux (2001), argue that media have resulted in the demise of childhood by exposing children to information that was previously kept from them; permanently blurring the boundaries between childhood and adulthood and disrupting established power relations (see Buckingham, 2000, for a thoughtful analysis of this). The internet has disrupted boundaries by providing young people with a gateway to the global world, something that parents and teachers worry will further destroy children and childhood. Fuelled in part by sensationalized reports in news media, these debates and panics about new technologies underlie public discourses. These are contradictory discourses that suggest on one hand that children need to have access to and be literate in new technologies in order to get ahead in a competitive global economy but on the other decree that young people also need to be protected from technologies that expose them to both commercial culture and sexual information before *adults* (the ones generating this discourse) are ready.

These public warnings, we argue, have been incorporated into the collective unconscious, skewing the ways childhood and youth are defined. The discourse surrounding the risks of children's exposure to digital media provides adults with a rationale for sheltering and protecting young people from media and technology (see Guldberg 2009). The rhetoric of protection serves as a justification to restrict and control young people. It is ironic that these restrictions serve to constrain adults too (Sternheimer, 2003). For example, Leslie Regan Shade's chapter examines public internet policy, which blocks access to all social networking sites from federally funded schools and public libraries. What adults forget is that the policies meant to protect young people will also affect them, subjecting adults to the same restrictions in those institutions. As scholars we cannot dismiss public views that promote the regulation of young people because they reveal crucial truths about how we (as a society) view technology and young people—both are valued, both are also mistrusted.

What About Gender?

The term, "gender" can be viewed as both an ambiguous, slippery concept and an ongoing process. It's an evolving social construction, a culturally bound set of role expectations, a contested classification system, an embodied reiterative performance, a cluster of sexualities, and more. In everyday life, it is also part and parcel of how people identify both themselves and others. Gender is a criterion according to which young children figure out where they fit into the social order, and, at some level, it becomes a vital part of how they think, feel, and act. Because gender is also linked to sexuality, it assumes particular significance during adolescence. We agree with scholars who suggest that the internet provides young people with spaces in which to express and test out their emerging gender identities (see Davies, 2004; Driscoll, 2002; Stern, 2004; Thiel, 2005; and Weber & Mitchell, 2008). While this book primarily examines the experiences of girls and young women, a few of the chapters focus closely on boys or include them in some way. These chapters contribute not only to a better understanding of girls' experience, but also allow us to be able to speak more generally about young people, childhood, and society. We think it important to consider girls and young woman as part of (and not always apart from) more general discussions of children and youth.

Perhaps because boys have had earlier and more frequent access to new technologies, and were thus the logical and available population to study, considerable research that theorizes about "children and technology," in fact, reports mainly or exclusively on boys' experience only. There is sometimes an implicit and perhaps unintended assumption that studying boys alone suffices to make general pronouncements about children. Our argument is simply that when writing about boys or children in general, a fuller and more useful understanding results from examining and including girls' experiences, taking them into account. It is for this reason, among others, that in a book that focuses more particularly on girls and young women, we include both male and female experiences in our reflections on technologies, looking not only for differences, but also for often-ignored similarities across gender.

Academics have expressed concerns that boys are more apt to play video games or engage with technology than are girls (Seiter, 2005; Walkerdine, 2004) reasoning that because girls are not playing as many video games, they are being excluded from important new ways of thinking and learning. This concern reflects the growing conviction (see Gee, 2003) that video games can function as important learning tools. Gee argues that video games provide an environment in which game players learn decision-making skills in a virtual domain, and later carry those generalizations into more complex decision-making processes. Games are perceived as bringing new innovative, playful, collaborative and democratic ways of thinking and learning to an old system, as children become producers of knowledge (overturning traditional hierarchical structures). So what might be the consequences if girls opt out of these new ways of learning? The chapters by Dixon and Weber, Pelletier, and Carr, suggest that it is not really a question of whether girls like to game (most of them do), as much as a question of how, when, and why they play. By and large, their participation has been understudied and under-valued, (see chapter One).

Play, Space, and Technologies

People often associate childhood with play. Just what constitutes "play" remains an open question to some, and the subject of much theorizing to others. Characteristics often attributed to play define it as voluntary, freely chosen, engaging, and pleasurable (Caillois, 1958; Huizinga, 1967; Smith et al., 1998; Sutton-Smith, 1997). What is seldom in dispute is that play is paramount for children (Scarlett et al., 2005; Smith et al., 1998). Though children's play varies, changing over time and from place to place as societies change, it is a constant feature of childhood. Perhaps it is the many and often exquisite ways in which digital technologies invite and facilitate play that makes them so appealing? Many of the chapters in this book re-examine play in the light of new technologies. Ultimately, this book goes beyond reflections on technology and digital culture to raise fundamental questions and theorize about broader constructions of childhood, play, sociality, embodiment, space, gender, and issues of power and control.

Researching Young People's Experiences of Digital Technologies

To give readers a clear sense of this book's underlying themes, questions, and research methods, we will conclude with short descriptions of the chapters.

Chapter One: Playspaces, Childhood, and Video games

The book begins with a chapter by Shanly Dixon and Sandra Weber, that explores children's imaginary play and critiques the intense nostalgia that has become associated with how adults think about children's play and childhood. The authors discuss children's play with video games, not as an isolated activity, but rather as play that is situated beside or even within other forms that children's play can assume. Different groups of children (boys and girls) are observed as they engage in imaginary play in a range of spaces: from pretend play in the woods, to video game play in the basement play room. The role of media in shaping children's play is examined as the players draw upon their media memories and experiences to create individualized play experiences. The authors emphasize the fluidity of children's playspaces, drawing on aspects of both cultural studies, play theory, and video game theory to conduct a close reading of the data.

Chapter Two: "I'm the One Who Makes the Lego Racers Go": Studying Virtual and Actual Play

Drawing on an in-depth microethnography of his two sons playing a Lego video game as well as with their Lego blocks, Seth Giddings documents and explores the ways in which video game play can be continuous with, but also transformative of, established children's toy and play culture. Focusing on the notion of "space," he argues that well-established discursive distinctions between virtual and actual space are of little significance to understanding play—children move fluidly between these realms, both creating new games within the video game virtual space and translating or interpreting that space (and its virtual physics) using their material toys. Giddings also raises questions about the nature of children's identification with action and characters in virtual and actual media and game-worlds.

Chapter Three: Girls' Adoption of New Technologies

Reporting on a longitudinal ethnographic study, Sandra Weber analyzes her niece's (and to a lesser extent her nephew's) experiences of technologies over a ten-year period. The study chronicles Julia's reactions to and experience of new technologies as they were periodically introduced into her home, reporting in Julia's own words how she viewed them and how her attitudes changed along with her needs. The author documents Julia's learning strategies and examines the ways she integrated digital technologies into many aspects of her daily life. All these things changed over time. This chapter illustrates how age, gender, sibling coaching, friendships, popular culture, as well as play opportunities can be important elements of technologies-in-use during childhood. Detailed accounts of multitasking and media-mix offer opportunities to rethink children's relationships to technology and cyberspace.

Chapter Four: The Girls' Room:
Negotiating Schoolyard Friendships Online

The theme of girls' agency in spaces produced by new media evolves as Kelly Boudreau provides a description of a school website created by a group of twelve-year-old girls. High-school girls in Montreal hurry home after school so that they can hang out together in the webspace that they have designed. It is a space in which they eagerly discuss the issues of the day: school, grades, teachers, friendships, crushes, and social events. They continuously and rapidly instant message each other, engaging in complex, multiple social interactions. As the chapter unfolds, the continuities and discontinuities between the off-line space of school and home and the online webspace are revealed. The nuances of girls' online sociality are explored as the complex webs of instant messaging are woven. Questions arise as to whether the girls cyber-sociality might provide an alternative means of hanging out for these urban girls whose opportunities to meet unsupervised in city space are often restricted.

Chapter Five: "I Think We Must be Normal . . . There are Too Many of Us for This to be Abnormal!!!": Girls Creating Identity and Forming Community in Pro-Ana/Mia Websites

In this chapter, Michele Polak explores questions of girls' online agency by turning badly needed attention to controversial sites that are run by girls for girls. Despite the intense debates sparked by Pro-Ana/Mia websites, it has been argued that they are nonetheless excellent examples of girls building autonomous online communities and expressions of agency. As more of these sites are shut down "for the public good," Polak suggests it is important to acknowledge that these sites offer marginalized girls a space where they feel safe and less isolated and provide a connection to a diverse community of identities. Girls trying to sort through the issues of disordered eating in relation to body image use Pro-Ana/Mia websites as a forum, combining guidelines for those wishing to maintain a disordered eating lifestyle with recovery narratives—a possible catalyst for girls seeking help in overcoming their disease. Despite their obvious, undeniably destructive potential, this chapter reveals the complex structure of these sites, which also provide a potentially positive, though always fraught space for expression, empathy, identification, and community-building.

Chapter Six: Private Writing in Public Spaces: Girls' Blogs and Shifting Boundaries

Brandi Bell examines the rapidly proliferating culture of girls' blogs, exploring questions such as who writes them and why? Are they forms of girls' private diaries gone public? What sorts of literacy are emerging in this genre and in what ways are blogs transforming or perpetuating girls' presentations of self? How does local context and popular notions of girlhood influence blogging? Weblogs are becoming increasingly popular and are international spaces for girls; spaces in which they journal their private lives and create online identities. This public posting of private material raises issues; private spaces and public spaces become problematized. As girls make their voices heard, questions are being raised concerning the potential significance of their blogs. Are they important modes of civic participation? Or are they simply diaries gone public? How the debates surrounding girls' blogs are resolved will have implications for their future online participation in the public sphere.

Chapter Seven: Consuming Fashion and Producing Meaning through Online Paper Dolls

Rebekah Willett studies girls engaged in discussions about competing discourses relating to girls and the media, discourses that suggest that girls are victims of media and fashion industries that position them as too sexualized too early, yet are also agents of "girl power"—confident, opinionated, and about to embrace their entrance to womanhood. The author researches girls aged twelve–thirteen as they both consume and produce dollmaker websites. Through visual data and interviews, the girls in the study position themselves in complicated ways (as innocent children, scornful teenagers, confident individuals, and as knowledgeable and savvy young women) and they seamlessly shift from one position to another as they appropriate and respond to surrounding discourses. Popular debates about girls as either subjects of negative effects of media images or as active agents who are employing media and fashion as cultural resources are both problematic. These critical positions overlook the complexity and internal tensions in girls' actual experiences. This chapter will explore how girls can be conscious and critical of the ways they are being positioned, yet also take pleasure in those positions, raising important questions for researchers and educators.

Chapter Eight: Producing Gender in Digital Interactions: What Young People Set Out to Achieve through Computer Game Design

Caroline Pelletier asks what happens when girls and boys are invited to develop their own games in the context of an after-school club whose activities largely focus on exploring game development software for children and youth. Stories based on close observations (videotapes) provide the basis for an analysis of the kinds of games young people make for themselves. Pelletier discusses the significance of these activities to broader notions of play, sense-making, and gender. This multimodal, observation-based research looks at the kinds of meaning the girls and boys of the club produce in designing games, the resources they draw on, and the notions of play they utilize. In describing the ways that young people explore game development software, the author analyzes the subject positions they take up through authoring and explores how girls and boys construct a gendered subjectivity. Drawing upon Judith Butler's work on performativity, this chapter examines the discursive and multi-modal construction of gender in texts about games and shows how these relate to dominant discourses about gaming, shaping social relations with adults and peers in the club itself.

Chapter Nine: Contexts, Pleasures, and Preferences: Girls Playing Computer Games

Diane Carr examines the computer games preferences of grade eight girls who joined a gaming club at a single-sex state school in South London. Through observations of the girls' choices and play on the computer, Carr found that gaming preferences are alterable and site specific. As this implies, preferences are not static—our choices depend on where we are and what we have had previous access to. They reflect what we know, who we know, what we've tried, or tired of, and what we will admit to. The question of "preference" is explored as it relates to a set of commercial games offered to a group of players in a particular context. This chapter unpacks the notion of preference itself, by cataloguing the various factors that impinge on users' choices, rather than merely reiterating that girls are predisposed toward particular game genres, or how their level of enthusiasm might compare with their male peers.

Chapter Ten: Adolescent Girls' Expression on Web Home Pages: Spirited, Somber, and Self-Conscious Sites

In this chapter, Susannah Stern reports on a qualitative study that describes adolescent girls' expression on their web home pages. Stern examines the potential of the internet to furnish new forums for girls' self-expression. Scholars concur that girls benefit from access to safe spaces where they feel comfortable expressing themselves, but such places have historically been sparse. The World Wide Web (WWW) allows those with access and the expertise to construct personal home pages to present their thoughts not only to their peers but also to a geographically removed, anonymous, and potentially global public. In addition to extensive description of the girls' home pages, Stern discusses the web's potential as a new "safe space" for girls' self-expression.

Chapter Eleven: Playing At and With Popular Teen Culture on "Girl" Websites: The Case of Alice

In this chapter, Jacqueline Reid-Walsh follows the lead of ten-year-old Alice as she explores a series of commercial websites designed to target

tween girls. Alice provides her own interpretation and critique of the
websites, while the researcher/author conducts a textual analysis of the
cluster of commercial websites that Alice has chosen. In her analysis,
Reid-Walsh juxtaposes and critiques the positions of the various interest
groups involved, including the researcher. The sites are often seen as
"information" sites by the child user or as a space for free online play.
From the point of view of the company, the websites are of secondary
importance and not intended to replace the product. An adult researcher
may see them only as a promotional vehicle or as a means to further
seduce or enmesh children into the commercialized world of play.

Chapter Twelve: Girl Culture and
Digital Technology in the Age of AIDS

How might new media provide badly needed information about sexuality and AIDS to girls? This question is the starting point for Claudia
Mitchell and Jacqueline Reid-Walsh's analysis of various popular culture
websites for girls. Popular magazine websites such as *Seventeen* open the
possibility for providing private information in public spaces. This is
particularly interesting when viewed through the eyes of girls in Africa,
where in some parts of the country HIV infection rates are between
20 and 30 percent, and where they are three or four times more likely
than boys of the same age to be infected with AIDS. Their views help
recontextualize and expand prevailing conceptions of the roles the
internet can play in girls' daily lives in different contexts.

Chapter Thirteen: New Girl (and New Boy)
at the Internet Café: Digital
Divides/Digital Futures

In this chapter, Claudia Mitchell and Grace Sokoya consider the ways in
which access to the internet may provide information and previously
unexperienced autonomy to a group of Nigerian girls as they set out to
visit a cyber café. The research revealed the girls' desire for knowledge
about their sexuality and the potential of the internet as a suitable
medium for providing that information to girls in Nigeria, notwithstanding the sociocultural factors mitigating against sexuality education
for girls in that country. The chapter is interwoven with quotes from
interviews with the girls, illustrating the ways in which rethinking technology has implications on how we look at girls' lives, their power, and
their bodies.

Chapter Fourteen: Contested Spaces: Protecting or Inhibiting Girls Online?

Leslie Regan Shade investigates the way in which the emergence of new media has typically elicited debate and polarized positions regarding children and the protection of childhood, particularly in so far as girls are concerned. As young people enthusiastically embrace social networking spaces such as *MySpace* (finding them to be an appealing method of communicating online with their friends and peers, particularly for girls whose participation in public space is often regulated), anxieties abound as concerned adults and policy makers attempt to curtail and regulate young peoples' participation in these spaces. Using a case study of MySpace and DOPA, this chapter examines recent public discourses around childhood and the internet as it relates to girlhood, exploring the interplay between public discourse and policy objectives, arguing that internet policy on issues of sexual exploitation is inappropriately "gender-blind."

Chapter Fifteen: Reviewing Young Peoples' Engagement with Technology

This final chapter by Weber and Dixon conducts a critical reading across the chapters, focusing on the most salient points raised by the contributing authors, and reflecting both critically and speculatively on the important issues that emerged. These include discussions of play, childhood, gender, transgression and regulation, the relationships of on and offline experience, media mix, public and private spaces, technologies in use, and modalities of participation and agency. Questions for further research are also posed.

Note

1. The term digital native was coined by Mark Prensky (2001) to refer to people born and raised surrounded by and comfortable with evolving digital languages. While we don't object to the term being used to describe the Net generation, we disagree with the oppositional term "immigrant," which he used to refer to the adult bridge or cross-over generation.

References

Bragg, S. & Buckingham, D. (2003). *Young people, sex and the media*. London: Palgrave MacMillan.

Brown, L. & Gilligan, C. (1992). *Meeting at the crossroads: Women's psychological development*. Cambridge, MA: Harvard University Press.

Buckingham, D. (2000). *After the death of childhood: Growing up in the age of electronic media*. Cambridge: Polity Press.

Caillois, R. (1958, 1961). *Man, play, and games* (M. Barash, trans.). New York: Crowell Collier.

Davies, G. (2004). Negotiating femininities online. *Gender and Education, 16,* 35–49.

Driscoll, C. (2002). *Girls: Feminine adolescence in popular culture and cultural theory*. New York: Columbia University Press.

Giroux, H. (2001). *Stealing innocence: Corporate culture's war on children*. New York: St. Martin's Press.

Gee, J.P. (2007). *What videogames have to teach us about learning and literacy*. New York: Palgrave Macmillan.

Guldberg, H. (2009). *Reclaiming childhood: Freedom and play in an age of fear*. New York: Routledge.

Huizinga, J. (1967). *HomolLudens: A study of the play-element in culture* (R.F.C. Hull, trans.). Boston: Beacon.

Kaiser Family Foundation (KFF). *Zero to six: Electronic media in the lives of infants, toddlers and preschoolers*. October 28, 2003.

Katz, J. (1997). *Virtuous reality: How America surrendered discussion of moral values to opportunists, nitwits and blockheads like William Bennett*. New York: Random House.

Mitchell, C. & Reid-Walsh, J. (Eds.) (2005). *Seven going on seventeen: Tween studies in the culture of girlhood*. New York: Counterpoint.

Mosco, V. (2004). *The digital sublime: Myth, power, and cyberspace*. Cambridge, MA: MIT Press.

Postman, N. (1994). *The disappearance of childhood*. London: W.H. Allen.

Prensky, M. (2001). Digital immigrants digital natives. *On the Horizon, 9,* 5.

Roberts, D. & Foehr, U. (2004). *Kids and media in America*. Cambridge, UK: Cambridge University Press.

Scarlett, W.G. et al. (2005). *Children's play*. Thousand Oaks, CA: Sage Publications, Inc.

Seiter, E. (2005). *The internet playground: Children's access, entertainment and mis-education*. New York: Peter Lang Publishing Inc.

Smith, P.K., Cowie, H. & Blades, M. (1998). Play. In P.K. Smith & M. Blades (eds.), *Understanding children's development*, 3rd edition, pp. 177–203. London: Blackwell.

Stern, S. (2004). Expressions of identity online: Prominent features and gender differences in adolescents' World Wide Web Homepages. *Journal of Broadcasting & Electronic Media, 48*(2), 218–243.

Sternheimer, K. (2003). *It's not the media: The truth about pop culture's influence on children*. Boulder, CO: Westview Press.

16   •   Sandra Weber and Shanly Dixon

Sutton-Smith, B. (1997). *The ambiguity of play*. Cambridge, MA: Harvard University Press.

Tapscott, D. (1998). *Growing up digital: The rise of the net generation*. New York: McGraw-Hill.

Thiel, S.M. (2005). I'm me. In S.R. Mazzarella (ed.), *Girlwide web: Girls, the internet, and the negotiation of identity*, pp. 179–202. New York: Peter Lang Publishing Inc.

Walkerdine, V. (2004). Remember not to die: Young girls and videogames. *Papers: Exploration into children's literature*, 14(2), 28–37.

Weber, S. & Mitchell, C. (2008). Imaging, keyboarding, and posting identities: Young people and new technologies. In David Buckingham (ed.), *Youth identity and digital media*. MacArthur Series on Learning and Media, pp. 25–47.

CHAPTER ONE

Playspaces, Childhood, and Video games

Shanly Dixon and Sandra Weber

Situating Video game Play within the Broader Context of Childhood

It has become a truism to state that children are growing up in an increasingly digital world. As greater numbers of young people engage in video game play, scholars, teachers, and parents endeavor to make sense of this leisure activity. Most of the focus, however, has been on video game play as an isolated activity cut off from the rest of childhood play forms and spaces. In contrast, like Giddings' micro-ethnography (see chapter two in this book), our research situates digital play amongst other forms that children's imaginary play can assume. Examining digital play alongside activities that occur in other playspaces such as the backyard or the neighborhood park enables us to make distinctions about digital play characteristics. It also serves to remind us that there is a fascinating continuity, flow, and ambiguity between various forms of play.

We will begin our consideration of playspaces, childhood, and videogames by framing these interrelated phenomena within a broader context, starting with a discussion of the intense nostalgia that currently surrounds children's play (see also *Boyhood spaces: play and social navigation through video games*, Dixon & Simon, 2005). After reviewing some of the literature on childhood, nostalgia, and play, we will more closely examine and reflect upon actual episodes of children at play. These ethnographic vignettes are based on extensive and unobtrusive observations of children in their natural settings, and are taken from a series of research projects we have conducted both separately and together over the course of more than fifteen years. The most recent data stems from research conducted for *The Digital Girls Project*, which we describe in the introduction to this book.

Nostalgia for Childhoods

In discussions about play with both adults and children, there appears to be a yearning for a form of play that is different from the play of today. In describing their own childhoods, for example, university students often reminisce about a simpler, more innocent, and less media-centered childhood experience. They remember playing games in the streets after dinner with neighborhood children, games such as "hide and go seek" or "capture the flag," until their parents called them in for bed. They tell stories of riding their bikes to the baseball diamond, the neighborhood park, or the local swimming pool; their parents seemingly unconcerned about risk from traffic or danger from strangers. This nostalgia pervades both popular culture and academic literature, and is based largely on the contrasts between what people think they remember and what their perceptions (or misconceptions) are of children's actual experiences today. This disappointment with the present has resulted in a flood of books that lament the disappearance of childhood (Elkind, 1981; Jenkins, 1999; Kline, 1993; Laumann, 2006; Postman, 1994).

Much of the concern that is expressed about childhood focuses on the potential threats to children's safety in both public spaces and in cyberspace (see Arthur, 2005; Giroux, 1997; and Walkerdine, 2001 for further discussion). There is also concern about what some are calling the assault on children's playspaces by consumer interests (Dale, 2005; Grimes & Regan Shade, 2005; Quart, 2003; Schor, 2004; Seiter, 2004). These panics regarding the changing nature of childhood translates into a nostalgia for a past that some scholars stipulate never actually existed. In her book *The way we never were* (1992), Stephanie Coontz suggests that the ideal family experience, and by extension, the ideal childhood as represented in "the golden age," does not hold up to rigorous analysis: "It is an ahistorical amalgam of structures, values and behaviors that never coexisted in the same time and place" (p. 9).

However, nostalgia is difficult to avoid. Even Henry Jenkins, renowned media scholar, engages in nostalgia; he portrays a childhood that he believes existed before media became so prevalent in children's lives. In his article "Complete freedom of movement: video games as gendered play spaces" (1999), Jenkins recounts a "Tale of two childhoods" in which he reminisces about his own childhood growing up in Atlanta in the 1960s. He talks about the freedom from supervision he experienced as he engaged in boyhood adventures exploring the neighborhood and nearby forests, which he claimed as his private play domains. He contrasts his own childhood with that of his sons growing up in an apartment complex with no available outdoor play areas. Constant supervision and lack of free space are characteristics typically associated with contemporary childhood. While many theorists bemoan the presence of new media in the lives of children, Jenkins suggests that virtual arenas are providing room for autonomous play, freedom, and adventure, which many contemporary young people are lacking. However, if Coontz is right and what we yearn for is an imagined and not an actual past, questions arise as to why we, as a society, collectively long for childhood as symbolic of a place, a feeling or an identity that never was. In her book *The future of nostalgia* (2001), Svetlana Boym explores how collective nostalgia can serve as an unconscious resistance to change.

> At first glance, nostalgia is a yearning for a different time—the time of our childhood, the slower rhythms of our dreams. In a broader sense, nostalgia is a rebellion against the modern idea of time, the time of history and progress. (p. xv)

Perhaps the nostalgia that characterizes this framing of childhood and the changing nature of children's play is not merely an individual yearning for one's lost childhood but a collective looking backward, possibly as an apprehensive response to a rapidly changing environment. But this looking back, as we have suggested earlier, simultaneously reflects a looking ahead, embodying concerns regarding an uncertain future that could harm our children. As Karen Sternheimer suggests in her book *It's not the media: The truth about pop culture's influence on children* (2003), the intense anxiety we express over the well-being of our children also reflects collective fears regarding social change and an uncertain future. In other words, in addition to representing our idyllic pasts, childhood now also symbolizes our concerns about the present, and worries for the future.

The public panic we have been discussing incites people to blame children's media culture and new technologies for robbing childhood of its innocence. Popular media are more visible than public policy and provide easy targets at which people can vent their fears; for example, people are more likely to get riled up about a controversial video game, such as *Grand Theft Auto*, than they are to express their concerns and frustrations by protesting public policy on video games (Sternheimer,

2003). Of course, as Leslie Regan Shade points out in this volume (chapter fourteen), when election time rolls around, public policy becomes more visible and thus more vulnerable to panic-inspired criticism.

The relationship between nostalgia for childhood and new technologies is not only about panics regarding children's safety and well-being. Adults can also be nostalgic for the possibilities that seemed to lie before them when they once stood at a technological crossroad; a nostalgia for the imagined roads not taken. When we remember our childhoods, we may see them as simpler and less complex, less centered around technology and media. Ironically, as each new form of media emerges, it is envisioned as embodying utopic potential for human enrichment and empowerment, but once the technology is adopted and its potential remains unrealized, we grow nostalgic for the promised possibilities that now seem unreachable (Mosco, 2004). Conceivably, the childhood for which we are nostalgic is an amalgamation of possibilities; a childhood that doesn't focus on media and technology or commercialism and materialism, but rather one that focuses on the possibilities of playing in spaces that are untouched by these influences.

In response to both panic and nostalgia, adults are increasingly organizing and regulating their children's play. Contemporary childhood is now constructed by adults as a space where children must continuously be engaged in activities that are productive. There is an expectation that play must serve some higher purpose: for instance, children play to learn, children play to burn off excess energy, children play for exercise. Play is no longer an objective in and of itself (Sutton-Smith, 1997). As a result of adults' conviction that children must continuously be regulated and supervised and that play should serve a higher function, much of children's play now takes the form of organized team sports and activities occur under institutional supervision. "Free play" is becoming an oxymoron rather than a logical coupling of complementary words. It's almost as if, after waxing nostalgic over lost childhoods and bemoaning the fact that their children's play can never be as innocent or carefree, adults now close all possible venues that might permit their children to experience a degree of the freedom they long for.

Nostalgia and Play Theory

Despite and alongside of all we have written earlier about increasing regulation of play, contemporary society seems to have much invested in maintaining the image of the purity of children's play. Dutch cultural historian, play theorist, and author of *Homo Ludens* (1961), Johan

Huizinga engages in a different form of nostalgia concerning play. He establishes the importance of play in social life, asserting that "Play is older than culture," and that "all culture is a form of play" (p. 1). Huizinga's emphasis is on a higher form of play, which he characterizes through two key features—play as a *contest* for something or as a *representation* of something (p. 13). The concept of play as a contest is evident in most games and sports, including those played by adults. What is interesting to us here, however, is Huizinga's concept of play as representation. For instance, children pretending to be pirates or princesses are creating a representation of something distinct from their usual selves; something more exciting, more daring, or more magnificent. Huizinga suggests that these imaginative experiences of play can fill children with delight, enabling them to be transported beyond the self to such an extent that they almost believe they actually *are* such and such a thing, without, however, wholly losing consciousness of "ordinary reality," an imaginative experience of the truest and most fundamental kind (p. 13). Huizinga asserts that children's play embodies play in its purest form, and that as children grow into adults, their play becomes increasingly complicated and hence corrupted. His nostalgia is not only for childhood, but also for the form of unadulterated play that he believes is fostered by this stage. He associates this play with the most heroic aspects of society and views it as a civilizing force, suggesting that in past societies where play was at its pinnacle, civilization itself was at its most noble. Conversely, Huizinga notes, as a society becomes increasingly complex, technological, and overburdened with rules and systems of knowledge, it becomes more serious and, as a result, play begins to assume a less important position.

In his book, *Man, play and games* (1961), Roger Caillois builds upon the work of Huizinga using his own classifications of play and games as a means for gaining insight into particular cultures. Caillois points to a contradiction that requires reconciliation in the analysis of play. Huizinga's theory suggests that culture is derived from play and therefore he accords a cultural significance to play; however, many theorists adopt a contradictory position suggesting that games are the cast-offs of adult culture, symbolizing that which was previously integral aspects of cultural institutions, now discarded and relegated to the realm of play and childhood. According to these theorists, play and games are no longer considered serious or important cultural endeavors. Caillois reconciles this difference by suggesting that "The spirit of play is essential to culture, but games and toys are historically the relics of culture" (p. 58). Whether one argues that play produces culture or that play *reproduces* culture, Caillois suggests that much is revealed about a culture by the games that are played. Games to some extent characterize the society in which they exist and, therefore, are a valuable source of information. As Caillois relates, "They necessarily reflect its culture pattern and provide useful indications as to the preferences, weakness, and strength of a given society at a particular stage of its evolution" (p. 83). Applying this reasoning to our present discussion of nostalgia, we suggest that the contradictions between the nostalgic yearning for the imagined innocent play of previous generations' childhoods and the current moral panic regarding media, technology, and related commercialization in contemporary children's play reveals much about our current society.

Childhood, Commodification, and Playspaces

From its very inception, childhood has been a social construction heavily influenced by commercial interests. In his book *The disappearance of childhood* (1994), Postman writes that childhood as a separate time and space emerged in the sixteenth century with the invention of the printing press and the subsequent rise in literacy and related need for an educated working class. Children were removed from the workforce and sent to school. But it was not until the late eighteenth century that childhood became a truly popular concept in Europe due to a developing middle class; people had newly acquired money and a desire to spend it (Postman, 1994). As families became smaller and modern capitalism resulted in children no longer being required to contribute to the family financially, having children became a conscious choice for the middle and upper classes (Dale, 2005). It was within the Victorian middle class that the idea of childhood became intertwined with the idea of consumerism. Children operated as "objects of conspicuous consumption" as adults purchased specially produced toys and clothes for their children in order to display their own economic prosperity (Du Boulay as cited in Postman, 1994, p. 44). It is perhaps this use of children as objects for conspicuous consumption that is pivotal in the Western construction of childhood. The role of children has changed; typically they no longer contribute economically to the family or to the marketplace. Young people have taken on the role of consumers rather than producers and as such they are immersed in popular culture, targeted by marketers, and inundated with media images.

Another reason that children's play has become so closely tied to media is the growing privatization and restriction of public spaces. The spaces of childhood are becoming increasingly concealed and protected whereas many public spaces have become adult-only spaces. This development has been explained in terms of two views that emerged from youth studies research around delinquency (Lucas, 1998): first, youth are thought to disrupt public space and so adults would rather they not be there; second, children are thought to be at risk in public spaces, it is too dangerous for them to be there (Jenks, 1996). This state of affairs evolved over the last century.

At the beginning of the twentieth century, it was not unusual for children to play unsupervised in the streets and empty lots. Children created their own private culture, with private spaces such as forts and clubhouses, frequently engaging in secret and forbidden activities such as gambling, fighting, drinking, and vandalism. In the second half of the twentieth century, adults began to bring children under stricter control by introducing playgrounds with commercial playground equipment; schoolyards began to be fenced in and organized clubs, such as boy scouts, and sports teams flourished (Sutton-Smith, 1997). More recently, as public spaces are viewed warily as dangerous places, children's play is becoming even further restricted, moving from streets and parks to organized, supervised activities and into domestic spaces such as bedrooms and playrooms. Adults equip children's domestic space with technologically enticing alternatives to public space in an effort to keep them safely inside (Buckingham, 2000). With this change in children's playspace, it thus becomes almost mandatory in Western society to purchase digital play equipment such as computers, video game consoles, MP3 players, things children think are fun or "cool." Households become what Kline (1993) calls "media saturated spaces." The marketing of new technologies targets young people directly, socializing them into "the attitudes and social relations of consumerism" (Kline, Dyer-Witheford, & De Peuter, 2003, p. 244). As play becomes increasingly privatized, regulated, and supervised, it also becomes increasingly commercial and digital.

Culture, Commodification, and Play

For centuries, childhood, and the toys that are associated with it, has been largely a commercial construction, one that draws deeply on the well of children's popular culture to commodify children's play, opening up markets for manufacturers, advertisers, and corporations. The pervasiveness of popular culture infiltrates and, perhaps to some extent, shapes children's play as they adapt images and take inspiration from multiple influences around them. We might even go so far as to suggest that popular culture in and of itself constitutes a playspace. Adults supply children with media images (old or new) that children then use to become creators of their own playspaces, piecing together elements and mixing media to individualize their play experiences (see Weber's chapter three in this book for a detailed discussion of this phenomenon).

Cumulative Cultural Texts of Childhood: Reading Children's Play

A useful way to analyze children's popular culture and deepen our understanding of children's play is to regard it as part of the "*cumulative cultural text of childhood,*" a text that can be "read." The concept of cumulative cultural text was described by Mitchell and Reid-Walsh (1993) and then expanded by Weber and Mitchell (1995) to refer to the culture of childhood, which carries vestiges of past images that link generations and popular images. The different, yet connected, versions of Barbie or NeoPets or Bratz Dolls or Snow White or Superman demonstrate how a strand of the cumulative cultural text of childhood evolves. Whether these "texts" begin as dolls, books, video games, movies, or toys, if they become popular, they get spun out into a series of related toys, media, and objects, each iteration adding to the popular text. This cumulative text becomes peopled by the generations of real and fictitious characters embodied in books, films, TV programs, comics, songs, toys, software, and so on. Composite contemporary representations of Barbie and Lara Croft take their place amongst previous versions, and alongside Paddington Bears, Peter Pans, Raggedy Anns, GI Joes, Rubber Duckies, Winnie the Pooh, Spiderman, and Batman, to name just a few:

> A multitude of familiar images thus feeds the wellspring of the popular culture of childhood into which we are born and in which we are raised. These images overlap, contrast, blend, contradict, transform, amplify, address, and confirm each other as they compete for our attention in an intertextual clamour. (Weber & Mitchell, 1995, p. 167)

The extended life enjoyed by many popular images is made possible through the intertextual and generative types of variation and serialization that, for example, transformed Barnie, a popular purple dinosaur, from a TV character to a series of books, dolls, movies, knapsacks, and computer software, thus giving him presence, longevity, and power.

> Both implicitly and explicitly, individual episodes and versions contextualize, influence, build on, and refer to each other, collaboratively constituting the cumulative text. A book begets a movie which begets both an audio track and a new edition of the book as well as a television series and computer games. But this serialization into multiple texts only happens if

there is something commercially viable in the initial representation— something that captures children's interest, which draws them in or addresses them in a meaningful way that sells. (p. 166)

In other words, popular texts such as the computer game *The Sims* or *Grand Theft Auto* wouldn't be pervasive unless they managed to tap into the particular desires of many child consumers. In that sense, they serve as a kind of mirror for childhood in our society, and reveal important truths to us about ourselves. As Caillois (1961) has suggested, the material culture of play has something to divulge about the culture within which it exists.

Returning now to our interest in video games, while it is impossible to say with absolute certainty that the text of a child's experience of video gaming can be read or interpreted in any one particular way, we find it helpful to frame play as a meaningful text that invites a reading between the lines. Moreover, situating children's video play within the wider context of the cumulative text of childhood culture enables us see how video game play might relate to other forms of play. How, we wonder, are social interactions and role-playing within the video game space similar or different from children's relationships through play in other spaces such as parks, playgrounds, and playrooms? How does the experience of playing video games shape (or how is it shaped by) the nature of contemporary childhood?

Observing and Describing Children's Play

Our collaborative reflections on digital childhoods and children's play is based, in part, on a series of longitudinal ethnographic case studies each of us has conducted of children at play. We have followed some of the children (from three to fifteen years old) for up to six years, and our data collection includes interviews and observations. We are now sharing and combining our data, reviewing and testing our interpretations, and looking for cross-case similarities and differences. From this large corpus, we have selected a series of vignettes reconstructed from fieldnotes, each one followed by some critical reflections. Our first comes from a study done by Weber more than fifteen years ago.

Playing at Snow White: Boys and Girls In and Out of Role

I am surreptitiously watching a mixed group of mainly six-year-old children playing outside. They have been kicked out of doors by their mums who said, "get some sunshine." Let's play "Snow White," one of the girls exclaims. Most of them have recently seen the Disney movie, which seems to have impressed them. There are cries of assent, followed soon by arguing over who is going to be Snow White, who is going to be the wicked queen, and so forth. One girl has dark hair and soon convinces people she should have the role because she looks like Snow White, although another girl claims that the fact she has a Snow White lunch box gives her an edge. An older boy suddenly announces that he wants to be the wicked Queen because he has a cape he could use as a costume. No one seems to want to be the prince. The children begin enacting the story, stopping and restarting, giving each other directions (no, first she has to ask the mirror, then the woodsman takes her out to the woods), and improvising many touches that bear little resemblance to the movie. The game stops and then starts up again as one child tickles another, or some-one calls attention to the mushrooms growing on the damp ground. Hilarity breaks out when one boy decides he is a deer who discovers Snow White asleep in the woods and tries to wake her by licking her. Suddenly, one of the children's mothers, who has come to fetch her child, intrudes upon the play space of the enchanted "forest." I notice that two of the children who were really "into" their roles seem startled, as if to say "what are you doing here? You're not in Snow White." One boy says "go away, we're playing." However, five minutes later, when another mother passes by and inquires, "What are you playing at," the same two children seem nonplussed and answer "Snow White." One of them says "I'm the wicked queen." "Oh, yes, I can see that you are," replies the mother gamely play-ing along. Snow White is called home by her mother—and another girl suggests her Barbie doll could take the part of Snow White. She proceeds to use her Barbie as a puppet, acting as ventriloquist for "Snow White Barbie." Another child goes along with this, but two others just sort of parallel play a different version of Snow White. The play keeps falling apart (to my adult observer eyes at any rate) changing directions, as a couple of boys engage in rough and tumble play, one child bursts into tears saying "I don't WANT to be Dopey," and so forth. And then the dwarfs start singing a popular song, "I'm too sexy for my shirt" and dancing around, while two girls decide the piece of cardboard they were using as the Mirror Mirror on the Wall is not very good, and announce they are going to make a "real one." When asked a few minutes after the play seemed to be grinding to a halt what they had been doing and how they had spent their afternoon, most of them said, "we played Snow White." Two of them told me "we were just playing outside." (Constructed from Weber's fieldnotes, August 1992.)

The children playing Snow White in the forest exemplify a form of childhood pretend, fantasy, or role-play that is familiar and ubiquitous, observed in children from one generation to another. Further, we see how children co-opt a variety of ideas and images to inform or guide their play, culled from various sources such as personal experiences, books, television, songs, and movies. Children adapt these images to the playspace and opportunities available to them—in this case, adapting the traditional story of Snow White to accommodate the roles the players wanted to adopt and making use of the props at hand. The play seemed to filter through *cumulative popular cultural texts*: their enacting of Snow White had an evolving script that was likely based not only on the movie but on the cumulative cultural text of Snow White that includes lunch boxes, figurines, Disney World characters, a variety of children's book versions, and so forth. It would perhaps be more accurate to say that the structure and "spontaneous" script of the children's play reflected their interpretations or responses to Disney and other forms of cultural texts. Through the children's active play, negotiations, and improvisations, the text was adapted, ignored, disrupted, and reconstructed. There was fluidity to the play despite a series of abrupt halts and changes of directions as the children moved in and out of the various roles that they had assumed.

Although the subject of the children's play (Snow White) was probably inspired by multiple sources of media and media experiences, it is nonetheless an example of the imaginary, make-believe play that many adults nostalgically reminisce about and want contemporary children to experience. This instance of play occurred unregulated and unsupervised by adults in an outdoor space. Since these fieldnotes are now fifteen years old, they may capture an experience of unsupervised outdoor pretend play that is becoming increasingly rare. And yet, as we shall see in more recent fieldnotes, children's play is not so different from contemporary examples of media-inspired play. At the time these notes were taken, movies and television (today's "old" and analog media) were still kind of "new."

Boys Playing Outside: Pretend Play and the Secret Spaces of Childhood

Eleven years later, Dixon conducted research on children similarly at play, but using video games as a play option; something that was not available to the children Weber observed playing Snow White. The following excerpt from her fieldnotes illustrates the children's play as it moves fluidly from an outdoor playspace to the world of a video game.

They crouch quietly, huddled close together, scarcely daring to breathe. The clouds are low and grey overhead. They have been waiting impatiently for what seems like hours. This is a secret place they come to in order to escape, safe from prying eyes. They discovered it last fall and made it their own; in the winter they enclose themselves with fortress walls of snow, and now in the spring, it's cool and dark where the high grass surrounds them and the wild bushes make a roof above their heads. From this vantage point they can watch the comings and goings in the alleyway that runs behind the apartment building where they live. The objects of their observations are none the wiser.

It's always been like this for as long as Rowan can remember. He and Tucker are the only eleven year old boys living on the alley so they have to stick together against all those girls. They have been waiting for the girls to come out and play so they can spy on them but they have waited in vain and now big wet raindrops are starting to fall. Tucker and Rowan abandon the "secret place" and run to get their "portable forts." They use these when the rain gets heavy. The portable forts consist of pieces of plywood that they have found and nailed to long sticks. They hold them over their heads running through the rain, chasing each other up and down the alley, splashing through the mud, laughing until Rowan's mother comes out and calls them inside. She hands them towels to dry themselves off and sends them down to the basement to play. (Constructed from Shanly's fieldnotes, April 2003.)

Playing Video games Inside

We now follow these same boys as they move to video game play indoors.

Rowan and Tucker sit in the tiny playroom that Rowan's father has built in the still-unfinished basement. It is a work in progress meant to keep Rowan and his friends and their noisy television and video games safely out of earshot of the adults. The apartment is small and Rowan's dad works from home so if Rowan wants to play inside, down to the basement he goes. The room is surprisingly bright, painted white with a colourful poster on the wall, a sofa and a standing lamp from which two Spiderman action figures are perilously dangling. The focal point of the room is the television and Rowan and Tucker are sitting on the floor in front of it, a bowl of carrot sticks between them. I am sitting on the couch; here to interview the boys about video games. They are excited at the prospect; eager to have the undivided attention of an adult who values their opinions, who regards them as experts on playing video games. They start off by showing me their selection of games. They begin to describe their favourite game, Pikmin.

Tucker: There's this guy from a planet and his name is Omar. Before he left on this journey he went to his wife who made him this soup with these carrots and when he left there was this asteroid who hit his ship and he lands down on this toxic planet and he finds a carrot and it's red and it's a carrot. He has oxygen for thirty days and so he has thirty days to recover all the parts of his ship so that he can return back home and so every day you finish you get time to picnic so you bring him to these onions and they have feet and there are these flowers and the Pikmin will destroy the flower so you actually have thirty days . . .

Rowan: (Impatiently) "So we play now?"

They begin to play the game.

Shanly: "What do you like about the game?"
Rowan: "It's an adventure but there is action too."
Tucker: "We like to search for the parts of the ship."

The planet in the game *Pikmin* acts as a playspace for the boys when they are unable to play outside. Their interaction on the virtual planet appears to be similar to their play in their secret hideout. In fact, at times they imagine the secret place as a spaceship, perhaps inspired from their play in the video game. The boys say that they play video games about three days a week, not all day long, but for a couple of hours and usually on weekends.

Comparing Outdoor and Indoor Playspaces

Although they describe themselves as "playing a lot of video games" when they relate the ways in which they spend their time, video games are one of many activities in which they engage. When asked if they play at the park, they respond that they don't usually because the park is full of "old people having parties and babies." The street in front of the apartments is too busy with traffic and so they prefer to play in the alley-way behind, where they can run freely and hide in their secret place and spy. When Dixon spoke to the boys' parents, they explained that they allowed the boys to play in the alleyway because many of the kitchen windows of the apartments faced into the alley. The children who played there could be easily watched by their parents who thus felt that it was a safe, supervised place for children to play in. The alleyway was enclosed by a fence at one end and a churchyard at the other, so there was no dan-ger from vehicle traffic, and because it was cut off, casual pedestrians rarely wandered through. The boys report that they prefer playing out-side rather than inside when the weather allows, but in winter, or when it is very rainy, or in the summer when it is hot and they are bored, they play video games.

In comparing the seemingly distinct playspace of the alleyway (an ostensibly classic childhood playspace) with the video game (a contemporary virtual playspace) there appear to be some similarities and even some fluidity between the spaces. Our interpretation is that both spaces serve to characterize the appeal of secret childhood spaces (van Manen, 1996): they both feel concealed and secret; they are spaces where a child might slip off alone escaping from daily demands; and they are places in which to fantasize and dream. They are also places where one might engage in social interaction with peers, away from prying adult eyes.

Girls Playing Video games: Fluidity of Play

The previous fieldnotes of boys at play reveals the permeability between the physical playspace of the alleyway and the playspace of the video game. The following vignette from Shanly's fieldnotes of 2004 portrays the fluidity of girls' play as it moves across digital platforms and playspaces.

> A group of four ten year old girls gathers around a video game console in Anna's playroom. They are playing a video game that they rented from the local video game store, Pirates; The Legend of Black Kat which features a female pirate described as:
>> Katarina de Leon, the "Black Kat" of the high seas possessing sailing and sword-fighting skills beyond compare and unflinching bravery in the face of extraordinary dangers.
> The girls spend their time in the game searching for treasure, navigating the pirate ship from island to island and fighting off pirates and giant crabs. The game is meant for a single player, but the girls take turns with the controller, advising each other on strategy and surfing the internet on Anna's laptop while waiting for their turn with the controller. They are engaged in multiple forms of play in the same space: instant messaging friends from school, listening to music, playing games online while simultaneously watching and coaching whichever girl currently has the controller. They are all invested in the success of the player, calling out encouragement or shrieking in dismay as the occasion requires. The game has captured their imaginations to such a degree that the play merges as they re-enact the adventure pretending to be pirates engaging in play sword fights and taking turns being Katarina.

Following is a short excerpt of dialogue from fieldnotes of the girls playing the video game:

> *Anna*: "This went so much faster than the 1st time but if I have to redo it again I'm gonna be so mad"

Anna hands the controller to Molly who explores the island looking for the treasure chest eventually encountering pirates.

Molly: "Pirates! Oh No!

I'm running through trees . . ."
Molly explores the island in the game looking for clues that will lead her to the treasure.

Molly: (handing the controller to Virginia) "Do you want to try"?

Virginia is the quietest of the girls. She is typically shy and timid on the schoolyard. She reluctantly accepts the controller.

Virginia: "You don't need to kill the monkeys cause they won't hurt you"
Anna: "Press 1, 2 right when the lock comes press 1, 2 go thru the door that opened"
Victoria: (Squealing) "Crabs, crabs, crabs, eww!" (She swipes wildly at the crabs with her sword, laughing and screeching)

In reviewing how the girls played and interacted with each other, it struck us that the video game was being "played" simultaneously both off and online—a flowing exploration through the permeable boundaries of the digital and the analog—as the girls played at, as well as played through and around the Pirate theme. Like Seth Giddings' sons in chapter two of this book, these girls seemed at times to be both *playing at playing* a video game and playing the game. There was a multiple layering or multitasking in the casual way they incorporated the pirate game into their play, cheering on the person playing, giving suggestions, and actually enacting or improvising around it.

Revisiting these girls four years after their pirate game play, we were curious to observe how video games fit into their lives now that they are teenagers. As one would expect, they no longer play games like *Pirates: The Legend of Black Kat*. Now they gather to play *Guitar Hero, Rock Band* and *Dance, Dance Revolution*. When *SIMMS 3* was released they celebrated with marathon weekend-long/slumber-party playing sessions. They socialize around and through the games engaging in the same collective imaginative play experience that was so evident in their play four years ago. As they move from childhood to teenhood, video games have simply become an accepted aspect of girlhood culture.

In terms of gender differences, some of the concerns that have been raised in the past were that by not playing video games to the same extent that boys do, girls might be excluded from new ways of learning and problem solving. However, in light of recent observations, it seems that girls do indeed play video games and engage with technology although perhaps in different ways than boys do. As girls become the new target market for video games, we suggest their engagement with digital culture warrants further research, particularly with regards to the affordances and contexts of the various games that girls are playing.

Reflecting Cross-Cases

The play represented in the video game episodes might serve to exemplify Huizinga's concept of play "as a contest for something" because indeed the children are playing a game and attempting to win. However, it may also be argued that they are also simultaneously engaged in Huizinga's "play as a representation of something." The video game play provides children with an opportunity to imagine themselves as something other than that which they typically are, as they pretend to be space travelers or pirates; in Huizinga's words, they are "transported beyond themselves in a playful imaginative experience." As Virginia plays the video game, she temporarily plays at being Katarina de Leon, pirate and legend of the high seas. Through this imaginary play she meets the criteria of Huizinga's definition: temporarily feeling magnificent, transcending the banality of the everyday, trying on identities (see Mazzarella & Pecora, 1999 for more on identity and video games). It is interesting to note that the same analysis could apply to the example of the reenactment of Snow White, so many years earlier.

In all of the episodes, the children's play was at least partially inspired by some version of a media-generated play "text": a bedtime story, a Disney movie or book, or a video game. There is often a bias against media-inspired play, a dismissal of such play as mere copying, not original or creative activity. Along with other scholars (e.g., Dyson, 1997; Kinder, 1991; and Seiter, 2004), we take issue with such a narrow interpretation and suggest that close examination of the kind of play we present here, reveals creativity and learning. In each of these vignettes the children adapt the text, altering the narrative in order to creatively accommodate their play intentions. The boys playing the video game *Pikmin*, for example, can choose not to play the game as the game designer intended. Instead, they often ignore the game objective of gathering parts for the spaceship; rather, they explore the planet, hanging out and fooling around. Similarly, the girls at times seem to be playfully incorporating Katrina characters and narratives into their talk and actions around the video game at the same time that one of them played the game itself—multitasking their play, as it were. This acting-out, inspired by the video game, in turn feeds back into the ways they subvert or alter the game. We agree with Dyson (1997) who states that media provide the "common story material" of childhood, and urges adults and educators to acknowledge that the creative ways children reinterpret and incorporate this material in their fantasy play constitutes a form of literacy (p. 7).

In Huizinga's analysis of play, he suggests that "with the increasing systemization and regimentation of sport, something of the pure play quality is inevitably lost" (Huizinga, 1967, p. 197). He laments that the adult professional player may have greater expertise but lacks the "play spirit" of the amateur player who plays purely for fun. He even goes as far as asserting that to really play, an adult "must play like a child" (p. 199). With this assertion Huizinga relegates pure play to the realm of childhood. However, it is questionable how much of children's play fits the criteria of pure play. Moreover, Huizinga's claim that play exists most purely in childhood raises questions regarding how much of his analysis is a romanticized reflection of how children *ought* to play. At the same time, although the play we have been observing may not exactly fit Huizinga's notion of pure play, our findings do suggest that media play can be highly creative and is an important venue or space for social interaction, problem-solving, and pleasure.

The children we observed are active agents, not passive spectators in their interactions with popular images. They turn the popular culture they consume into material for their imaginative play, and use it, we would argue, to construct their own private playspaces. This interpretation of children's interaction with media is gaining currency as we revise the older and, in Seiter's (2004) opinion, classist notions that media consumption is inevitably passive mind-numbing (for in-depth discussion on this point, see Buckingham and Sefton-Green, 2004; Ito, 2007; Jenkins, 2006). This is not to say that the children's play is not shaped by media or that all play is creative. Their play is both limited and encouraged by the design possibilities (affordances) of the material at hand (see Weber & Mitchell, 2007). Like all human activity, we view the children's interaction with media as dialectical, a sense-making interaction with the environment through which they learn about the world, each other, and themselves. Through fantasy or narrative play, they are representing and interpreting their understanding of various aspects of the culture that surrounds them.

Even more important in terms of our topic of playspaces is the way that children's play flows easily on and off line, in and out of roles, weaving back and forth from the imaginative to the actual. It is in this blurring of boundaries between physical and cyberspaces, between the virtual and the actual that children create playspaces for themselves—spaces that those few scholars who still insist on separating the virtual from the "real" ignore. Most of us now argue that all play is part of real-life experience, something that is hard to deny even when we observe play media-generated spaces such as video games. As we suggested earlier, video game play is, perhaps in part, a consequence of adult regulation of children's outdoor playspaces. Through their anxiety and desire to monitor children at all times, adults have greatly diminished the opportunities for children to play privately with their peers. Where can a child go to carve out a secret hiding place? It is most ironic that the type of play adults long for in their romanticized past has moved to the spaces we are most concerned about; our children are finding safe harbor in the spaces created by technology and media, where in many respects, they continue to play in ways not that different from generations past. When they grow up, we wonder, what childhoods will they be nostalgic for?

References

Arthur, L. (2005). Popular culture: views of parents and educators. In J. March (ed.), *Popular culture, new media and digital literacy in early childhood*, pp. 165–182. New York: RoutledgeFalmer.

Boym, S. (2001). *The future of nostalgia*. New York: Basic Books.

Buckingham, D. (2000). *After the death of childhood: Growing up in the age of electronic media*. Cambridge: Polity Press.

Buckingham, D. & Sefton-Green, J. (2004). Structure, agency, and pedagogy in children's media culture. In J. Tobin (ed.), *Pikachu's global adventure: The rise and fall of Pokémon*, pp. 12–33. Durham: Duke University Press.

Caillois, R. (1961). *Man, play, and games*. New York: *The Free Press*.

Coontz, S. (1992). *The way we never were: American families and the nostalgia trap*. New York: Basic Books.

Dale, S. (2005). *Candy from strangers: Kids and consumer culture*. Vancouver: New Star Books.

Dixon, S. & Simon, B. (2005). Boyhood spaces: Play and social navigation through videogames. Presented at the International DiGRA Conference: *Changing Views: Worlds at Play*, June 16–20, Simon Frasier University, Vancouver, BC, Canada.

Dysan, A.H. (1997). *Writing superheroes. Contemporary culture popular culture, and classroom literacy*. New York: Teacher's College Press.

Elkind, D. (1981). *The hurried child: Growing up too fast too soon*. MA: Addison-Wesley.

Giroux, H. (1997). Are Disney movies good for your kids?. In J. Kincheloe & S. Steinberg (eds.), *Kinderculture: The corporate construction of childhood*, pp. 53–68. Bolder, CO: Westview.

Grimes, S. & Regan Shade, L. (2005). Neopian economics of play: Children's cyberpets and online communities as immersive advertising in Neopets.com. *International Journal of Media and Cultural Politics*, *1*(2), 181–198.

Huizinga, J. (1961). *Homo ludens: A study of the play-element in culture* (R.F.C. Hull, trans.). Boston: Beacon.

Ito, M. (Forthcoming). Mobilizing the imagination in everyday play: The case of Japanese media mixes. In S. Livingston & K. Drotner (eds.), *International handbook of children, media, and culture*.

Jenks, C. (1996). *Childhood*. London: Routledge.

Jenkins, H. (1999). Complete freedom of movement: Videogames as gendered play spaces. In J. Cassell & H. Jenkins (eds.), *From Barbie to Mortal Kombat: Gender and computer games*, pp. 262–297. Cambridge: MIT Press.

———. (2006). *Convergence culture: Where old and new media collide*. New York and London: New York University Press.

Kinder, M. (1991). *Playing with Power in Movies, Television, and VideoGames*. Berkeley: University of Berkeley Press.

Kline, S. (1993). *Out of the garden: Toys, TV and children's culture in the age of TV marketing*. London: Verso.

Kline, S., Dyer-Witheford, N., & de Peuter, G. (2003). *Digital play: The interaction of technology, culture and marketing*. Montreal: McGill-Queen's University Press.

Laumann, S. (2006). *Child's play: Rediscovering the joy of play in our families and communities*. Canada; Random House.

Lucas, T. (1998). Youth gangs and moral panics in Santa Cruz, California. In T. Skelton & G. Valentine (eds.), *Cool places: Geographies of youth cultures*, pp. 145–160. New York: Routledge.

Mazzarella, S. & Pecora, N. (eds.) (1999). *Growing up girls; Popular culture and the construction of identity*. New York: Peter Lang.

Mitchell, C. & Reid Walsh, J. (1993). "And I want to thank you Barbie": Barbie as a site of cultural interrogation. *The Review of Education/Pedagogy/Cultural Studies*, *17* (2), 143–156.

Mosco, V. (2004). *The digital sublime: Myth, power, and cyberspace*. Cambridge, MA: MIT Press.

Postman, N. (1994). *The disappearance of childhood*. New York: Vintage Books.

Quart, A. (2003). *Branded: The buying and selling of teenagers*. New York: Perseus Publishing.

Schor, J. (2004). *Born to buy*. New York: Scribner.

Seiter, E. (2004). *The internet playground: Children's access, entertainment and mis-education*. New York: Peter Lang.

Sternheimer, K. (2003). *It's not the media: The truth about pop culture's influence on children*. Boulder, CO: Westview Press.

Sutton-Smith, B. (1997). *The ambiguity of play*. Cambridge, MA: Harvard University Press.

Van Manen, M. (1996). *Childhood secrets: Intimacy, privacy and self reconsidered*. New York: Teacher's College Press.

Walkerdine, V. (2001). Safety and danger: Childhood, sexuality, and space at the end of the millennium. In K. Hultqvist & G. Dahlberg (eds.), *Governing the child in the new millennium*, pp. 15–34. New York: RoutledgeFalmer.

Weber, S. & Mitchell, C. (1995). *Reinventing ourselves as teachers: Beyond nostalgia*. London: RoutledgeFalmer.

——— (2008). Imaging, keyboarding, and posting identities: young people and new technologies. In David Buckingham (ed.), *Youth identity and digital media*. MacArthur Series on Learning and Media, pp. 25–47.

CHAPTER TWO

"I'm the One Who Makes the Lego Racers Go": Studying Virtual and Actual Play

Seth Giddings

I had picked up a free pack of computer games on CD-ROM from PC World, a promotion for NVidia graphics chips (each game uses 3D graphics). One of the games, *Lego Racers 2*, quickly became a favorite with my two sons, Jo (aged four) and Alex (three). They both enjoyed the novelty of seeing and controlling Lego cars and "men" on the computer screen and the humorous elements of the game that link the virtual world with the actual world of familiar play with plastic toys. As a media researcher (as well as a parent) fascinated by video games, I began to notice some unexpected and intriguing aspects of their play. I picked up the family video camera and began recording them, unwittingly embarking on what was to become an in-depth study with important implications.

What is going on when children incorporate video games in their everyday domestic play? This chapter draws on detailed participant observations of my two sons playing at home with Lego: the bricks *and* the video game. It explores and documents the ways in which video game play can be continuous with, but also transformative of, children's established toy and play culture. I begin by questioning the usually firm distinctions often made between virtual and actual space. Following that discussion, I describe a video recording of the two boys at play, tracking their movement between virtual and actual play realms. As the chapter progresses, what started out as a small-scale improvised microethnography ends up raising unexpected but fundamental questions about children, play, and new technologies.

The research on playing video games tends to fall into one of two broad categories that indicate different approaches, foci, or conceptual frameworks:(i) some studies concentrate mainly on the social or communicative contexts and practices of new media, which frame and inflect playing (Alloway & Gilbert, 1998; Ito, 1998; McNamee, 1998; Wright, Boria, & Breidenbach, 2002) reflecting an ethnographic concern for describing and understanding observable, lived experience; (ii) other research tends to focus much more closely on the use of theories of subjectivity to examine the complex nature of the relationships between humans and media ("technological intimacy"). Studies in the latter kind of research tend to echo cybercultural studies (or film theory) in that their theorizations or cybertextual analyses are based on assumptions about the nature of interaction and "immersion" (the idea that users of the internet or players of video games are somehow present—or feel themselves to be present—within cyberspace) rather than on any observation of actual, lived interaction (Friedman, 1995; Lahti, 2003; Morris, 2002).

This is not to argue that either of these approaches is wrong, but rather that there is a gap between ethnographies that say little about the detailed nature of human/media technological intimacy, and theories of subjectivity that address these issues but neglect ethnographic concern for observable, lived experience. A synthesis is needed between theoretical work on new media/technoculture and ethnographic work with more familiar research objects: domestic space, everyday life, established media and toys, familial relationships, and children (Facer, Sutherland, & Furlong, 2003; Flynn, 2003; Green, Reid, & Bigum, 1998; Ito, 1998; Sefton-Green, 2004; Walkerdine, 1999). In this chapter, I hope to bridge the gap, at least partially.

To examine how the game as software, and PC as hardware, facilitate emergent practices and meanings in children's lived media culture, I use a research approach that takes technologies (both hardware and software) and media images as its objects of study. Or, more precisely, an approach that describes an "event" constituted by the circuits of agency, affect, and play between human and technological participants. However, as I hinted earlier, it quickly became clear that any microethnography of popular technocultural events such as video game play should also address the operations, effects, aesthetics, and kinesthetics of the video game-in-play; it should, after Espen Aarseth, develop a *cybertextual analysis* (Aarseth, 1997; Manovich, 2001).

A Microethnography of Virtual and Actual Play

The Lego video game that I brought home to my sons was played on a PC in the living room. The machine is used by the whole family for game-playing, word-processing, internet access, photo-viewing, and web design work. Jo played a range of games on the PC, including Flash games for young children on the BBC website, "edutainment" CD-ROMs, and commercial video games, often based on media worlds and characters he was already familiar with (e.g., *Scooby Doo, A Bug's Life, Buzz Lightyear*). The commercial strategy of cross-media licensing is well-established in children's culture (Kinder, 1991; Kline, Dyer-Witheford, & de Peuter, 2003), and this game is not unique in making links between media forms and genres and toys (other successful recent examples include, of course, *Pokémon*, and games based on the films of *Harry Potter, Star Wars*, and *James Bond*). However, *Lego Racers 2* makes direct and witty links between the gameworld and its objects, and the physicality of Lego as a toy. For example, the player at the start of the game is given the option of building his/her own car and driver. A menu system offers ranges of virtual bricks from which figures and vehicles can be built. In the game proper, crashes result in bricks breaking off from the cars. Whilst the cars in the game are controlled in ways familiar from other racing games, they are represented explicitly as Lego cars, built from bricks and—implicitly acknowledging the pleasures of play that constitute the flipside to Lego's promotion of its toys as for *construction*—destructible back into bricks.

I initially resisted picking up the video camera as I did not want my pleasure in watching my children's play to be invaded by "work." However, my attention was caught when the boys recreated the world of the game's first level ("Sandy Bay") with actual Lego bricks, replicating the features that most excited them in the game. They built steep mountains and drew a beach and sea on a sheet of paper to lay on the floor beneath the mountains. The boys constructed cars and drivers from actual Lego and raced them around the living room, making engine noises and shouting, before arriving at their plastic and paper gameworld. The "race" itself was non-agonistic, driven by their enthusiasm for the dynamics and noise of speeding virtual cars, not competition.

The improvised replication or performance of settings and environments from literature and media in children's play is hardly new. Spatial elements such as topographies, maps, and architectures also shape games and play—from Lego and dolls houses to board games and theme parks. However, it was apparent that this particular translation was a response to the specificity of computer-generated gameworlds as a spatial and kinesthetic form. The boys were not merely constructing a backdrop for their translated play of the computer game, they were constructing it *as* space, and as an actualization of a dynamic *virtual* space with its own simulated physics (friction, gravity, acceleration). The topography of the mountains, beach, and sea was not only animated by the actions and dramas of driving toy cars; this space and action were animated by both video game form and a translation of the kinesthetics of Sandy Bay's virtual physics. For example, when the race was over they began to drive their Lego cars up and down the mountains, but (and I did not notice this until I watched the video footage later) in the tractile dynamics of the cars, they simulated the low-gravity physics of the video game environment. This "virtual physics" allows cars to drive up cliffs that would, in the actual world, be far too steep. On the other hand, if cars are driven off cliffs, they tumble more slowly (and with less damaging results) than vehicles in the actual world. Watching this movement is a little like watching footage of astronauts and moon buggies on the moon. The car must have some momentum to make such a climb and, as it bounces up the slopes, must make enough contact with the ground to maintain this momentum. To play this ascent–descent game the player must implicitly understand this simulated but real relationship between the momentum of the car, the friction afforded by the topography, and the gravity of the gameworld. This lunar gravity then, and the kinesthetic pleasures it offered, led the boys to repeatedly propel their virtual vehicles off cliffs into exhilarating descents, the cars bouncing slowly yet inexorably downward toward the sea. For a time this offered sufficient pleasure in itself, an exploration of both the extremes of the gameworld's landscape, its hyper-real gravity, as experienced through the control of the car/avatar. Their translation of this virtual phenomenon into *actual* movement and dynamics, as they shifted their plastic cars between the breakneck velocities of the living-room circuit and the slow-motion bounce and plummet over the brick mountains, highlighted these virtual operations.

To best understand these translations, it is necessary to think through how virtual and actual playspaces and their players constitute each other. This microethnography needs to draw on, and factor in, something of the structure, operations, and effects of the video game as virtual space and popular media software. The video game as hardware and software is an agent or set of agents in this event alongside the children.

Cybertextual Analysis of the Video game

The *Lego Racers 2* interface uses a third-person viewpoint—a mode of representation common to a number of the most popular genres of contemporary video games. The avatar or player-controlled agent on the screen is positioned immediately in front of the virtual camera in the bottom half of the screen. The term "third-person" is defined in opposition to the "first-person" virtual camera of the tremendously popular genre that is to a significant degree defined by this characteristic: the first-person shooter. Car racing games (and many adventure games such as the popular *Tomb Raider* series) almost always use the third-person perspective as a default, the player's point-of-view/virtual camera angle always hovers immediately behind the avatar as the avatar is directed through the three dimensions of the gameworld—down paths, through tunnels, and up hills and structures. However, many do allow the option of a first-person viewpoint (e.g., the player's point-of-view in looking at the on-screen events is contiguous with the view out of a car windscreen from a driver's point-of-view).

This terminology (third- and first-person perspectives) is adapted from film theory's notions of subjective camera positioning. As we will see, the ways in which a video game organizes its interface between player and code (through the presentation of its virtual world and the operations of its virtual camera) are often considered key to the player's subjective engagement or "identification" with the gameworld and its characters.

In "adventure" mode, the *Lego Racers 2* player has to first construct the driver and car. Following the logic of actual Lego construction, the driver/avatar is made up from a selection of bricks "printed" with various faces and indications of clothing. Constructing the car is more complicated. Side-scrolling menus at the top of the screen offer a range of types of bricks, and submenus offer particular bricks within these ranges. When a specific brick is chosen by the player (left and right arrow keys slide the menu left and right and the return key is struck once the required brick rests in the middle of the screen) its image hovers over the car under construction. The player positions it over the car and hits return to drop it into place. There do not seem to be many restrictions on the style or number of bricks thus added, and whilst the completed construction subsequently appears in the game, the design itself has no effect on the performance of the car or on the behavior of the driver.

Once the design has been completed, the game itself begins with a tutorial. An animated Lego figure (in close-up) instructs the player via panels of text. For example the player's first task is to drive the car to a beach to meet the instructor again. The green arrow points the way, and through this simple task the player learns how to direct the car and something of the kinesthetics of the car and the gameworld. Whilst the movements and speech/text of this instructor are pre-rendered, the contingent avatar car/driver as constructed by the player are also visible in these sequences.

At this point in the description it becomes clear that methods of textual analysis drawn from media and film studies cannot fully account for the operations and aesthetics of video games in play. One of the most immediate differences between video game play and other forms of screen media consumption is the requirement for the player to possess or acquire the relevant skills or competencies needed to play. These include motor skills, knowledge of game conventions, intellectual skills of deduction, experimentation, and problem-solving. Any description or analysis of the video game in play must factor in the cybernetic feedback loop between player and software in particular events of gameplay. For example, Jo quickly found that the "preferred" or expected arcade mode of racing against the competing computer-controlled vehicles (non-player characters, or NPCs) was no fun; his motor skills of hand–eye coordination were not yet adequate to compete with the computer in a race. Taking bends with mathematical accuracy, the NPC cars disappeared from sight almost immediately. However, it soon became apparent to Jo that his car was not restricted to the track, or its immediate borders, as is usually the case in racing games. Rather, the Sandy Bay track loops around a fully explorable island with a beach, a town, and mountains with no marked distinction in virtual friction between track and other surfaces (the latter a common device in racing games for guiding players on the game's preferred trajectory). The player can therefore leave the track and explore at will. From this revelation on, the game changed. It first became a game of exploration. Jo adopted a free-roaming, exploratory approach to the game, finding tunnels and tumbling down cliffs. Thus, as well as establishing constraints (of ability and experience) on the player, the software also offered different modes of play and facilitated alternate virtual activities and pleasures. Certain repetitive patterns of activity became apparent within this overall exploration, notably the ascent–descent game discussed earlier.

Games within Games

Though such vertiginous manoeuvres generally had little effect on the car/avatar, beyond a few bricks shed on particularly spectacular impacts, it soon became apparent that the car/avatar could be destroyed if driven or dropped into the sea. Usually "death" in a video game marks failure—temporary or terminal—and results in frustration for the player. However given that Jo's exploration had no set goal and the fact that the game was configured to allow infinite numbers of lives, this repeated death became a simple game in itself, one in which he delighted. Jo would begin with the car/avatar at the race start, then deliberately veer it off the track to pursue the shortest route into the sea and hence into momentary death. The car/avatar would then reappear instantly, in a swirl of stars reminiscent of graphic conventions from comics and cartoons of minor head injury. A new variation emerged. Jo found that driving the car slowly and carefully into the sea allowed a more nuanced experience of drowning than that offered by plunging off a cliff. The car could be directed into the water and gently nudged deeper, until, just before its uppermost point (usually the top of the driver's head) was submerged, it "drowned." The motive of this new game then was the identification of, and the edging around, the precise point at which the game switched between life and death. The cars lurched up the cliffs, teetered at a vertex where dwindling virtual momentum succumbs to the faint but insistent pull of virtual gravity, and fell back, slowly, bouncing down to the beach. Down here the drowning game was reenacted, the car and driver held over the drawn sea, hovering, descending, then emerging again. The video game world's liminal state between land/life and sea/death was, therefore, replayed out in an actual game environment, where the point of death (like the momentum/gravity vertex) was determined by an embodied articulation of video game kinesthetics.

On watching video footage of Jo playing (often attended and encouraged by his younger brother) it became clear that these improvised games were constituted by the complex interactions among the gameworld's physics; the affordances of software elements (notably those of the car/avatar); the transmedial suggestions and humor of this particular game (linking it to prior knowledge of the Lego franchise in its actual instantiations); and the characteristics of more traditional children's play with toys, notably the pleasures of exploration and creative destruction. For example, one of the game's funniest features is that if a car suffers a particularly powerful collision then virtual bricks will fall off it. Enough collisions and the car will eventually be stripped down to a chassis (with no apparent effect on its capabilities as a vehicle). One more crash, however, and (deliciously) the player is left with the "man" on his own to steer around the gameworld running delightfully on stiff little legs. We were all disappointed to find out, after much effort and experimentation with collisions and suicidal leaps into the path of non-player cars, that the game does not allow the man, as Jo put it, to further "break into two legs."

This feature offers visual pleasures (the familiar form of knee-less Lego legs are now more hilarious in their frantic animation) but it also highlights the operations of vehicular affordance in the game. It is an unusual and perhaps unique device. Games such as the *Tomb Raider* and the *Grand Theft Auto* series periodically encourage or require players to guide humanoid avatars into vehicles, shifting control from the manipulation of human-shaped capabilities to motor-vehicle-shaped capabilities. In these other games there are instrumental reasons for this (shape) shifting between different kinds of control/movement, and specific affordances are granted or denied as part of the design of the gameplay.

The visual pleasures made possible by the car-less driver and by Lara Croft as popular screen media characters are, in play, inseparable from their transmedial circuits (through films, toys, posters, advertisements), their playful–instrumental affordances in the gameworld, and their kinesthetic characteristics. A swift button press and Lara gracefully executes a somersault and roll, to face in the opposite direction, Uzis primed. Hold ↑ in Sandy Bay and the car-less driver runs as fast as his little legs will carry him. He lacks Lara's elegant knees, but each get where they/their drivers want to go.

Whilst noninstrumental in terms of progression through the game proper, the little game of playing with the car-less driver is still motivated by the specific nature and operations of game software and the pleasure they offer. Jo's delighted attempts to "break myself into a man" demonstrate, first, the potential of the video game to facilitate emergent play through possiblities and potentials embedded in the design rather than "rules." His subsequent attempts to "break myself into two legs" clearly highlight that these possibilities are not infinite (the software/ designers did not anticipate or facilitate the real-time configuration of a player with a full sense of the surreal possibilities of play with Lego). Second, this feature offers a micro-spectacle, a sudden change in a main character is (initially at least) hilarious and clearly linked to both the high-impact aesthetics of cartoon animation and to a familiarity with the connective/ destructive nature of actual Lego bricks. Third, the kinesthetic elements of the game (as a piece of software or virtual world) and its aesthetic elements (screen images of living toys in vivid environments) are inseparable; they are articulated in the moment at which Jo/Lego/man/car is broken into a man. The pleasure in running the little man up and down the mountains is, instantaneously and inseparably, a visual delight ("Look at him run!") and kinesthetic play (*feel* him run, feel the play between his response to ↑ and the resistance from the virtual gravity) (Giddings & Kennedy, 2007; Salen & Zimmerman, 2003).

Translations or Transformations—From the Video game to the Living-Room Floor

This cybertextual analysis begins to articulate the relationships between affordance and exploration that facilitate emergent and exploratory play in some video games. I will explain how these relationships and circuits loop out into the actual games with toys and paper mentioned earlier. Two key loops between the virtual and actual worlds that I will concentrate on here (in addition to the translation of the kinesthetics of virtual gravity and friction into an embodied kinesthetics of actual play already described) are the translations of distinct video game conventions (menu systems, e.g.) from the virtual to the actual; and, less obviously, how agency is translated between children, software, and other agents (both human and technological) (Latour, 1992).

Once they were familiar with the video game, the boys began incorporating and translating the videogameworld and its conventions into their off-screen play. My younger son, Alex, for example, adapted characteristics from the videogameworld into his own well-established ludic universe of playing with swimming creatures and dramas in the bathroom sink. In particular he developed the dramatic (and presumably psychic) possibilities of immersion: he had found another way to "drown" the car driver, fusing his ongoing fascination with toys and water with the video game-suggested event-horizon of life/death. Not only were the images and actions of the computer game being played out with real toys, but *the ways* the boys played with their actual Lego blocks was now quite different from how it had been before their experience of the computer game. The boys were not only continuing the game of racing Lego cars begun on the computer screen (its characters, scenarios, and dramas), they were also playing with actual Lego as if it *were* a video game. They were, on one level, *playing at playing a video game*. For instance, the actual Lego cars and drivers were constructed through a translation of the video game's menu-driven start-up processes.

Invited by the boys, not least because of the attention I was giving them, to join in their play (or rather, take direction from them), I was instructed to choose the cars and figures to be played with from a range they had built. Initially this choice was made as they were creating the vehicles, but later the process was repeated more formally, with cars and drivers neatly laid out on the table. The process of selection was incorporated into well-established patterns of their off-screen play: on-screen, no qualitative or quantitative value is placed on any selection, whilst in our living room the boys offered me a choice of two menus; each comprised of vehicles they had built individually. A familiar sibling/parent politics of attention-seeking and turn-taking was brought to bear: the eldest boy was most insistent, so his car was chosen first; his younger brother was keen to keep his menu in play though, asking, "later, can you choose this one?"

Initially I was able to observe these translations of agency because of the way I was positioned by the boys in relation to their actual game: I was not offered the chance to give any input into the design or construction of the actual cars (even for the one decision I was allowed—whether one driver should wear his baseball cap forward or backward—it was made clear to me that "backward" was a preferable choice). Clearly I was not the empowered agent, or so it seemed. However, from studying the video record it appears that my role in these games did prove instrumental to opening a whole complex of actions, choices, and translations arising from the peculiarities of the video game medium and its articulations or channeling of agencies. It became clear that an entirely unexpected set of shifting identifications and transformations were at play in these shifts from screen to living room and back.

As the boys careened across the floor, racing each other, crashing into and leaping over the mountains, I was instructed to "use the keyboard." I was expected to play the role of the "player," "clicking" (with my fingers on the arm of a chair or on a book) imaginary keys to make the Lego Racers go "forward!" and "faster and faster!." Of course my role was in some senses redundant—my finger movements had no influence on the direction or velocity of the Lego Racers (human or plastic)—yet the passion with which I was remonstrated when I stopped my performance indicated that this participation was, in some way, significant to them.

My role, then, was an apparently contradictory passive performance of interactivity. The video game dyad, the circuit between player and avatar, was simultaneously collapsed and expanded: the boys and their cars were the avatars "in the game," the agency of the player assimilated into the new boy/car/avatar and the residue (the empty performance of key pressing and looking on) displaced to another, "interpassive," body. The sheer complexity of these circuits, translations, and feedback loops was brought home to me with the following sequence of events: at the start of the actual game, once cars and drivers had been selected, Jo asked me to write my name ("D.A.D.D.Y.") on a piece of paper, a translation of the familiar entering of the player's name or nickname at the start of the video game.

This activity was consistent with my passive player role, but when I asked Jo why he wasn't writing his own name, he replied, hesitantly, "I don't have to . . . I'm the one who makes the Lego Racers go . . ." I tried to draw him on this, excited at the implications of this for theories of identification in video games. That is, Jo might be identifying himself (through role-play) directly with the computer or computer game rather than the characters, the Lego car, or man. He was not the player and so he didn't "sign in" but neither was he simply the "avatar." It is then the game itself, perhaps thought of as the game software or engine, that actually "makes the Lego Racers go." I asked Jo if he *was* the game, and he hesitantly answered "yes." I realized though that I was pushing him and that if he was "playing *as* the game" in the sense I suspected, he wasn't aware of it—at least not in the terms I was using. I stopped asking questions in this way.

For film studies, the concept of "identification" between (human) spectator/viewer and the screen text's (human) protagonists is frequently taken to be the key process by which spectators are positioned by, engage with, and make meaning of these texts (Metz, 1985; Mulvey, 1989). Game studies has drawn on these theoretical approaches to explore the relationship between the player and avatar. For some game studies scholars then, it is this process of identification that is key—and is perhaps even more significant given the player's "control" over their avatar (Lahti, 2003; Rehak, 2003). Yet, in this microethnography it becomes apparent that something more complicated is going on in the translation of the player's agency in the virtual world to the actual game. Jo, as "the one who makes the Lego Racers go," unselfconsciously adopted a play role that could not be mapped onto: the video game avatar (the Lego man/car), the actual toy Lego man/car, or the human player of the video game. The children's translation of the virtual game into actual space provokes a set of interesting questions: what does it mean to "identify" with the computer or with the processes of software? How does this identification operate if, as is apparent, it is not at the level of straightforward make-believe ("I'm a computer") or the product of cybercultural musings on the status of the relationship between human and computer? At the very least, the term identification tends to assume that a coherent, bounded subject can become identical with a coherent, bounded object. Jo's statement that he is "the one who makes the Lego racers go" strongly suggests that this identification is premised as much on the video game's material distribution of agencies and positioning of agents as in imaginative role-play or ideological interpellation and hence exceeds the concepts of identification and subjectivity.

So, Jo's refusal to write his name in the actual version of the video game's signing-in screen because he was "the one who makes the Lego Racers go" was not motivated by any mirroring identification with the computer or game-as-system. He was positioned or disposed by the game event's translations of agency of which he was an integral part. He had to be an agent, but not the player (delegated to another human component) or the avatar (he was still driving the car/driver avatar). The game is the only agent left. An imaginative event was, therefore, configured by a real relationship between agencies and entities. In the virtual game Jo was playing *with* the whole gameworld/system, in the actual game he was playing *as* the gameworld system, not one character within a screen fiction, but rather the whole universe that makes the Lego Racers go.

Conclusion

In this microethnographic study of boys' incorporation of features of computer video game play into their off-screen play, it became apparent that the established distinctions between the virtual and the actual across the diverse conceptual frameworks of new media studies are inadequate. Through play these boys shifted across these two spaces with ease, their play adapting to the different environments, environmental resources, and the capabilities and possibilities they afforded. The virtual space in this event of gameplay was neither an ideological illusion, nor a transcendence of the everyday and embodied. The virtual and the actual were each contained within the other, intertwining, each inflected by the other.

The virtual space of *Lego Racers 2* subjects its players to a range of simulated physical forces. Most notably, the boys quickly, and apparently unconsciously, acclimatized themselves to the effects and possibilities of weakened virtual gravity. The playful and vertiginous kinesthesia coded into the gameworld made new kinds of games possible within it (e.g., the repetition of ascent and descent, or the exploration of the cusp between the avatar's "life" and "death" in the sea) and outside it (through the transformations of play and movement between children's bodies, toys, and domestic space "suggested" by the gameworld).

Even in this small study, conventional notions of spectatorship or identification with screen characters are undermined. The shifting of players' identification with screen images is driven more by the demands of the various games in play here, than any sense of ideological investment by a subject positioned in relation to a fictional protagonist. These boys slip between a number of "identifications": being the virtual Lego men and being the virtual Lego car-driver dyad; being the constructors of these men and car-men; being at once the child playing with the actual Lego car-men, and coextensive with the car-men they are propelling around the room; being the player of a video game and being a meta-player (perhaps the computer or game-system itself) in an actual game. Other agencies are imaginatively displaced onto other human participants in the shift from play in virtual to actual worlds.

Reflecting on the findings of this little study, it became apparent to me that my "microethnography" is not just a variant of an existing set of methods, but rather that it facilitated, indeed necessitated, a more fundamental rethinking of the proper objects of ethnographic research. The micro-events and relationships identified here cannot be separated out into familiar dynamics or entities. It becomes clear, for example, that video game players are acted upon as much as they act, that they must work out what the machine wants them to do (or what it will allow them to do) as well as engage with it imaginatively. A key term to understanding children's play on and off-line is thus "agency" (rather than subjectivity), an agency that cannot be restricted to discussions only of the human participants. We must also inquire as to who or what the agents are in these circuits, and develop conceptual resources that can be called upon to allow new media studies to identity and study them. However, this emphasis on describing and theorizing the operations, agencies and effects of nonhuman partici-pants in children's video game play should not lead us to disregard concerns about human desires, anxieties, identifications, and investments as players in these media technocultural events. As we saw earlier in this chapter, the different games were spun into being through the tastes, personalities, and abilities—technicities—of the two boys as well as the material affordances of computer hardware and software simulacra (Dovey & Kennedy, 2006). If code and information must be understood as real, material, of the world, then so too can the intangible yet real, embodied yet distributed, mon-strous, operations of human factors—perception, imagination, creativity, anxiety, play—without always already reducing these to the reassuring sin-gularity of "identity" or "subjectivity." The multiple translations, varia-tions, and transformations of the Lego video game both on and off-screen that we have been examining in detail in this chapter, reminds us of the wide range of possibilities and the complexities in children's play and in the varying networks that facilitate but also shape that play.

References

Aarseth, E. (1997). *Cybertext: Perspectives on ergodic literature*. Maryland: The John Hopkins University Press.

Alloway, N. & Gilbert, P. (1998). Videogame culture: Playing with masculinity, violence and pleasure. In S. Howard (ed.), *Wired up: Young people and the elec-tronic media*, pp. 95–114. London: UCL Press.

Dovey, J. & Kennedy, H.W. (2006). *Game cultures: Computer games as new media*. Milton Keynes: Open University Press.

Facer, K., Sutherland, R., and Furlong, R. (2003). *Screenplay: Children and com-puting in the home*. London: Routledge.

Flynn, B. (2003). Geography of the digital hearth. *Information, Communication and Society*, 6(4), 551–576.

Friedman, T. (1995). *Making sense of software*. Retrieved June 11, 2000, from http://www.duke.edu/~tlove/simcity.htm.

Giddings, S. & Kennedy, H. (2007). Little Jesuses and fuck-off robots: On aesthetics, cybernetics and not being very good at *Lego Star Wars*. In M. Swalwell & J. Wilson (eds.), *Gameplay: Pleasures, engagements, aesthetics.* Jefferson NC: McFarland.

Green, B., Reid, J., & Bigum, C. (1998). Teaching the Nintendo generation? Children, computer culture and popular technologies. In S. Howard (ed.), *Wired up: Young people and the electronic media*, pp. 19–42. London: UCL Press.

Ito, M. (1998). Inhabiting multiple worlds: Making sense of SimCity 2000™ in the fifth dimension. In R. Davis-Floyd & J. Dumit (eds.), *Cyborg babies: From techno-sex to techno-tots*, pp. 301–316. London: Routledge.

Kinder, M. (1991). *Playing with power in movies, television and videogames: From Muppet Babies to Teenage Mutant Ninja Turtles.* Berkeley: University of California Press.

Kline, S., Dyer-Witheford, N., & de Peuter, G. (2003). *Digital play: The interaction of technology, culture and marketing.* Montreal: McGill-Queen's University Press. Lahti, M. (2003). As we become machines: Corporealized pleasures in videogames. In M. Wolf & B. Perron (eds.), *The videogame theory reader*, pp. 157–170. London: Routledge.

Latour, B. (1992). Where are the missing masses? The sociology of a few mundane artefacts. In W. Bijker & J. Law (eds.), *Shaping technology/Building society: Studies in sociotechnical change*, pp. 225–258. Cambridge MA: MIT Press.

Manovich, L. (2001). *The language of new media.* Cambridge MA: MIT Press.

McNamee, S. (1998). Youth, gender and videogames: Power and control in the home. In T. Skelton & G. Valentine (eds.), *Cool places: Geographies of youth cultures*, 195–206. London: Routledge.

Metz, C. (1985). *Psychoanalysis and cinema: The imaginary signifier.* London: Macmillan.

Morris, S. (2002). First-person shooters: A game apparatus. In G. King and T. Krzywinska (eds.), *ScreenPlay: Cinema/videogames/interfaces*, pp. 81–97. London: Wallflower.

Mulvey, L. (1989). *Visual and other pleasures.* London: Macmillan.

Rehak, B. (2003). Playing at being: Psychoanalysis and the avatar. In M. Wolf & B. Perron (eds.), *The videogame theory reader*, pp. 103–128. London: Routledge.

Salen, K. & Zimmerman, E. (2003). *The rules of play: Game design fundamentals.* Cambridge MA: MIT Press.

Sefton-Green, J. (2004). Rites: A small boy in a Poké-world. In J. Tobin (ed.), *Pikachu's global adventure: The rise and fall of Pokémon*, pp. 141–164. Durham: Duke University Press.

Walkerdine, V. (1999). Video replay: Families, film and fantasy. In S. Thornham (ed.), *Feminist film theory: A reader*, pp. 180–195. Edinburgh: Edinburgh University Press.

Wright, T., Boria, E., & Breidenbach, P. (2002). Creative player actions in FPS online videogames. *Playing Counter-Strike, Game Studies, 2*, 2. Retrieved July 9, 2004, from http://www.gamestudies.org/0202/.

CHAPTER THREE

Girls' Adoption of New Technologies

Sandra Weber, with Julia Weber

In too many places in the world, including parts of North America, there are girls and young women who do not have dependable access to food, shelter, and health care, let alone access to the internet (see Seiter, 2005 for concerns about this growing digital divide in North America and Livingston & Bober, 2004 in regards to the United Kingdom). For the more fortunate, everyday life increasingly includes a digital dimension, one in which various combinations of computers, cell phones, telephones, MP3 players, console and handheld games, portable DVD players, software, video, digital cameras, and so forth are part of daily experience (Ito, 2003). This technological cornucopia, however, seems to be part and parcel of a childhood that is nonetheless restricted (Buckingham, 2000).

Young people's movements are increasingly regulated, largely as a result of parental concerns about real or imagined dangers lurking out in the street, a panic that seems to center more on girls than on boys. The ever-increasing load of homework doled out by teachers also encourages young people, especially girls, to stay in. Consequently, when they are not being shuttled around to organized activities and lessons, many girls spend a lot of their after-school and weekend time in the domestic space of their homes (see chapter one for an in-depth discussion). This, of course, does not necessarily mean that they are under the supervision of their parents, many of whom work late hours. Being home alone, however, does not necessarily mean *feeling alone*: if she can find access to the internet, a girl can "hang out" with others in the public venues of cyberspace, as Julia does in the opening quote of this chapter (see also Danah Boyd, 2007 and chapter four in this volume).

In this age of increasing parental and public panics and pressures, how are girls coping? What does their digital engagement look like? Peek into many a residence, whether it be a house, apartment, flat, or townhouse, and what you are likely to see is girls actively engaging in a number of popular culture/media activities at once, participating in what Henry Jenkins (2006) calls a "convergence culture," blending new media forms with old. This chapter will examine important aspects of girls' digital culture by focusing in detail on a longitudinal case study I conducted in collaboration with Julia, my niece, whose adoption of digital media technology I observed from birth to age twelve (she is now sixteen). As a family member who is welcomed into her home, I have the kind of access and contextual knowledge that few ethnographers can achieve. Without being limited to the formal research protocols or institutional timelines that usually frame periods of observations in these kinds of studies, I am free to seize opportunities to observe her interactions with digital media as they occur naturally—a real advantage when documenting everyday experience is the goal.

Introducing the Study

Through a lens provided by Julia (who helped me write this chapter)[1] and her friends, I will examine girls' everyday "domestic" use of digital technology, tracing how it evolves over time as new technologies are introduced into the home. The case of Julia is a narrative report based on an initially informal "in-house" longitudinal ethnography that became slightly more formal and a lot more collaborative as Julia grew older and noticed that I was observing her intently.

Although I had been videotaping her since she was two years old, it was only when she was about five that I explained to Julia my desire to better understand digital girlhood, partially because my own girlhood was very analog and I was curious. She, in turn, seemed intrigued by my interest and somewhat surprised to learn that my university career could have something to do with her everyday life. As she grew older, we experimented with ways to document and reflect on Julia's digital world together, and we began including her friends because so much of her life involved them. Our collaboration resulted in activities such as videotaping, interviewing, writing, and, subsequently, making a brief documentary (Weber, Mak, & Weber, 2002). Writing this chapter enables us to further organize and reflect on her experience and work toward a shared understanding of it. All of this "life material" we collected (van Manen,

1990) gives rise to a sense of narrative and layered nuance that is conducive to a literary or storytelling genre of reporting as Julia and I try to give readers a feel for what her experience is like. What stands out about this research is the degree of child–adult collaboration and its longitudinal aspect—a rare chance to glimpse how children adapt to and take up evolving technology as they grow up online. Although the project tapered off by the time Julia was thirteen, in writing this chapter, we took into account the way media technology has evolved since then, especially in terms of cell phone use.

Julia: A Brief Digital History

Julia's Experiences of Media Technologies before Computers: The Study Begins

When Julia was born (in the 1990s), her older brother, Evan, was already four years old. By the time Julia was two, under his casual, unintentional tutelage, she was using the remote control for both the TV and VCR like a pro—she would blithely insert and then watch one taped episode after another of the ubiquitous purple dinosaur, *Barney*. As their godmother and aunt, I hung out with them often (and still do to this day). This "hanging out" gradually turned into a longitudinal case study of how they reacted and interacted with their increasingly technological world.[2]

I noticed, for example, that while her parents slept or cooked or worked elsewhere in the house, Julia spent a lot of time downstairs in the basement family room, drawing pictures or playing with other toys while her chosen show or video played, switching tapes or channels as she wished. For two-year-old Julia, changing television channels and playing and rewinding videotapes were as natural activities as filling a pail with sand in the backyard sandbox, just a normal part of toddlerhood and childhood—no big deal. Whenever she tired of watching, she would just walk away and ignore the screen as she played at something else, the television screen fading into some form of wallpaper or background "musak." This written snapshot of Julia and the TV/VCR contrasts starkly with her parents' memories of their own childhoods when the VCR was a very new gadget to be used by children only under adult supervision, if at all. And in my early childhood, there was no television whatsoever: it had just been invented.

Growing Up In Front of the Digital Camera

When Julia was two years old, the family computer had not yet arrived in their modest suburban household, although most of the neighbors on her street had at least one, and some even had two. The reason Evan and Julia had no home computer access at that time was partly financial, but parental convictions played a big role too. They had definite ideas about what children do and do not need to do, about how best to raise children, and about what they perceived as the advantages and disadvantages of home computers and other digital technologies. Consequently, it was the digital video camera more than the computer that had priority on Julia's parents' shopping list (especially for her mother who is an amateur photographer). Both children became used to living their lives in front of a video camera and watching the results afterward on the VCR—a visual record of family life they took for granted. By the time she had a cell phone and her own camera a few years later, the notion of casually snapping digital photos had become part of Julia's repertoire.

Digital Games Arrive in the Household: The Gender Gap Widens

Although there still was no computer in the house when Julia turned three, Nintendo Game Boy, and console video games had quickly become part of the entertainment available to the children in the family room, subject to rules and limits placed on the amount of time they could spend playing with them. Julia and Evan's parents felt that homework (Evan was already in school), socializing outside, organized sports, art, family time, and activities such as music lessons or drama club should be given priority over playing video games. This was initially disappointing to Evan who would have played forever if not chased off the console by his sister or parents. Julia would occasionally play *Nintendo* too, when she was able to get access—something that entailed a lot of nagging, pleading, and appealing to her parents when her brother was reluctant to give up control. At times, though, Evan was remarkably patient and cooperative with Julia (who is four years his junior), showing her how to play the games and watching her play in case she needed help (or perhaps simply waiting for her to tire so he could resume his play!). Although no one but Julia would likely have recognized it, there seemed to be an unspoken view in the family that video games were Evan's domain—a male activity, or at the very least, something for older children. Julia was certainly not encouraged to play video games. However, this did not stop her from spending hours upon hours *watching* her older brother and his friends play *Sonic, Super Mario*, and, a year or so later, *Pokémon* game-boy-to-game-boy tournaments, at which Evan became very adept. The older boys usually tolerated her presence with good humor as long as she did not disrupt the play, and occasionally, they even let her make suggestions or have a go.

When Julia managed to get the video game console to herself, she would sometimes half-heartedly play alone with *Barbie's Car* video game (borrowed for her because it's "a girl's game") or with her brother's discarded *Sonic* game, but the struggle to gain access didn't seem to interest her nearly as much as watching the more sophisticated play of the older boys did. Was all this watching a manifestation of stereotypical female passivity and acquiescence in the face of more powerful males? Or was it, as it appears to both Julia and me now in reviewing the videotapes I made of their play, more a matter of trying to learn game rules and strategies she had not yet mastered through careful observation from the sidelines? For many players of all ages, male and female, watching others is a normal part of learning how to play. As Dixon and Weber demonstrate in describing an episode involving a group gathered around a video game, watching attentively from the sidelines is one of several ways to actively participate in "gamer culture," and a great way to pick up useful moves or tips. Perhaps the desire to be with others was a factor as well. For Evan, video games were frequently a mode of hanging out with his friends who came over, something that was not yet happening for Julia. Whatever her reasons, she seemed to be making the best of the situation, turning disempowerment into a form of self-empowerment through learning, finding a way to be with the boys, to be part of the game.

Initial Contact with Computers

When Julia was three going on four, her father bought the eagerly awaited computer that soon challenged the television for dominance in the family room. The rationale for this purchase was to support the children's learning and schoolwork as well as to help Julia's parents organize their own work. Evan took to it almost instantly and intuitively, needing only a bit of demonstration and help from adults.

Deciding one day that she wanted to play with the computer too, Julia instinctively picked up the mouse, as if it were a TV remote control, and confidently pointed and clicked it at the computer, trying to turn the machine on by applying what she knew about remotes and VCRs—a lovely example of how even very young children transfer what they learn in one situation to another. When her brother demonstrated how to boot the computer and load games, Julia did not seem to be awed or intimidated. She simply started clicking away at will, calling on her brother and father for help whenever she was stuck. After overcoming the initial novelty of marveling at what the computer could do, and learning to deal with the frustrations of frequent crashes and glitches, Julia, like so many other children, began treating it as just another toy or machine—a normal part of her everyday life.

Julia's parents, on the other hand, were not so sure that that computer was "just another machine," which is partly why they waited longer than many North American suburbanites to buy one. They established some guidelines for their children to follow, especially after a computer virus wiped out their hard drive.

Initially, I did witness a fair amount of parental supervision, some of it in response to their children's frequent calls for technical help, some of it simply to ensure that the children weren't breaking anything. There was also an effort to teach them safe use of the internet. This consisted of making sure the children weren't spending too much time online, show-ing them how to avoid "adult" content sites and viruses, and warning them about the potential dangers of chatting with strangers. They also chose a service provider that offered the option to block out sites deemed unsuitable for children. As the children's expertise and confidence grew, quickly surpassing that of their parents, supervision diminished markedly. What hasn't diminished is Julia's interest in the computer. The older she gets, the more time she spends online, especially during the school year when she is indoors more often.

An Afternoon in the Digital Life of Julia

The following narrative is excerpted from the script for a documentary called *Digital Girls: Part 1. Julia*, which was based on interviews and observations of Julia and her family, especially those that took place as I videotaped Julia and a friend one afternoon when Julia was nine years old.[3]

> Julia's dad turns on the T.V. The man on the telly says parents better watch out. Perverts are lurking out there in cyberspace, waiting to pounce on unsuspecting young girls in chat rooms, ready to lure them out of the safety of their parents' homes with promises of candy, gifts, or adventure. Why, just look at what happened to that nice young girl in England who ran off to France with an American soldier! Julia's dad shakes his head.
>
> Upstairs, seated at the kitchen table, Julia's mom reads in the newspa-per that parents should not let their girls use computers unsupervised. They're wasting their time and not learning much. And who knows what kind of mischief they might get into, what with all that "porn" floating around and internet predators lurking. During an interview, Julia's mother seems unconcerned. She has given her daughter strict guidelines, she says.

What she doesn't mention (perhaps because she didn't realize it) is that their service provider's content filters and blocks that used to be active have been removed, and that, should they choose to use it, the children now have the same access to the web that their parents do.

For her part, when questioned about the dangers of chatting with strangers on the net, Julia adamantly shakes her head and says "I am NOT STUPID—no offence to the girls who were fooled and go to meet strangers they met online—I would never do such a thing. If someone tries to chat with me who I do not know, I don't answer and I block them immediately."

According to Julia's mum, Julia doesn't have much interest in computer game software (a claim Julia vehemently disputes, saying her mother just doesn't notice how often Julia uses her favourite software). Both agree that Julia's favourite uses of the computer these days are creating cards, writing original stories, poems and paintings, and chatting with her friends online using MSN text messaging—often all at the same time! Her mum worries that MSN is becoming addictive, interfering with homework, household chores, and family time.

(Aside: This parental nagging of Julia to get off the Net reminds me of being nagged to get off the telephone when I used to run home from school and immediately call up my friends to chat for hours.)

Meanwhile, Julia has brought the portable telephone into her bedroom so that she can chat with her friends in privacy. She invites one of them over to play videogames on the computer. Half an hour later, the two girls are seated alone downstairs at the computer, giggling as they simultaneously chat with several people on MSN while, at the same time, they design wallpaper or animate audio/video sequences using *Kid's Picks Deluxe 2*. The mouse gets handed back and forth whenever one or the other requests it, but there is clearly a "leader"—Julia. The television situated near the computer, is on, tuned to—*The Simpsons*. No one seems to be watching it. Julia also has a portable telephone nearby, and occasionally, uses it to call a friend with whom she is instant messaging. It was getting too frustrating to type out all that she wanted to tell her, she says. Her mouth was getting the job done faster than her fingers could (That soon began to change as Julia's keyboarding efficiency increased by leaps and bounds).

Later, after her friend has left, Julia shows me some of her favourite websites: these include *Neopets* and *My Scene*—two very different sites, the latter highly commercialized with mass consumer appeal to the stereotypical fashion tween. At nine, it wasn't so much the fashions or the urge to shop that motivated her visits to *My Scene* as much as it was the games and activities (dress up a doll, fill out a poll, decorate a bedroom) and the thrill of being "cool" or "grown up." It's where the cool girls go, she explained seriously. She also wanted to make it plain to me that she now loves to play videogames, both online, at whatever sites she visits, and especially off-line, for example, the Harry Potter CD ROM she received as a gift.

Three Years Later, Julia at Twelve

For a while when she was ten, Julia preferred to call herself JulZ, a very net-influenced spelling. By the time this book is in print, Julia will be a teenager who no longer plays *Harry Potter* and laughs affectionately at her younger self when reviewing those older video tapes. Her ideas of "cool" have changed too. While seemingly aware that she is being targeted as a potential consumer, she maintains that she is pretty much immune to the lure of fashion cool as she cruises the many websites to play games constructed for girls by advertisers of name-brand fashions. Her penchant for name-brand sportswear, running shoes, and the latest costume jewellery, however, might suggest otherwise. That the web is a major source of media advertising that targets young people's consuming habits is clear (Lindstrom & Seybold, 2004; Quart, 2003; Schor, 2004), and I am not as confident as Julia is that it does not affect her consumer taste and ambitions. But she says that although all the fashion media stuff is sometimes fun, it is also ridiculous, and she is not very much into being "all girly girly," as she puts it. In other words, she views herself as in control, an active agent rather than a dupe, yet at the same time freely takes pleasure in consuming "cool" (see, e.g., Kline, Dyer-Witheford, & de Peuter, 2003).

As Julia ages, I also note that she spends more time trawling online for information. She is an expert "Googler" who knows how to use Boolean code and so forth to delimit and narrow a search to find just what she wants. For example, while asking me to suggest artists whose work I thought she might like to research as part of a school project, Julia rapidly conducted web searches and downloaded information and images of the works of art I had in mind almost before I could mention them (we were standing near the computer, she wasn't even seated!). In other words, her use of digital technology evolves to reflect and fulfill her emerging needs and skills.

Another development in Julia and her friends' digital lives was their rapid creation and abandonment of websites, along with their growing desire for privacy from adult eyes. In the course of interviewing Julia and a group of her friends ranging in age from eleven to twelve, it quickly became evident that their individual websites served at least three purposes (see Weber & Mitchell, 2007 for an in-depth analysis of girls' website construction processes, and chapter ten in this volume):

1. *Communication and friendship:* Foreshadowing *Facebook*, which had not yet taken hold, the girls frequently modified their personal websites which they sometimes used as a means of communicating and keeping up to date with each other. They would admire each others' sites and take pleasure both in agreeing and disagreeing with each other on tastes in music and style. It seemed as if, from the girls' perspective, the sites formed a sort of cluster, a manifestation of their friendship-group. Now, almost four years later, this use of personal webpages has migrated to *Facebook*, which has become more central and permanent to their everyday way of expressing themselves and communicating with their friends. What is interesting to note here is how naturally Julia and her friends, like other young people, adopted and adapted whatever new formats, genres, and affordances became available. Their evolving tastes and needs, and a sense of what their peers deemed "cool" seemed to dictate the ways they modified their use of digital media.

2. *Public space as personal private diary:* It was also made very clear to me by the girls that there was a tacit expectation that parents and adults were not supposed to snoop and read or post on their site. In the girls' eyes, such behavior would be a violation of net etiquette. Adults should know better, they said! To the girls, even though their websites were there in public cyberspace, their sites constitute a private play or meeting space just for them (see chapter ten as well). They seldom voiced these implicit expectations to their parents however, more or less assuming that adults would treat the sites (if they indeed were even aware of them) like a diary, respecting the sanctity of the girls' privacy. I spoke to Julia about this again more recently, asking her if she posts with potential adult readers in mind. "No," she replied:

> It's not that I used to put things on my site that would shock anyone or that I would be really embarrassed about—but it's not for adults. If my mum went to my site, it would be sort of like—well, it's as if I were talking to my girlfriends in our basement and my mum suddenly appeared and started listening. It's not so much that we have something to hide, it's just that it would feel weird. We would either change the way we talk—or no—probably we'd go to my room to be private. Or like, if I was talking on a phone with my friend, it just wouldn't feel right if my mum picked up the extension and started eavesdropping. I would be really annoyed. You don't talk to your friends the same way you talk to adults, especially your parents.

This statement reflects young people's growing awareness of social codes, an acknowledgment that we adjust our communication to suit our audience.

3. *Expression of self, working through identities:* The girls take pride in standing out from each other, in making their own sites unique in some ways, even in terms of what they borrow from other sites. In reporting on research to investigate home-page use by another group of similarly aged young people, I suggest that through designing and posting on their own and each other's websites, young people create and post identities (see Weber & Mitchell, 2007). Choices of photos, images, music, links, fonts, formats, and wallpaper can all be viewed as representations of how the girls see themselves or how they might like others to see them (see Mazzarella, 2005, and chapter ten in this volume). In changing their posts frequently, they may be experimenting with self-image, trying on identities, although not necessarily consciously. Like all people, through their words and activities, they reveal aspects of themselves, even as they may try to conceal others.

Cell Phone Ambivalence and Digital Communication Preferences

While conducting a group interview about cell phones several years ago with five of the girls when they were age eleven, I noted that only two of them had phones. In comparison to today's tweens who have widespread access, cell phones were relatively late acquisitions for Julia's circle of friends, coming into their lives long after computers were part of their daily routine. In fact, some of them had MP3 players before they were given phones.

It was interesting to note that what the girls liked about the phones was not so much that they could be used to call someone (that was "old" technology), but rather that they could be used to send text messages as well as to take and view photos with the built-in digital cameras. This led to a discussion about consumerism and family attitudes toward children's material acquisitions. It turned out that most of these girls had overheard their parents on several occasions disparage other parents who "spoiled" their children by showering them with goods. Cell phones, at that time in Canada (a country very slow to adopt them), were a relatively new status symbol for pre-adolescents and teens, much less ubiquitous than they are now, a source of bragging rights in some circles, a source of embarrassment in others (embarrassment in terms of not wanting to seem spoiled or snobby). Nowadays, it is not so much whether or not you own a cell phone as *what kind* of cell phone you have, with Blackberries and I-phones currently commanding the highest status. It is no longer only the brand of footwear or jeans you wear that signify your worth in tween and teen circles, but also owning the latest in cool technologies. In other words, in addition to acting as tools used to market consumer goods to young people, digital devices have *in themselves* become objects of desire and signifiers of status and cool.

Cell Phone as Parental Care and Control

The parents of the "cell phone girls" worked outside the home and viewed the cell phone as a way to keep tabs on their children. As we saw in the earlier discussion, this gave the girls a handy explanation to justify their possession of this relatively new technology. However, in conversations with some of them a year later, it became clear that the girls had quickly caught on to the fact that although the phones gave them freedom to talk to their friends (only if their parents had prepaid for enough talk time), it also meant that they had to live under their parents' ever present "digital eye." Instead of giving them greater freedom, most of the girls said that the phones deprived them of opportunities to disappear from the radar, putting them more securely than ever under their parents' thumbs. One of the girls, however, pointed out that she felt she now had more freedom because her mother allowed her to go to places she would not normally have consented to before, confident that she could reach her daughter and her daughter could reach her. The cell phone thus seems to become a proxy for some parents, an extension of their care and presence sent out to accompany their children.

Cell Phone as Security

Linked with the earlier discussion of surveillance is concern about children's security. Some parents buy cell phones for their children in the hope that a phone will somehow keep them safe, or at least get them speedy help if they need it. Media hype about school shootings and kidnappings feed parental fears that their children are not safe outside the home. In this panic mode of thinking, a cell phone becomes a necessity, not a luxury or status symbol. Some children who I have interviewed in the context of another study told me that they too feel safer having a phone with them, even in relation to each other. One eleven-year old,

Jennifer, for example, told me that when a friend of hers unexpectedly had to walk home from school because her parents couldn't pick her up, Jennifer "accompanied" her home virtually by text messaging her back and forth all the way. The cell phone, she told me very earnestly, helps her keep track of her friends to make sure they are safe.

About a year after the initial cell phone interviews, when Julia was twelve, I asked her if she used her cell phone often. Her reply: "I never use it anymore—except to call my mum or to get calls from her. When I'm home I mainly use instant messaging to talk to my friends while I'm on the computer; it's faster and more convenient." Quite a turnaround from the nine year old who used to pick up a phone if she had a lot to say to her friends, because using MSN was too slow!

Skills and ease of use influence the extent to which people use technologies. But *affordance*, what you can actually do with the technology, is important too. As communication and media access continue to converge around the cell phone, it has become vital to Julia and her friends, now ages fifteen and sixteen. Young people who spend more time out in the community see a greater need to use the cell phone rather than the computer for their messaging. Its mobility makes it more practical. Studies done with teenagers in England, Finland, Japan, and Denmark suggest that for many of them, the cell phone is a precious object, one they decorate and value, almost an extension of themselves (see, e.g., Katz & Sugiyama, 2006; Weber & Mitchell, 2007).

Theorizing Julia's Experience: Further Close Interpretations

Julia's experience is of course her own, and not necessarily that of other children and tweens, particularly those whose material and/or social circumstances preclude access to digital technologies. Nonetheless, what this study points to are possible experiences and theoretical points of departure. As Holloway and Valentine (2003) point out, we need many detailed accounts of what children are actually doing in order to test the largely theoretical or survey-based research that dominates the field of children and technology. To conclude this chapter, I will discuss the major themes arising from this longitudinal study, which may contribute to a deeper understanding of young people's experiences of technologies.

Multitasking and Relating to Peers through Cyberspace is the "New Normal"?

As Julia's story illustrates, many young people are growing up in what Kline, Dyer-Witheford, and de Peuter (2003) call "media saturated households," ones in which children come to expect, as a matter of course, that there will be an ever-changing succession of new technologies, which they integrate into their everyday activities. The often-fluid interactions and adaptations that we saw in Julia's reactions to digital technologies as they were introduced into her life over the years give us cause to critique views that online and off-line worlds, or modes of being, are discrete and that digital technology is somehow more foreign or artificial than other toys and machines. Julia's story lends support to research done by Plowman (2004, 2005), validating the claim that digital and non-digital toys and modes of interaction have a lot more in common than we realize, and that children have unique ways of adapting, subverting, and integrating technologies to suit their own play and communicative purposes. Julia's initiation into the culture of convergence, described by Jenkins (2006), seemed to her, in her own words "just a normal part of growing up."

The older Julia becomes, the more computer time is devoted to instant messaging her friends while simultaneously cruising the web to find information for homework or looking for cool websites to share and discuss via MSN with her friends. At the same time, she often has a Microsoft Word window open to work on an assignment. She may also be downloading music onto her computer (often when Evan is the user) with the television on as a background media input. In the same way that previous generations of parents (e.g., Julia's grandparents) would shake their heads in confusion while watching their children doing homework in front of the television or studying for exams with a stereo blaring, Julia's parents shake their heads in amazement as they watch this multitasking evolve.

What to make of all this concurrent activity? Is this behavior evidence of cognitive dissonance or inability to concentrate? Or are children like Julia creatively enacting their own version of media convergence—integrating functions and tasks even before new technology has brought these different media together digitally and before their parents or teachers have mastered these nonlinear ways of learning and doing? Do meanings change in the unique and ever-changing juxtapositions that result as they juggle and move back and forth between one media message and another? How might all this "digital dancing" be reshaping the nature of girlhood? Even if their digitally rewired brain cannot multitask as efficiently as young people may think, there is also the possibility that while they are busy multitasking, young people cannot be so easily duped or become too absorbed in any one popular media or content, since their attention is simultaneously focused on other content. This phenomenon of multitask learning and production requires more research, but research doesn't dictate behavior. My speculation is that young people crave efficiency and will naturally do whatever seems fastest and easiest. A further update from Julia as this book went to press illustrates that what is fastest and easiest does not always and necessarily involve multitasking. "I don't use MSN any more, and I don't have a million windows open at the same time the way I used to. I now find it easier just to text or call my friends."

Gender Issues: Access, Preferences, and Styles of Using Technology

Scholars such as Seiter (2005) and Goldstein, Buckingham, and Brougére (2004), and Dixon and Weber in this volume discuss how digital media are transforming playspaces. And, as is only hinted at in Julia's story, these playspaces like all social spaces are gendered. Mitchell and Reid-Walsh (2002) explore the notion of digital "bedroom culture" demonstrating, among other things, the complex ways in which girls treat the public arena of the net as an extension of their private "bedroom" spaces. For Julia, this cyber bedroom is *not* in her actual bedroom in the same way that her parents and Evan have TV and video game technology in their physical bedrooms. Everyone must go into the family room to use the computer. It is important to remember that this room (and hence the computer) is in *the basement*, not in the kitchen, or living room, or dining room on the main floor of the house. Seldom is the whole family down there at once. For Julia and the other members of the household, having the computer in the basement means that it has to somehow function as a private space within the more public space of a common family room. All these private/public, individual/family functions are fluid—the privacy of a digital bedroom (which is a psychological and existential sort of privacy within the paradoxical very public open realm of the internet) can quickly turn into a shared family activity, and a once-shared activity can live on as a private one. But, as we saw in the girls' reactions to adult visitors on their personal sites, privacy and rules of online conduct have to be negotiated, either tacitly or explicitly, with results not always to girls' satisfaction.

Despite learning to use technology in the shadow of her older brother, Julia never viewed the technology itself as "not for girls," even though accessing the computer did (and sometimes still does) require a certain amount of assertive negotiations with a parent or brother. This necessity to fight for time and control seemed to be empowering in an odd sort of way, fostering Julia's emergence as a formidable debater who now defends her rights very ably. It is interesting to note, however, that her brother seldom had to argue for online access, perhaps not so much because he is a boy, but that he is older and appears more compliant than his vociferous younger sibling. What made matters more unfair, in Julia's eyes, is that Evan was given a television, game console, and DVD player for his own bedroom. He can quietly retire there (which he often does) to make whatever use he wishes of the technology—except for the internet, which is still only accessible in the family basement room; a significant caveat.

Many of the different uses Julia and Evan have made of technology conform to the sorts of gender differences already noted by scholars such as Cassell and Jenkins (2000). Evan prefers games that involve competition, puzzle solving, strategies, and combat-style rapid action. Julia is more attracted to games and sites that involve creative drawing and designing, storylines, chat, and nurturing or caring for animals. But there is also a lot of gender convergence. Like Evan, Julia enjoys games of logic and puzzle solving. And like her brother, she loves *The Simpsons* and *Survivor*, a reality show that actually became an integral part of family time for a couple of years—everyone snuggled on the king-sized bed in their parents' bedroom to watch the show together (see Christensen, James, & Jenks, 2001; Papert, 1996).

Technology as Extension of Self and Control of Presentation of Self

Perhaps more than anything else, the role of digital technology in Julia's life seems to amplify or help her actualize who she is. She uses it not so much to isolate herself from the world, as to socialize in a way that is comfortable for her. One of Julia's most constant uses of the internet was for instant messaging, a form of communication that allows her, when she feels like it, to change her username as often as she changes her clothes. This allows her to control who she interacts with (usernames not on her chat list are blocked and she can remove or add people as she likes to her chat list) and facilitates or mediates a playfulness in how she presents herself. According to Thiel (2005), tweens typically engage in messaging, name-changing, and playing out identities online—Julia is not unique in her activities.

The tentative ways that Julia both critiques yet also lingers or indulges in the "girly" online sites that feature the pleasures of dress, fashion, and rites of heteronormative womanhood seem to indicate that she is feeling out, playing with, or testing possible grown-up female identities. As Driscoll (2002) points out, however, this playing with identity through popular culture that may initially seem so empowering to girls could easily give way to a re-inscription of more stereotypical dominant discourses of beauty and femininity that tend to be confining and passive.

While boys are busy gaming and being targeted by game developers whose products seem to be designed to try to perpetuate macho, misogynist, and patriarchal stereotypes, girls are visiting an increasing number of commercially sponsored websites, such as myscene.com or www.gurls. com, where empowering messages may be encoded surreptitiously in conservative clothing. More often than not, cultural reproduction is disguised as radical chic.

Whatever else she does online, Julia's chief use of the internet remains to communicate and hang out with her friends. The importance of the computer to Julia's daily life is possibly best summed up by the following conversation we had when she was only nine:

> *Sandra:* "If for some reason you absolutely had to give up either the television or the computer, which one would you give up? I know you wouldn't want to do without either of them, but if you had no choice and had to let one go . . . ?"
>
> *Julia:* (Groan, hand goes to forehead, long pause.) "That is REALLY hard . . . but if I had to, I guess I would give up the television."

The fact that media technologies are continually evolving and enabling us to do a variety of things in different ways seems for Julia, who was born at the cusp of the emergence of digital childhood, just a normal, taken-for-granted aspect of life—nothing that would warrant a collection such as this book!

Notes

1. There is no way I could adequately express my appreciation to Julia, her parents, her brother Evan, and her friends for allowing me such candid and free access to their digital lives. You guys are the best!
2. Part of this research was funded by the Social Sciences and Humanities Research Council of Canada. I am very grateful to them for their ongoing support.
3. A fourteen-minute video, *Digital Girls: Part I. Julia*, documents much of the information presented here. The video is described, and eventually will be accessible online at www.iirc.mcgill.ca.

References

Boyd, D. (2007). Why youth (Heart) social network sites: The role of networked publics in teenage social life. In D. Buckingham (ed.), *Youth identity and digital media.* MacArthur Series on Learning and Media (pp.119–142). Cambridge: M.I.T Press.

Buckingham, D. (2000). *After the death of childhood: Growing up in the age of electronic media.* Cambridge: Polity Press.

Cassell, J. & Jenkins, H. (eds.) (2000). *From Barbie to Mortal Kombat: Gender and computer games.* Cambridge & London: MIT Press.

Christensen, P., James, A., & Jenks, C. (2001). Home and movements: Children constructing "family time." In S.L. Holloway and G. Valentine (eds.), *Children's geographies: Playing, living, learning.* London: Routledge. pp. 139–155.

Driscoll, C. (2002). *Girls: Feminine adolescence in popular culture and cultural theory.* New York: Columbia University Press.

Goldstein, J., Buckingham, D., & Brougére, G. (eds.) (2004). *Toys, games, and media.* New Jersey & London: Lawrence Erlbaum Associates.

Griffiths, V. (1995). *Adolescent girls and their friends: A feminist ethnography.*

Holloway, S. & Valentine, G. (2003). *Cyberkids: Children in the information age.* London: Routledge.

Ito, M. (2003). *Intertextual Enterprises: Writing alternative places and meanings in the media mixed networks of Yugioh.* Retrieved September 2004 from http://www.itofisher.com/mito/publications.html.

Jenkins, H. (2006). *Convergence culture: Where old and new media collide.* New York & London: New York University Press.

Katz, J. & Sugiyama, S. (2006). Mobile phones as fashion statements: Evidence from surveys in Japan and the US. *New Media and Society, 8*(2), 321–337.

Kline, S., Dyer-Witheford, D., & de Peuter, G. (2003). *Digital Play: The interaction of technology, culture and marketing.* Montreal: McGill-Queens University Press.

Lindstrom, M. & Seybold, P.B. (2004). *Brand Child: Remarkable insights into the minds of today's global kids and their relationship with brands.* London: Kogan Page.

Livingstone, S. & Bober, M. (2004). *UK Children go online: Surveying the experiences of young people and their parents.* London: London School of Economics and Political Science.

Livingston, S. & Drotner, K. (eds.) (Forthcoming). *International handbook of children, media, and culture.*

Mazzarella, S.R. (ed.) (2005). *Girlwide Web: Girls, the internet, and the negotiation of identity.* New York: Peter Lang.

Mitchell, C. & Reid-Walsh, J. (2002). *Researching children's popular culture: The cultural spaces of childhood.* London & New York: Taylor and Francis, Routlege.

Papert, S. (1996). *The connected family. Bridging the digital generation gap.* Atlanta: Longstreet Press.

Plowman, L. (2004). "Hey, hey, hey! It's time to play." Exploring and mapping children's interactions with "smart" toys. In Goldstein, Buckingham, & Brougeres (eds.), *Toys, Games and Media,* pp. 207–223.

Plowman, L. (2005). Getting the story straight: The role of narrative in teaching and learning with interactive media. In P. Gardenfors & P. Johansson (eds.), *Cognition, Education and Communication Technology*, pp. 55–76. Mahwah, NJ: Lawrence Erlbaum.

Schor, J. (2004). *Born to Buy*. New York: Scribner.

Seiter, E. (2005). *The internet playground: children's access, entertainment, and mis-education.* New York: Peter Lang.

Thiel, S.M. (2005). 'I'm me' identity construction and gender negotiation in the world of adolescent girls and instant messaging. In S.R. Mazzerella (ed.), *Girlwide web: Girls, the internet and the negotiation of identity.* pp. 179–202. New York: Peter Lang.

Van Manen, M. (1990). *Researching lived experience: Human science for an action sensitive pedagogy.* London & Ontario: Althouse Press.

Weber, S. & Mak, M. (2004). *Digital girls. Part one: Just Julia.* 24-minute DV CAM video. Directed by S. Weber & M. Mak. Based on research by S. Weber & J. Weber. Taffeta Productions, Montreal.

Weber, S. & Mitchell, C. (2007). Imaging, keyboarding, and posting identities: young people and new technologies. In D. Buckingham (ed.), *Youth identity and digital media,* pp. 25–47. MacArthur Series on Learning and Media. Boston: M.I.T. Press.

CHAPTER FOUR

The Girls' Room: Negotiating Schoolyard Friendships Online

Kelly Boudreau

Introduction

After a day spent sitting in classrooms, taking notes, gossiping in the school bathroom ("the girls' room"), and dishing about "top styles" in the hallways, there is little for a girl to do but meet up with her friends after school to relive it all over again! Whether at the local soda shop in the 1950s or the neighborhood mall in the 1980s, for generations (Bernard, 1961; Childress, 2004) girls have regrouped after school to chat, hang out, and feel a sense of belonging among their peers. So where are girls meeting after school today? For a group of junior high-school girls who attend a Montreal alternative school, online is the new mall. As the girls get off the city bus and walk through their front doors, you can imagine them all hurriedly throwing off their knapsacks, tossing their lunch bags in the kitchen, and rushing to turn on their computers as they settle into an afternoon of music, homework, and catching up on the latest daily news.

For these city girls, after-school social interactions occur primarily online in the *Girls' Room*, a message board website they created collectively. This cyberspace offers teens a sense of freedom from the highly scheduled leisure time that often characterizes their postmodern childhoods (Dixon, 2004). In this space, they can interact with their peers at virtually any time of the day or evening from their own homes. Cyberspace offers a place where they are in control of their activities, often multitasking homework, talking to their friends, and surfing various websites. How does this new social space shape group dynamics in their daily lives? What impact, if any, do their online interactions have on their schoolyard friendships? This chapter examines the experience of a group of teenage girls who share a forum website. Drawing on the girls' postings and the comments they made during interviews, I will describe how they negotiate their schoolyard friendships in a networked world and reflect on the broader implications of their experience. I will also compare message boards to instant messaging systems in order to evaluate the differing contexts these communication tools provide for teens. Finally, this chapter will position the analysis of girls' digital social experience in the larger spectrum of literature on contemporary networked girlhood by touching on some of the dominant threads that appear concerning the digital nature of contemporary adolescence and girlhood. These include: technology as a tool of empowerment for girls (Maczewski, 2002; Shade, 2002); the internet as a space for self-discovery and as a testing ground for identity (Gross, 2004; Turkle, 1995; Valkenburg, Schouten, & Peter, 2005); and how the internet provides social circles for girls who might not otherwise have access to them in their "everyday lives" whether resulting from rural isolation or shyness (Convertino, 2002; Maczewski, 2002).

Description of the Study

This research was inspired by one of my daughter's typical homework sessions in which a group of her school friends came to our house to work on a science fair project. Since our home computer space is in the living room and consists of three computers grouped together, the girls were able to conduct individual research and still chatter together. They discussed the information they were finding and what might be best for the project as a whole. One of the most interesting observations I made while watching the girls work collectively was that each of them kept clicking on the same forum website, skimming the titles of the threads and looking for any new posts on the site. When I asked the girls what they were doing, they explained to me that it was a website that they had created and posted to regularly. The site, they explained, centered on their daily school activities, both formal and social. Interestingly, although the girls were in the same room, they posted quietly to the message board. After they posted, they would wait for each other to reply so that they could read the active thread while interacting with other friends who were not in the room or online at the time.

Shortly afterward, I contacted five of the girls who actively participated on the forums (age thirteen–fourteen), including its technical creator, inviting them individually to engage in informal interviews that could be characterized as casual conversations. These guided conversations included discussion of schoolyard and hallway activities, how the girls felt about their social circles during school hours, and any other school-related conversation they felt was relevant to their forum discussions. Each member also took part in three unstructured group conversations. Due to the fact that the girls were personal friends of my daughter, access and rapport had already been established; therefore, the conversations were relatively open and direct as the girls were eager to discuss what their website meant to them and how they felt it impacted their daily interactions during school hours. This "snowball" method is commonly used in small ethnographic studies (Hines, 2005; Merchant, 2001), because it poses significant benefits such as instilling a level of comfort from the respondents that would not otherwise be there in a random sample environment. Since each respondent is referred by another, the snowball method usually begins with a description of the research, and interview process, creating a form of rapport prior to the initial research. However, this method also presents potential ethical issues such as the ambiguity of informed consent during casual conversations (Platt, 1981).

I addressed this challenge by posting a notice on the message boards explaining my research, in order to gain permission to passively observe the girls' online interaction. Each girl who participated on the message boards were asked to post whether they agreed to be observed or not in order to respect the privacy of their online space (Jacobson, 1999). Parents were also informed of both the interviews and online observations. I collected observational data by spending four weeks reading the website's content twice a day for a total of fifty-six viewings. I then printed and coded the content for various elements, including length of the active threads based on how many posts were in one discussion, amount of views or "hits" per thread, and frequency of posting per member. This allowed me to map the social hierarchy found on the message boards. This data was then compared with their perceived social status during school hours to see if there was a difference between face-to-face and online interactions among the same group of girls. The goal of this comparison was to understand how the girl's physical social space impacted their online social space and vice versa.

From the Schoolyard to the *Girls' Room*

Montreal, an urban center with a population of almost 3.5 million people,[1] is an active city with its fair share of malls, coffee shops, and parks. Yet, the most common meeting place for this group of girls after school is not found in the urban planning of the city, but rather, online, at an undisclosed World Wide Web address shared only with its participants. The local fine arts school that the girls attend extends geographically beyond a traditional school district; therefore, students live anywhere from a five-minute walk to a two-hour drive away from each other. This makes it difficult for many students to get together spontaneously, outside of school hours without having coordinated their social time with their parents' schedules. The internet seems the most convenient place for these girls, and teens in general, to congregate after school hours. As Grinter and Palen (2002) iterate, "logging in after school [offers] continuity to the day's events" (p. 24).

School days are filled with a variety of classes, and as a result the girls only see each other briefly in passing. Morning breaks are usually rushed, as they run between floors to get their books for the next class. During those five minutes at their lockers, the girls talk hurriedly to each other, trying to squeeze thirty minutes of talk into five. Lunchtimes are often crowded with extracurricular activities that have the girls running off in different directions. Molly described a day where she barely had a chance to drop off her books in her locker, ate while she ran up the stairs to the music room, and had violin rehearsals during dinner time.

Molly: "Sometimes I really hate having to run around all day its like . . . um, like never having much time to talk to my friends really . . . I mean, I like playing the violin, but we always have to practice at lunchtime . . . that's the part I really don't like since I miss out on everything at lunch you know?"

However, this frustration at missing out on the day's lunchtime conversation is short lived. As Molly tells me about the *Girls' Room*:

Molly: "That's one of the reasons why we started the Girls' Room you know . . . I can log on when I get home and read what I missed at lunch. It's cool—even though I wasn't there, I can still chat about it later after I've read the threads and catch up on who said what and stuff you know?"

After arriving home and settling in, each girl turns on her computer and logs into instant messenger. Several chat windows later, the girls are catching up with each other, detailing their days' events in real time. Typical for this age group, instant messaging among peers is the primary mode of digital communication (Tyler, 2002). Conversations are often informal, and used to make social plans for later. Much like the chatter in the hallways and over phone lines, instant messaging is often fast and light (Boneva et al., 2006). Yet for these five girls, instant messaging is only one of their online spaces for after-school socializing. They prefer to spend most of their time logged into the *Girls' Room*. Although they cannot chat in real time through the message boards, something they are able to do via instant messaging, they can nonetheless see if there are other registered users on at the same time.

Inclusion through Language

Perhaps not so surprising in a bilingual city where the majority language is French, the content of the message boards is completely in French, even though all of the girls participating in the study speak mainly in English at home and could just as easily have conducted the forum in English. When asked about the choice of language for the boards, the girls explained that for the most part, they do not really think about what language they are using, they just *write*. Since they speak French at school all day, it seems like a natural extension of their day to continue in that language. Moreover, by communicating in French on the message boards, the girls open up the possibility for their French-speaking peers who are not a part of their group of friends to visit the *Girls' Room* website and add their comments to the discussions too. This demonstrates the girls desire to have students outside their immediate friendship circle participate in their online sociality.

Creating the Girls' Room Site

What made the *Girls' Room* special, was not only the fact that the girls could communicate with each other after school without being online at the same time, catering to each one's different schedule, but also that it was a space that they had created together. Unlike many websites with topics and images determined by market researchers, or sites with a corporate agenda on which teens reportedly are spending most of their time (Duncan & Leander, 2000), the site's content was not readymade. Nor did it fall under the category of "personal homepages," which are often seen as spaces that teens create to explore their identities through text, images, and links (Stern, 2004). Instead, the *Girls' Room* was a space that was solely dedicated to their own group interests.

Like a custom designed house, the colors and the layout for the *Girls' Room* were carefully selected collectively by the girls. From color scheme to content, there were no unwanted pixels infringing on the girls' collective experience. They boast proudly that they created the website themselves. Although the site follows a standard message board style,[2] following a predetermined process for selecting and uploading the colours and layout, font, and so on, Sarah[3] tells me that they worked hard to make sure their site looked different from the more common boxy ones with only two colors. They wanted something that reflected not only who they were as a group, but also the distinct tastes of each of the girls. During one of our group conversations, the girls chimed in that this "collective identity" (my words, not theirs) was important given that during school hours, they often felt they didn't stand out—sometimes feeling "lost in the crowd." Jenn and Molly put it this way:

> *Molly:* "Sometimes, there is just so much going on . . ."
> *Jenn:* (Interrupting Molly) "Ya! There are always so many people around . . . the hallways are always so crowded! With the Girls' Room, it's just nice to know that we are the only ones there—that
> *Molly:* (Interrupting Jenn) "That we are the ones everyone wants to hang out with when they come to our site . . . not like we have to fight for everyone to hear us like at school."

After they determined what colors they wanted—deciding on a monochromatic blue scheme to contrast the white and grey walls of their school's hallways—and inserted selected photographs found online of old schools, they created the individual discussion threads. Besides the obligatory public forum that allowed visitors to pop in and post their hellos, the majority of the site consists of private, registration-required, permanent threads. There is a thread for tutoring and homework help, a thread discussing various teachers, and another discussing rumors and highlights of the day. Here, the girls feel free to post what they really thought, instead of feeling the need to be guarded as they often do during conversations in school hallways, fearing intrusion might be right around the corner. Sarah, the site administrator, has sole moderating privileges. Luckily for Sarah, she is not often in a position where she has to intervene and has thus far only interceded a couple of times. For the most part, those who post are relatively respectful of others, which is sometimes difficult to do when dishing on the girl who was seen holding hands with the boy you have a crush on.

Conversations posted within the threads on the message boards offer the girls an opportunity to bond outside of school hours, preparing them for the day ahead. For Sarah, her digital aptitude awarded her a recognition that she may not have otherwise received, boosting her schoolyard social status. Schoolmates who had heard of the *Girls' Room* over the semester were curious about the site, its creation, and its content, often stopping by the public threads to say hello and offer a contribution to the site.

Working Out Social Hierarchies

Although not part of the "popular" crowd, the girls know everyone in their grade from sharing classes, working on class projects, and theater productions together. Sometimes, they sit with other classmates in the cafeteria, or share space with them on the lawn on the campus next to school, but the hierarchical social lines are visibly drawn out nonetheless. The girls still fall victim to rumors and snickers on the schoolyard or in the hallways. Always hearing the chatter but never quite making out the words, the girls are sometimes excluded from schoolyard news. For them, the *Girls' Room* provides a place to utter their own whispers. During the interviews, the girls suggested that by posting on their own site, they have some sort of control over how much they let the whispering bother them. In some ways they feel empowered by the site forum because the typed words make their reactions seem more permanent than face-to-face interactions can, and stand to remind them of what they had felt and said about any given topic, on any given day.

Building Community and Group Identity

If "popularity of IM among teens is a result of their need to socialize while confined to their homes" (Boneva et al., 2006), then the drive to participate in an asynchronous forum could be a result of a desire to feel part of a community. This sense of community is often possible even when no one else is online after school. While most urban teens' time is regulated by parents, responsibilities, and other controlling factors, online activities and conversations are rarely monitored, despite all the media hype about the dangers.

Unlike instant messaging, online message boards allow adolescents to communicate one-to-many—from themselves to the readers of the boards, while maintaining a sense of one-to-one communication. Posting in asynchronous time while others are off-line is a more solitary experience. This means of communication, as opposed to chatting in real time via instant messages, offers the individual time to reflect on their post, correct it, and contemplate what it is they want to say, how they want to say it, and so on. The opportunity for reflective communication has the potential to deepen the content of the posts, enabling the girls to feel that they are adding to more than just a random, topical thread. In a sense, they are writing a sort of collective online journal that intertwines each girl's daily physical and emotional lives. If we look at instant messaging with friends as an extension of face-to-face conversations, then message board participation in a stable online environment can be seen as a form of interactive narrative creation. However, what is the result of such interactive (re)creation of events? And how does the permanence of the content posted online affect the girls' social life at school?

According to Boneva et al. (2006), "IM boosts adolescent's group identity and is so popular because it simulates spending time with an offline group of friends, without the rigidity of the acceptance rules of adolescent offline peer groups" (p. 613). If instant messaging boosts adolescent's group identity, one can speculate that message board participation, which carries an element of permanence, reinforces such collective identity. This in turn enhances a girls' sense of belonging to a real-life peer group, such as those found among the members of the Girls' Room.

Building Community
In many ways, a message board creates a sense of community through its permanence, and because the girls who interact on the board must be members. It occupies a fixed space; a location with an address that the girls can repeatedly visit, hang out in, and where they can leave their mark. Scholars (Boneva et al., 2006; Bryant, Sanders-Jackson, & Smallwood, 2006) have suggested that buddy lists function as communities. I would suggest that message boards are even more highly developed communities. IM buddy lists are unique and individual to each girl while the membership list to a message board is the same for everyone on the list, and although conversations in instant messaging are archived, they are not accessible collectively between "buddies." Another differentiating element is that a message board can be stumbled upon on someone's journey through cyberspace—an instant message cannot; the result of this is that people outside the original group of girls can be drawn in to join their community, whereas Instant Messenger buddy lists are added to strictly by direct social relationships.

The larger significance of the *Girls' Room* is that what began for the girls as a place to continue the day's socializing and chat about the day's events inadvertently has become a space that gives them a sense of belonging, a belonging they did not find solely through their schoolyard conversations and face-to-face interactions. The *Girls' Room* has become a virtual community of sorts where they can discuss things about school that they might not otherwise do face-to-face, between friends and across schoolyard social cliques.

The Permanence of Posting:
A Double-Edged Sword

The girls enjoyed divulging their more articulated thoughts on the forums to me. However, they soon realized that the writing they were engaged in was not solely a one-way stream of communication. What was said on the message boards, unlike an instant message session, was permanent. The threads could be visited and revisited and past words rehashed and remembered, even brought to life again. This was not without consequence as is demonstrated by the following account of Jenn's experience.

Jenn told me of an incident where she learned the hard way that there are different consequences to chatting about peers online as opposed to talking about them in passing conversation. She told me what happened to make her think twice about what she posted:

Jenn: "When it happened, at first, I didn't think much of it . . . I mean, we all say things we don't mean and stuff, I mean, its like . . . well, one day we were all hanging out on the message boards, it was a Saturday I think, cause we weren't at school that day . . . anyways . . . we were all talking about this one girl cause she was starting to change her look you know?
. . .
So ya, some of us weren't being very nice about it, kind of making fun of her but not to be mean, but you know . . . just kinda talking about how she dressed more . . . older and stuff and sometimes it was just funny. We kinda forgot about it and talked about other stuff—boys and stuff you know?
. . .
But the week after that, at school, things weren't going so well one day I can't remember what it was about really . . . probably something at lunchtime. But I got into an argument with one of the girls who hang out in the Girls' Room with us and I cant remember why, what it was . . . but some of the girls took her side, and then when I got home from school there was a few mean emails in my email . . . I didn't know why, but some of the girls sent the girl from school my posts from the thread from the weekend—you know, the one where we were making fun of that girl and her new style and stuff . . . and I couldn't believe it, I mean we were all saying stuff that day, but that's not what it looked like you know?"

Although the rest of the girls had also "dished" and Jenn's comment was made in context of the larger conversation, someone vengefully singled out her particular message and passed it on.

Since a viewer must be registered to read and post on the forums, the person they were talking about did not have access to the entire thread, therefore absolving the other girls of responsibility for the words they too had posted. It was then, Jenn tells me, that she realized that she had to be a bit more diplomatic when ranting online. She learned that what happened online had social repercussions in the schoolyard.

Interpretations and Implications

Where does this study fit into the larger scope of literature on the internet as a social space for connected teens, and girls in particular? What are the sociological implications for girls' online interactions in terms of their impact on their everyday lives? While early literature often defined the internet as an isolating social space (Kiesler et al., 1998; Sanders et al., 2000), it is becoming apparent that online social interactions do not necessarily replace "real life"[4] interactions with friends and family, but complement them. As the *Girls' Room* demonstrates, the internet can engender a deeper sense of belonging among peers in a real life setting.

The task of defining the boundaries and terms of online communities and determining whether they are to be perceived as "real" communities or not (Matei, 2005; Rheingold, 2000; Ward, 1999) is quickly becoming more and more complex. As the *Girls' Room* demonstrates, digital technologies, the internet, and the spaces created there are interwoven into individuals' daily lives. When technologies strengthen and reinforce social relationships that originate on- or off-line, they foster a sense of belonging among peers and create community. In this respect then, the *Girls' Room* can be recognized as a collectively imagined community among teens in cyberspace. Many young people, it would seem, are carving out spaces for their own communities online to maintain the everyday relationships in their lives. As evidenced by the *Girls' Room*, message boards can strengthen girls' self-esteem and sense of place within a social group, as well as among the larger complex social organization of the schoolyard.

In many ways, what makes these relationships flourish online is not only the often documented utopian potential of online communication (Pruijt, 2002; Wellman, 1997), but also the fact that these interactions also carry off-line consequences. For the girls, the message boards could provide a haven among friends, or prove to be a hazardous space where rumors run rampant. Either way, they learn that what happens in one social space influences behavior in another, creating a relative process of social identification between on- and off-line social groups.

In conclusion, this chapter has demonstrated that although girls use the internet for communication purposes among peers, there is more to the technology than simply being an extension of the telephone. Indeed, the internet and the message boards that girls create online can provide a place to which they feel they belong: like a soccer team or a social clique, enabling them to feel connected to each other even when they are physically disconnected. The *Girls' Room* is the kind of place where girls can share the day's events while offering their insights and ideas to create an archived, collective memory of their school year. Together they test, create, and re-create their own narratives into their teen years. In a world where urbanization is sprawling, "the global" envelops the local, and children roam virtual digital fields to explore friends, self, and life; technology offers these girls the opportunity to build their own digital fields in which to play.

Notes

1. http://www.montreal.worldweb.com/TravelEssentials/PeoplePopulation/8-122.html
2. Although there are many forum sites, the girls used the templates found at http://www.forumactif.fr/
3. Names have been changed to protect the girls' anonymity.
4. I use the term "real life" loosely as a reference to the distinction often made between online interactions as "virtual" and interactions that occur off-line as "real." Merchant (2001) among others also defines this distinction within his work.

References

Bernard, J. (1961). Teen-age culture: An overview. *Annals of the American Academy of Political and Social Science, 338, Teen-Age Culture* (November), pp. 1–12.

Boneva, B.S., Quinn, A., Kraut, K.E., Kiesler, S., & Shklovski, I. (2006). Teenage communication in the instant messaging era. In R. Kraut, M. Brynin, & S. Kiesler (eds.), *Computers, phones, and the internet: Domesticating information technology*, pp. 201–218. New York, NY: Oxford University Press.

Bryant, J.A., Sanders-Jackson, A., & Smallwood, A.M.K. (2006). IMing, text messaging, and adolescent social networks. *Journal of Computer-Mediated Communication, 11*(2), article 10, 577–582.

Childress, H. (2004). Teenagers, territory and the appropriation of space. *Childhood, 11*(2), 195–205.

Convertino. G. (2002). *Teenagers: The internet use and groups on-line and off-line.* Retrieved July 15, 2006, from http://br.endernet.org/~akrowne/courses/2002/fall/dc/all_papers/gregorio_convertino/project.pdf

Dixon, S. (2004). *Heterotopic spaces of childhood*. Master's thesis, Concordia University, Montreal, Canada.

Duncan, B. & Leander, K. (2000). Girls just wanna have fun: Literacy, consumerism, and paradoxes of position on gURL.com. [Electronic version.] *Reading Online, 4*, 5.

Grinter, R. & Palen, L. (2002). *Instant messaging in teen life*, presented at CSCW '02, November 16–20, 2002, New Orleans, Louisiana, USA.

Gross, E.F. (2004). Adolescent internet use: What we expect, what teens report. *Applied Development Psychology, 25*, 633–649.

Hines, C. (ed.) (2005). *Virtual methods: Issues in social research on the internet*. Oxford: Berg Publishers.

Jacobson, D. (1999). Doing research in cyberspace. *Field Methods, 11*(2), 127–145.

Kiesler, S., Kraut, R., Lundmark, V., Mukopadhyay, T., Patterson, M., & Scherlis, W. (1998). Internet paradox: A social technology that reduces social involvement and psychological well-being? *American Psychologist, 53*(9), 1017–1031.

Maczewski, M. (2002). Exploring identities through the internet: Youth experiences online. *Child & Youth Care Forum, 31*(2), 111–129.

Matei, S. (2005). From counterculture to cyberculture: Virtual community discourse and the dilemma of modernity. [Electronic version.] *Journal of Computer-Mediated Communication, 10*, 3, article 14.

Merchant, G. (2001). Teenagers in cyberspace: An investigation of language use and language change in internet chat rooms. *Journal of Research in Reading, 24*(3), 293–306.

Platt, J. (1981). On interviewing one's peers. *British Journal of Sociology, 32*(1), 75–91.

Pruijt, H. (2002). Social capital and the equalizing potential of the internet. *Social Science Computer Review, 20*(2), 109–115.

Rheingold, H. (2000). *The virtual community: Homesteading on the electronic frontier*. Revised edition. Cambridge, MA: The MIT Press.

Sanders C.E., Field, T.M., Diego, M., & Kaplan, M. (2000). The relationship of internet use to depression and social isolation among adolescents. *Adolescence, 35*(138), 237–242.

Shade, L.R. (2002). *Gender & community in the social construction of the internet*. New York: Peter Lang Publishing.

Stern, S. (2004). Expressions of identity online: Prominent features and gender differences in adolescents' World Wide Web Homepages. *Journal of Broadcasting & Electronic Media, 48*(2), 218–243.

Turkle, S. (1995). *Life on the screen: Identity in the age of the internet*. New York: Simon & Schuster.

Tyler, T.R. (2002). Is the internet changing social life? It seems the more things change, the more they stay the same. *Journal of Social Issues, 58*(1), 195–205.

Valkenburg, P.M., Schouten, A.P., & Peter, J. (2005). Adolescent's identity experiments on the internet. *New Media & Society, 7*(3), 383–402.

Ward, J. (1999). Cyber-ethnography and the emergence of the virtually new community. *Journal of Information Technology, 14*(1), 95–105.

Wellman, B. (1997). The road to utopia and dystopia on the information highway. *Contemporary Sociology, 26*(4), 445–449.

CHAPTER FIVE

"I Think We Must be Normal . . . There are Too Many of Us for This to be Abnormal!!!": Girls Creating Identity and Forming Community in Pro-Ana/Mia Websites

Michele Polak

I open this chapter with an excerpt from the website *Beauty of the Bones*:

> Ana, let me see the error of my ways, the flaws of my mind, and the imperfections on my body. Give me the self-control to change, and the strength to satisfy your every command. Remind me every day of my inadequacy [. . .] If I cheat on you and procreate with Ronald McDonald, I will kneel over my toilet and thrust my fingers deep in my throat and beg for your forgiveness. (Pledge to Ana, 2006)

Variations of this Pledge to Ana, along with a Letter from Ana, "I follow you throughout the day. In school, when your mind wanders I give you something to think about. Recount your calories for the day. It's too much" (Letter from Ana, 2006), appear in one form or another on countless websites across the internet. These websites are part of a cyber community called Pro-Ana. Followers of the pro-ana movement identify with each other by claiming that their disordered eating is a *lifestyle choice*. They refuse to acknowledge medical classifications, which categorize eating disorders as a psychological disease (e.g., anorexia and bulimia). In addition to the Pledge to Ana, Letter from Ana, Ana Creed, and Ana Commandments, pro-ana sites include personal reflections and journaling about living with an eating disorder, motivational quotations supporting the pursuit of a pro-anorexia lifestyle, dieting tips and tricks, recipes for low-calorie meals, medical information, and hundreds of pictures of women of various weights.

In August 2001, Yahoo, internet host to GeoCities where many of the pro-ana websites were housed, removed over one hundred pro-ana websites in one day. They continue to monitor and shut down pro-ana sites as often as they are posted, as does Angelfire, Tripod, and AOL: all free servers like Yahoo, where pro-ana followers have built their sites. During the span of my research into the pro-ana movement, more than half of the sites I analyzed have been deleted from their servers; by the time you read this chapter, *Beauty of the Bones* may already be defunct. Every time I return to my research, I have to revisit internet search engines for new sites from which to collect my data. The search does not take long; in minutes, I am back inside the pro-ana community where sites seem to spring up almost as quickly as they are taken down.

The National Eating Disorders Association (NEDA) believes that as many as ten million women in the United States alone are fighting an eating disorder. Of all psychiatric disorders, anorexia nervosa has the highest mortality rate. Data collected by NEDA also revealed that at least "42% of first to third grade girls want to be thinner" (Statistics, 2002). This suggests that the disease may originate in childhood, progressing through adolescence and therefore is not specific to mature women. It was once believed that eating disorders affected only young, white women because "relatively little research had been conducted utilizing participants from racial and ethnic minority groups" (Eating Disorders in Women of Color: Explanations and Implications, 2002). Many eating disorder specialists now recognize that the disease is also not specific to race, that "all socioeconomic and ethnic groups are at risk" (Dawkins, 2005). As one young feminist writes, "Eating disorders are the famine mystique of my generation" (Martin, 2005, p. 59), the most topical issue that plagues contemporary girls and young women.

As a scholar investigating girls' online discourses, I could not avoid encountering the issues of pro-ana websites since the sites hold such a controversial space in discussions of online technologies. Whether or not I reference them, I am asked about pro-ana at every conference presentation I make about girls' online activities. I find I am conflicted about the pro-ana movement: as a rhetorician, I value the possibilities of an online space that provides opportunities for girls to speak to a variety of audiences in an array of textual forms. As a feminist, I value the unrestricted space that online discourse provides for girls and young women, allowing for alternative viewpoints and voices of female resistance. But the pro-ana movement—a very young subculture that has only just picked up momentum in the last five years—is more powerful than anything I have ever seen before online. The written texts by pro-ana followers are sometimes both shocking and disturbing, as are the artwork and other visual elements, such as photographs. However, there is also poignancy to these online texts as they create identity, form community, and even encourage recovery among users. The pro-ana movement continues to thrive despite being constantly decimated by host servers and media critics and in the face of shattering clinical statistics on eating disorders. Members simply rebuild sites and find new servers. As Lena (2003) writes in the site *House of ED*: "They can label me, but they'll never understand me!" This adaptive and defiant behavior on the part of the users demands a closer reading of the texts of the pro-ana movement, so that we might better understand these "chosen" identities. This will be the focus of the remainder of this chapter.

Pro-Ana Girls Online

Public access to the internet as a form of communication has helped rework the geophysical spaces in which girls have historically been defined. Constructions of gender have traditionally placed masculinity in "the public world of social power" and femininity in "the privacy of domestic interchange" (Gilligan, 1982, p. 69). Harris (2004) argues, "public space is by default adult space" (p. 98), and she joins many other girl studies' scholars in citing the private space of girls' bedrooms as sites of growth for young women. The notion of an existing idealized space in which girls are able to explore their identity and form community outside of the domestic sphere becomes possible with the emerging concepts of public online space. The arguments that boys are allowed to roam public spaces more freely while "girls are usually associated with [more private and domestic] space inside the home and boys with space outside" has been contested by Reid-Walsh and Mitchell (2004) as they assert, "the space of the Web and the homepage may 'unsettle' and, indeed, begin to overturn this opposition" (p. 181). With technological literacy part of the ideology in which contemporary girls have been educated, coupled with the pull and familiarity of popular culture, the shift to a "virtual bedroom culture" (p. 174) was almost inevitable. Internet space allows girls to escape from the traditional confines of their homes to the social and public arena of cyberspace, all while playing with ideas of private space in their online discourse.

Pro-ana websites are very much like any personal website created by girls and young women. They range in design: from simple, framed templates created through web design software programs to elaborate presentations of visual and textual elements. Stern (2002) defines girls' personal home pages as a "digital showroom replete with autobiographical information, self-reflection, critical commentaries, creative poetry, and diverse imagery" (p. 233). Reid-Walsh and Mitchell (2004) note girls' use of space on the internet as "semiprivate places of creativity and sociality" (p. 174). And Takayoshi (1999) argues, "rather than remain silent and withdrawn, legions of articulate, thoughtful, and strong girls are actively creating and maintaining progirl home pages" (p. 95). Girls and young women have found a space to be vocal in a visual and textual way using new forms. Contemporary girls, unlike those of previous generations, are well-versed in new technologies. The digital spaces that they occupy provide new and crucial space for identity processes to unfold and be tested. There are more choices and more ways to envision oneself. It isn't as if the issues that plagued generations of women before have disappeared, but rather, as Harris (2004) asserts, "a variety of ways of being young and female have become bound up together, such that new spaces can be occupied with old and new meanings attached simultaneously" (p. 103).

The construction of personal websites allows for a merging of private and public space and site creators are not only aware of this fact but use it to define their sites' purpose. Reid-Walsh and Mitchell (2004) maintain that "web sites constructed or designed by girls are one of the few spaces under their control" (p. 174), and the continual additions, updates, and revisions of site content and structure will attest to the dedicated attention of website creators. Girls claim ownership of their sites and profess their identities through site design and inclusion/exclusion of content. Personal websites created by girls and young women are spaces of "self-disclosure" told in narrative form, 'stories that are very personal, intimate, and immediate' (Stern, 2002, p. 224). The structures of pro-ana sites include the usual autobiographical information, personal writings, blogging, and posted pictures that can be found on most personal websites. The purpose for pro-ana sites, however, is to identify with others as supporters of disordered eating as a lifestyle choice. It is rare that a pro-ana follower does not identify with one of the categories that create the pro-ana discourse. Community members in fact spend much of their time finding and defining which category of disordered eating they may fit into.

Inside the Pro-Ana Site

In clinical terminology, an eating disorder was originally defined only as anorexia nervosa: self-starvation and excessive weight loss. This term has been made into an acronym by pro-ana followers who use it as part of the regular discourse of the pro-ana movement (anorexia = ana). The number of medically recognized eating disorder categories, however, continue to increase and are also included as part of the discourse on pro-ana sites: bulimia nervosa, secretive binging and purging is identified as pro-mia and binge eating disorder or compulsive overeating (uncontrolled, impulsive, or continuous eating without purging) is identified in the pro-ana movement as COE. The most recent category added to the medical classification of eating disorders is eating disorder not otherwise specified, which combines several of the clinical features of eating disorders. The identifying pro-ana term is EDNOS. Ironically, EDNOS "is the most common category of eating disorder seen in outpatient settings yet there have been no studies of its treatment" (Fairburn & Bohn, 2005, p. 692). In addition, because many pro-ana followers also identify as self-injurers (SI), pro-SI is also a common category. Self-injury constitutes a variety of self-inflicted acts of pain including cutting, burning, and branding. While an all-encompassing term may be pro-ED (pro-eating disorder), pro-ana is the reference most familiarly found through internet search engines.

By appropriating for themselves the language of the clinical terminology that defines eating disorders, followers of pro-ana are able to create new identities that are often explored within the pro-ana community. While the internet is certainly a viable place for exploration in many ways due to the anonymity of users, language specifically relating to eating disorders is one of the unique features of pro-ana sites, which might not be found on other personal websites. Pro-ana sites include a glossary of terms defining both the language used by those that identify as pro-ana and the language used by medical specialists that research eating disorders in clinical environments. Site creators compose very specific descriptions of the various categorizations of disordered eating and pay great attention to the detail of such descriptions. In a pro-ana site *(not otherwise specified)*, for example, users may find information about the site owner by clicking on the link marked "patient." Posted by the site owner herself, users can guarantee an understanding of pro-ana by reading a personal narrative in a discourse that is familiar to pro-ana community members. There is a shared language here, with stories about familiar experiences related to living with, and managing, an eating disorder. Medical terminology is defined: "In my terms, ketosis is a condition in which the body uses its own muscle and/or body fat as an energy source instead of food. In technical terms, ketosis is a condition brought on by a metabolic imbalance" (ketosis, 2006), breaking down such clinical terms into a language that members may understand and apply if needed. By creating a space for community members to learn and discuss the language of the medical establishment, those that identify as pro-ana are able to gain control over their identity exploration.

The depth of research that can be found in pro-ana websites is staggering. On many sites, not only are there calculators and charts for figuring body mass index and calorie intake, but sites also break down medical jargon for users and address various health issues in relation to disordered eating. On the site *Feast or Famine*, for example, a listing for side effects of eating disorders under "Health Risks" include (but is not limited to): cardiac problems, anemia, dental decay and discoloration, liver damage, pancreatitis, depressed immune system, hypoglycemia, and kidney damage/failure (Health Risks, 2005). There are corresponding definitions for each listing. Several sites list links to pages of "thincouragement," quotes in relation to perseverance and staying thin: "It's not deprivation, it's liberation" (Quotes, 2004) or "Think smaller, a stone lighter, a size slimmer" (Quotes, 2005). By listing dichotomies such as health risks and encouragement, pro-ana community members are left to pick and choose which information is most suitable for their needs. As with other personal websites, many pro-ana sites include some form of personal writing by the site creator. In the case of pro-ana, it is the constant struggle of living with an eating disorder; through this relating of personal experience, community members may find themselves in another's story. By reading and understanding this shared connection, the real exploration for the pro-ana member may begin.

Much of what has caused critics to lash out at pro-ana sites, aside from the textual representations of supporting disordered eating, is most likely the sites' forums of "thinsperation." The visual text here is represented through posted pictures of models and other celebrity icons walking down the runway or posing on the red carpet. There is a canon of respected women among pro-ana followers; model Kate Moss is popular, with the recent eating disorder admission by Mary-Kate Olsen moving her to the top of the list, as the body that represents a personal goal for many that identify within the pro-ana movement. There are two divisions of thinsperation photos: those that display posed photos of well-known celebrity icons, and "bone pictures," photos that depict female bodies in various forms of emaciation. Bone pictures are inarguably the most disturbing content to view on these sites and they cause an array of discussion among members of the community. Not all sites carry bone pictures and not all pro-ana followers strive to emulate the bodies displayed in these photos. However, the use of such pictures is significant: many are manipulated in photo software programs to depict bodies thinner than they actually are (on some sites, passing the cursor over a bone picture will show the user both the original photo and the graphically manipulated reworked version). The irony is that most pro-ana followers are aware of this photo manipulation; yet, because of their fascination with the pictures, they do not remove them from their sites or eliminate them as topics of discussion.

It is these differences within the pro-ana community that fuel debate within these sites. Choices in posting bone pictures, for example, or choosing which eating disorder category members may identify, even noting "trigger" components—a picture or a comment that may spur someone in recovery or someone new to pro-ana into an eating disordered lifestyle—are all issues that can be found and explored in pro-ana websites. I argue that such disagreement is healthy as it prompts community members into discussion and away from (and out of) silence. The collective conversations are issues of disordered eating itself: how to identify, how to maintain, how to navigate health risks. Above all, the sites emphasize that being part of the pro-ana community means maintaining an eating disorder as a lifestyle choice. Members of the community are careful to hold onto an identity that links them to disordered eating through choice and warns against entering the community without such recognition: "CAUTION: THIS SITE IS NOT INTENDED TO PROMOTE ANY DISORDER OR THE BEHAVIOR! [. . .] If you are in recovery for any eating disorder, or are under the age of 18, it is advised that you leave this website now. You have been warned" (xcigaretteTHEIFx, 2005). Likewise, users are warned against entering pro-ana sites for reasons other than to find support within the community: "If you come here it means you have a real ED and you're not some ED poseur or looking to lose weight fast" (ana_life6, 2005). To be part of the pro-ana community and reap the benefits of the community, users who enter pro-ana sites must be prepared to identify as pro-ana. This means understanding what entails being pro-ana and being prepared to engage with the community. Such interaction with members involves sharing both support and personal experiences. Without such vocal presence, users are often "trolled out," or ignored as viable community members. The pro-ana community is not one of silence but of active, participatory exploration.

Creating Identity and Forming Community

Creating identity inside a community that has established a discourse of like-minded interests is certainly not specific to the pro-ana community, but it does seem to be a crucial aspect for them. While the visuals that structure thinspiration forums may be shocking to non-members, pro-ana is defined by such imagery. Members may agree or disagree on how the body should look but they expect some sort of visual representation to accompany the discourse. These are references for the pro-ana follower, a guide that helps direct them toward their pro-ana identity. I find that girls well-versed in adapting online space for their personal space manage to utilize the webpage as a whole; visual components are as important to page design layout as the textual elements: "Mere attention to the words on a Web page will not suffice, since the images are so important to textual meaning" (Warnick, 1998, p. 76). While I see evidence of a symbiotic relationship between the visual and textual elements at work in most online spaces created by girls and young women, I find it more evident in pro-ana sites. The connection to the visual representation of the body must exist in order to help create the pro-ana identity. This is a constructed identity under the authorship of any given site creator; the possibilities of multiple discourses and multiple readings, resulting in an array of created identities. In their research into how women represent themselves online, Hawisher and Sullivan (1999) discovered that "women begin to forge new social arrangements by creating a visual discourse that startles and disturbs" (p. 287). There is certainly proof for this argument in the pro-ana web community.

With pro-ana, I find very few limitations on how the body may be constructed. Members create images of how their eating disorder can contribute to their identity. Despite the communal discussions of health risks, identity is up for exploration. As members enter, they begin to situate themselves inside a discourse that layers and intertwines textual and visual elements in relation to something very real to the user. Doheny-Farina (2001), in his work on networked communities asserts, "the networks present the attractive possibility of finding new places that transcend the mundane physical spaces restricting our daily lives" (p. 49). This is the possibility for construction of self: "the postmodern self: a self that is fragmented, ever changing, ambiguous, and perhaps even liberated" (p. 65). Since online interaction involves an identity that has been constructed out of visual and textual elements with no "paralinguistic cues such as voice, facial expressions, and dress" (Hawisher & Sullivan, 1999, p. 269), girls are free to play with self-representation, claiming a space that is defined on their own terms, constructed by their own sense of a newly created identity.

What is found in many of the pro-ana sites is identification with community members in disordered eating. Members are not only interactive participants but are also able to create a personal identification that allows each member to navigate through the various stages of their eating disorder in ways that affect them, according to their own needs. Many of the sites in the pro-ana movement use electronic message boards to communicate. It is on these boards that personal goals with body issues are discussed, thincouragement is exchanged, thinsperation photos are analyzed and the categories of pro-ana/mia/COE/EDNOS or SI are chosen, realized, and confronted. Here, users voice their appreciation for the community as a place that offers less isolation for eating disorder sufferers:

> (Hugs Jen) Just like you've stood by me every step of whatever I was doing, whether it be SI, starving, exercising till I pass out, or just venting about life—I'll stand by you. [. . .] You really mean a lot to me having these boards, I dont know if you know that. (Hug) (Empty, 2005)

Postings on message boards are in a familiar language to many of the members within the pro-ana community. Not only are postings in the discourse of internet chat language complete with misspellings and word substitutions, but also with the common acronyms and issues used within the community:

> "I think most people are ednos because its hard to fall into one little category. At least thats what its like for me." (Ophelia, 2005)

> "When I was 13 I was a classic Ana—then when I was about 15 I was Ana and Mia, then for a while I was just Mia, now I'm sometimes Mia and ALWAYS a COE. IT just changes all the time. You're going to manipulate your disease to whatever way it suits you best." (kate, 2005)

It is this use of space for community recognition and identity formation that seems most overlooked by critics of the pro-ana movement. The NEDA has this to say about pro-ana sites:

> The National Eating Disorders Association actively speaks out against pro-anorexia and pro-bulimia websites. These sites provide no useful information on treatment but instead encourage and falsely support those who, sadly, are ill but do not seek help. These sites could have a severe negative impact on the health of those who consult them and encourage a "cult" type destructive support system that discourages people from the treatment they so desperately need. (NEDA's Position on Pro-Ana Web Sites, 2002)

In an October 2001 Oprah Winfrey show, Oprah tells her audience: "There are pro-anorexia Web sites and they are so disturbing that, when we were talking about doing or not doing this show, we debated about whether or not to even talk about them, but we decided that you as parents need to be aware" (Winfrey, 2001). Producers then proceeded to show screenshots from various pro-ana sites while audience members watched in shock. However, Oprah failed to discuss the deletion by Yahoo of the many pro-ana sites only months before.

About Recovery

Criticisms of pro-ana sites are easy to find and media attention has shifted to the pro-ana movement through many different venues. Ferreday (2003) argues, "The mass closure of pro-ana home pages is partially a response to a proliferation of articles in the press expressing consternation and demanding that something be done about the 'problem' of pro-ana" (p. 288). In reality, studies have not found "major differences in body weight, duration of eating disorders, number of missed periods or bone density between anorexics who visited the sites and those who didn't" (Song, 2005, p. 57). And as Nagourney (2005) reports, "some experts wonder whether they are doing a better job of getting their message out than do the sites intended to promote recovery from eating disorders," offering that perhaps, "the sites might serve as no more than a support community, and not as a source of encouragement to continue destructive behavior" (p. 6).

The more I read pro-ana sites, the more I question the acts of deletion by server sites such as Yahoo. I think about Gilligan's (1982) argument concerning women's psychological development, "the truths of psychological theory have blinded psychologists to the truth of women's experience" (p. 62). When Ferreday (2003) asserts, "The anorexic body [. . .] is what members of the community have in common, both as an ideal and as lived experience" (p. 285), I wonder if critics in opposition to pro-ana are actually *reading* the sites. The site creator of *(not otherwise specified)* writes,

"I think the bashing of pro-ED websites is unbelievably hypocritical coming from the same media and magazines that highlight page after page of underweight actresses and models as role-models." (in general, 2006)

Pro-ana followers are critical analysts of their disorder and of the culture in which they exist. The assumption that members are too immersed in their disorder to think objectively about the issue does not allow for the growth that *does* occur in pro-ana communities, the conversations that *do* happen. Hero at *no place to hide* writes, "But at 5 foot 5, I know that I can't be as obese as I look in the mirror. How do we know ACTUALLY how skinny we're getting?" and "damnit, at what point does the line between 'fat' and 'thin' come to be? Size eight? Size one?" (Hero, 2005). What I believe might be overlooked by most critics is the amount of attention that pro-ana sites give to recovery. In many of the pro-ana sites I have analyzed, there has been reference to recovery, either through a link to a new page or as a message board forum. Here is yet another example of community support that pro-ana offers. Many members that write within recovery forums have been with the community for some time; seldom does a user enter a pro-ana community just for recovery purposes. They enter in the process of creating their identity as pro-ana. Members have already spent time forming friendships and sharing intimacies about their disorder, so by the time the entry into recovery occurs, the community knows the struggle that is ahead and offers support accordingly. As Song (2005) argues, "If there's one thing teens respond to, it's the rallying cry of other teens, something lacking on sites dedicated to recovery" (p. 57). While recovery sites do exist within the medical eating disorder community, they are seldom pro-ana. Recovery sites are often linked to medical institutions or doctors that have written books on eating disorders. Where recovery is concerned, recovery sites are not frequented nearly as often as pro-ana sites.

Within pro-ana, personal interaction concerning dialogue around recovery can occur without censorship or chastisement or being labeled as a bad girl or a sick woman. The key element here is support. I have never seen a member post her desire for recovery and not receive support from the community. At *Not just a Disorder*, in a thread entitled "Two Days No Binging or Purging Challenge," jesse writes, "You might think two days??? that little, well yeah, since I'm not doing a very good job at the moment, I thought this is the thing to do. Who ever wants to join, please do!!" (jesse, 2004). To which PinkFlipFlop responds,

"Hey Jesse—mind if I join you on the no binging thing? [. . .] I want to go the whole week without binging—right through next weekend. I am so sick of these weekend binges! So I am going to challenge myself not to for the whole week and then when I do that I will just keep going. I think it's the first week that's the hardest—so I just need to get through that! We can do this!!" (PinkFlipFlop, 2004)

Communal support is always available for the pro-ana member when they are ready for recovery. Many pro-ana sites are very informative toward issues surrounding recovery. It is common to find just as much research and dedication to recovery issues as pro-ana members give to every other aspect of disordered eating. The site *(not otherwise specified)* offers an entire page of links to topics such as stopping binging, stages of recovery, recovering independently, and personal experiences with such suggestions as, "My best advise is to write [. . .] Once you can be honest with yourself about your emotions and feelings you can start to express them through mediums like talking or writing to people other than yourself" (recovering independently, 2006). It is the need to share in the common struggle with disordered eating that brings girls and young women to search for pro-ana communities. As Ferreday (2003) concludes, "by encouraging sufferers to talk about their conditions, they disrupt the medical model of anorexia and challenge the distinction between the public and private" (p. 292), bringing the argument back to the value of these online spaces.

Conclusion

In pro-ana sites, followers have found a space to create, revise, and play with identity. Here are spaces where they can feel less like outsiders and realize they are not alone. There is an explorative process that occurs in this space, one that travels through various identity formations. Pro-ana is a disturbing and undeniably difficult subculture to navigate. When Gilligan (1982) argues that we must "notice not only the silence of women but [accept] the difficulty in hearing what they say when they speak" (p. 173), I consider how often critics of the pro-ana movement shut down the space that a pro-ana girl has created for her exploration of self. I weigh the arguments that pro-ana websites lead girls and young women to a lifestyle of disordered eating against the positive option for allowing explorative space that encourages communal discourse. Recognizing and not censoring the online space of pro-ana enables girls to give voice to these controversial issues instead of remaining silent: unidentified and unheard. As the creator of *Lollypop Playhouse* writes, "Call me Jenny. Yes, I'm mia, but I'm not sick or suffering. I'm simply enduring and existing" (Jenny, 2004).

References

ana_life6. (2005). *Homepage.* Retrieved August 5, 2006, from http://www.freewebs.com/liteasafeathersuccession/.

Dawkins, A. (2005). Eating disorders crossing the color line. *Eat Right.* Retrieved October 1, 2005, from http://www.banderasnews.com/0503/hb-eatright.htm.

Doheny-Farina, S. (2001). *The wired neighborhood.* New Haven: Yale University Press.

Eating Disorders in Women of Color: Explanations and Implications. (2002). *Eating disorders info.* Retrieved August 8, 2006, from http://www. nationaleatingdisorders.org/p.asp?WebPage_ID=286&Profile_ID=73571.

Empty. (2005). *Message board forum.* Retrieved August 5, 2006, from http://noplacetohide.proboards107.com/index.cgi?board=Mia&action= display&thread=1126123753.

Fairburn, C.G. & Bohn, K. (2005). Eating disorder NOS (EDNOS): An example of the troublesome "not otherwise specified" (NOS) category in DSM-IV. *Behaviour Research and Therapy, 43,* 691–701.

Ferreday, D. (2003). Unspeakable bodies: Erasure, embodiment and the pro-ana community. *International Journal of Cultural Studies, 6*(3), 277–295.

Gilligan, C. (1982). *In a different voice: Psychological theory and women's development.* Cambridge, MA: Harvard University Press.

Harris, A. (2004). *Future girl: Young women in the twenty-first century.* New York: Routledge.

Hawisher, G. & Sullivan, P. (1999). Fleeting images: Women visually writing the web. In G. Hawisher & C. Selfe (eds.), *Passions, pedagogies, and 21st century technologies,* pp. 268–291. Logan: Utah State University Press.

Health Risks. (2005). *The Basics.* Retrieved August 5, 2006, from http:// famine.brokensanity.org/.

Hero. (2005). *Message board forum.* Retrieved August 8, 2006, from http:// noplacetohide.proboards107.com/index.cgi?board=Mia&action=display& thread=1123731238.

in general. (2006). *the site.* Retrieved August 5, 2006, from http://lexusine. candyandrazorblades.net/thesite/general.html.

Jenny. (2004). *Homepage.* Retrieved August 8, 2006, from http://www.freewebs. com/lollypop_playhouse/index.htm.

jesse. (2004). *Message board forum.* Retrieved August 5, 2006, from http://p202. ezboard.com/fnotjustadisorderfrm44.showMessage?topicID=68.topic.

kate. (2005). *Message board forum.* Retrieved August 5, 2006, from http:// noplacetohide.proboards107.com/index.cgi?board=ednos&action=display& thread=1123712589.

ketosis. (2006). *disorder.* Retrieved August 5, 2006, from http://lexusine. candyandrazorblades.net/eating/ketosis.html.

Lena. (2003). *Homepage.* Retrieved August 5, 2006, from http://www.freewebs. com/houseofed4me/index.htm.

Letter from Ana. (2006). *Beauty of the Bones.* Retrieved August 5, 2006, from http://beautyofthebones.bravehost.com/Letter.html.

Martin, C. (May–June 2005). The Famine Mystique. *Off Our Backs,* pp. 59–62.

Nagourney, E. (June 2005). Web sites celebrate a deadly thinness. *The New York Times,* p. 6.

NEDA's Position on Pro-Ana Web Sites. (2002). *Press Room.* Retrieved August 8, 2006, from http://www.nationaleatingdisorders.org/p.asp?WebPage_ ID=779.

Ophelia. (2005). *Message board forum*. Retrieved August 5, 2006, from http://noplacetohide.proboards107.com/index.cgi?board=ednos&action=display&thread=1117347752.

PinkFlipFlop. (2004). *Message board forum*. Retrieved August 5, 2006, from http://p202.ezboard.com/fnotjustadisorderfrm44.showMessage?topicID=68.topic.

Pledge to Ana. (2006). *Beauty of the Bones*. Retrieved August 5, 2006, from http://beautyofthebones.bravehost.com/toana.html.

Quotes. (2004). *Homepage*. Retrieved August 5, 2006, from http://fadingobsession.houseofthin.com/.

———. (2005). *Homepage*. Retrieved August 8, 2006, from http://www.freewebs.com/feedmeonempty/quotes.htm.

recovering independently. (2006). *recovery*. Retrieved August 5, 2006, from http://lexusine.candyandrazorblades.net/recovery/independently.html.

Reid-Walsh, J. & Mitchell, C. (2004). Girls' web sites: A virtual "Room of One's Own"? In A. Harris (Ed.), *All about the girl: Culture, power, and identity*, pp. 173–182. New York: Routledge.

Song, S. (July 2005). Starvation on the web. *Time*, p. 57.

Statistics. (2002). *Press Room*. Retrieved August 8, 2006, from http://www.nationaleatingdisorders.org/p.asp?WebPage_ID=286&Profile_ID=41138.

Stern, S. (2002). Virtually speaking: Girls' self-disclosure on the WWW. *Women's Studies in Communication, 25*(2), 223–253.

Takayoshi, P. (1999). No boys allowed: The World Wide Web as a clubhouse for girls. *Computers and Composition, 16*, 89–106.

Warnick, B. (1998). Rhetorical criticism of public discourse on the Internet: Theoretical implications. *Rhetoric Society Quarterly, 28*, 73–84.

Winfrey, O. (October 2001). Girls who don't eat. *The Oprah Winfrey Show*. Chicago.

xcigaretteTHIEFx. (2005). *Homepage*. Retrieved August 8, 2006, from http://www.freewebs.com/sickly_yours/.

CHAPTER SIX

Private Writing in Public Spaces: Girls' Blogs and Shifting Boundaries

Brandi Bell

> With the weblog the public is invited into the privacy of the diary of an individual [. . .] In some manner, the writer is putting his or her daily experiences into a larger context, discussing micro events in relation to the wider universe of events. The weblog connects the public arena with that of individuals.
>
> Mortensen & Walker, "Blogging thoughts"

Introduction

As the quote at the start of the chapter suggests, weblogs are often conceptualized as spaces where the private and public overlap or converge. In this chapter, I will explore the phenomenon of weblogs, focusing specifically on the participation of adolescent girls as weblog authors. Following a description of weblogs and their history, I will discuss how these relatively new spaces provide a means for some girls (those with access to technology, specific skill sets, and leisure time) to post personal thoughts and feelings in what many consider to be public spaces. Drawing on Habermas' and Warner's writings on the public sphere, I will argue that it is important to consider how girls' blogs operate as means of constituting audiences of readers.

Adolescent girls represent a large portion of weblog authors (Lenhart & Madden, 2005). While there is evidence of increasing interest in examining girls' blogging activities (see, e.g., Bortree, 2005; Cadle, 2005), there continues to be a general dismissal of girls' blogs in many scholarly and popular discourses. Herring, Kouper et al. (2004) have argued that there is "a gender and age bias in contemporary discourses about weblogs" such that we rarely hear about girls' blogging activities in popular media or in the blogging community itself. Many researchers also continue to "marginalize the activities of women and teen bloggers, thereby indirectly reproducing societal sexism and ageism, and misrepresenting the fundamental nature of the weblog phenomenon" (Herring, Kouper et al., 2004). This marginalization of girls' blogging activities might be due, in part, to how we conceptualize blogs as spaces. Much of the writing on blogs thus far has considered them within the framework of "public space," focusing on how blogs are effective as alternative outlets for amateur writers and journalists, or as spaces for political commentary. This has resulted in a devaluing of the personal style and private focus of many other blogs, those associated with young women in particular. Yet, as this chapter will demonstrate, girls' blogs are very significant. They represent spaces that problematize notions of private and public and, consequently, challenge traditional notions of girlhood and childhood.

Defining Weblogs

As with other relatively recent phenomena and trends, weblogs (or blogs, for short) are difficult to define considering that the conventions of their form, use, and content continue to evolve as users adapt them to their needs. A review of popular and academic writing reveals a number of different approaches to defining weblogs. The two most common ways of describing blogs highlight very different uses and content: one view focuses on blogs mainly as personal writing in the style of a journal or diary, while the other approach defines blogs more in terms of gathering internet links and information. For those who define blogs as an online journal or diary, importance is placed on the personal nature of blog entries and the use of blogs to write about opinions and daily experiences. Those who view blogs as places to gather and share information and internet links (see Kahney, 2000, e.g.), define a blog as "a regularly updated list of links and commentary to interesting material on the Web." For these writers, it is the blog author's commentary on the information that is important. This form of personal writing is conceptualized as a critique of information as opposed to personal opinions and descriptions of one's everyday life.

A broader and more useful view of weblogs is as a combination of journal-writing and the collection of information and internet links.

Mortensen and Walker (2002), for example, define weblogs in terms of content, while also highlighting some of the common formatting elements of blogs:

> Weblogs, or *blogs* as they are affectionately termed, are frequently updated websites, usually personal, with commentary and links. Link lists are as old as home pages, but a blog is far from a static link list or home page. A blog consists of many relatively short posts, usually time-stamped, and organised in reverse chronology so that a reader will always see the most recent post first. (p. 249)

It should be clear that these different perspectives on the role and content of blogs fall along the lines of private and public, thus placing blogs at the center of an ongoing shifting and redefining of the boundaries between the two, as will be discussed later.

Thus far, the majority of studies done regarding adolescent girls' blogs have primarily addressed content and style, helping us to situate girls' blogs within the different perspectives. Huffaker (2004) performed a content analysis of 184 randomly selected blogs authored by both female and male adolescents between thirteen and seventeen years of age and found that "the content of blogs typically reflects what is expected to impact a teenager's life, such as school, intimate relationships, sexual identity and even music" (p. iii). This was supported by Lenhart and Fox (2006) who found that "younger [Internet] users were among the most likely to say that they blog to document and share their lives" (p. 7). In an interesting study of the use of blogs in college classes, Brooks, Nichols, and Priebe (2004) found that "first-year students [. . .] were not particularly interested in the academic potential of weblogging, but they were interested in the personal and expressive dimensions." This suggests that the capacity of blogs to provide a space for personal writing about one's daily experiences is an important motivator for blogging, particularly for adolescents, and it also indicates that girls' blogs are typically of a private nature, focusing more on diary-like entries than on gathering of topical information or web links.

History of Weblogs

Though a comprehensive history of weblogs is beyond the scope of this chapter (see Blood, 2000; Carl, 2003; Jensen, 2003), it is useful to provide a brief overview of how weblogs have developed. It is generally argued that blogs, as they currently exist, began in the mid to late 1990s. Since the term "weblog" was coined in 1997/1998,[1] a number of developments have led to the increasing popularity of blogs. The most important of these, perhaps, was the release, in 1999, of a number of blogging tools, such as Pitas (www.pitas.com) and Blogger (www.blogger.com), which made the act of blogging more accessible to internet users. Following their release, the number of blogs began to increase more quickly.

As more people created blogs, the mainstream media began to take notice and blogs were more frequently discussed in the popular discourses of journalism, politics, and culture: "As the number of blogs has exploded, so has their presence in the cultural landscape" (Drejer, 2003). Reporting about blogs has now moved off-line and expanded beyond the technology-focused pages of *Wired* and *PC Magazine* with stories in *Time Magazine* and on National Public Radio (NPR), for example. The growth of the blog phenomenon has also resulted in more academic attention, and studies that focus on adolescent girls' blogging activities, some of which will be discussed here.

Blog Authors

As the popularity of blogs increases, they are becoming an important topic of discussion in popular and academic writing, and many people are speculating about the roles they may play in social and cultural life. Because it is relatively easy to author a blog and write whatever you like (if you have internet access), blogs are generally thought to be democratic and open to all. It is hard to back up those assertions, however, because the actual number of blogs, and the demographics of bloggers are difficult to determine and are constantly changing.

In a study of blogging conducted in early 2006, the PEW Internet & American Life Project estimated that "8% of internet users age 18 and older, or about 12 million American adults, report keeping a blog" and "about 57 million American adults, report reading blogs" (Lenhart & Fox, 2006, p. 2), indicating that the popularity of blogs continues to rise. Surveys such as this have begun to explore who bloggers are and a number have concluded that "blogs are currently the province of the young, with 92.4% of blogs created by people under the age of 30" (Henning, 2003). More recent data suggest that this early trend continues: "One in five online teens (19%), or roughly 4 million young Americans, have created their own blog" according to a study conducted in late 2004 (Lenhart & Madden, 2005, p. 4).

Within the context of this chapter, it is important to note that survey results of blogs have revealed that many bloggers are adolescent girls: "As with other online communication activities, older girls again lead the charge into blogging in the teen cohort. A quarter (25%) of online girls ages 15–17 blog, compared with 15% of online boys of the same age" (Lenhart & Madden, 2005, p. 5). While these statistics continue to change as the phenomenon evolves, they currently point to the importance of considering the role of blogs in the lives of adolescent girls.

Researching Girls and Blogs

Given the claim that adolescent girls are actively blogging, it is surprising that their blogging activities have not been researched more thoroughly. Preliminary work in this area (Herring, Kouper et al., 2004; Herring, Scheidt et al., 2004) stresses the need for continued research. As Herring, Kouper et al. (2004) argue, "women and young people are key actors in the history and present use of weblogs, yet that reality is masked by public discourses about blogging that privilege the activities of a subset of adult male bloggers."

Since that call for research, a few more studies of girls' blogs have been reported. Bortree (2005), for example, conducted a general examination of forty teen blogs and an in-depth analysis of six by teen girls, followed by a set of thirteen interviews with other girl bloggers. She characterizes girls' blogs as monologues rather than discussions and through an explanation of girls' blogs provides a good introduction to the phenomenon. Her findings, which will be drawn upon in this chapter, indicate that girls use a number of strategies to present themselves through their blogs and that girls are generally aware of the potential public audience for their writing. In her doctoral thesis, Cadle (2005) provides an in-depth look into four girls' blogs. She discusses the links between blogs and other forms of personal writing particularly focusing on the gendered nature of personal writing, as I will discuss later. Cadle's (2005) main concern is to understand how blog writing may affect identity and literacy with a central focus on the application to pedagogy. Her thesis raises a number of important issues pertaining to girls and blogs, such as the relationships between gender, writing, public space, and technology, themes that will be highlighted throughout the remainder of this chapter. Other commentaries and studies have also been written concerning girls and blogs (see, e.g., Scheidt, 2006, on the issue of audience and performance), helping to redress the existing gender inequalities in the researching of blogs.

Despite the research being done on girls' blogs, however, we still do not know much about girls' actions or the significance blogs may have for their lives. Research conducted by Stern (1999, and chapter ten in this volume) on adolescent girls' online authoring and their motivations for creating home pages and blogs is beginning to explore this important area. What has become clear from early studies on blogs is that the content and style of blogging differs depending on gender and age: "The journal-type is dominated by teen females (and is favoured by females in general), whereas adult males predominate in the creation of filter-type (e.g., news and politics-oriented) blogs and k-logs [knowledge-logs]" (Herring, Kouper et al., 2004).

The Blog as Diary?

The potential of blogs as spaces for writing about personal experiences and feelings has led many scholars to comment on the similarity between journal-type blogs and traditional paper journals. Miller and Shepherd (2004) argue that journals and diaries are one "branch of the blog family tree." They describe the traditional diary as "understood to be written in the present and about the present; to be written serially, in installments; and to refer to the actual experiences of the writer, whether external or intrinsic." This, they argue, brings the genre of the traditional diary in line with blogs. Similarly, Cadle (2005) discusses the "roots" of the weblog in personal journals and diaries, pointing to the gendered nature of such writing.

There is an important body of work on personal forms of writing such as the journal or diary, which provides much useful insight when examining girls' blogs. Historically, and in contemporary Western culture, personal writing in the form of journals, diaries, and autobiographies has played an important role. For example, as Cadle (2005) argues, "journals in paper form have long been the writer's friend inside and outside the classroom," as well as being part of published literature (p. 11). There are a number of parallels between paper diaries and girls' blogs, most obviously their tendency to focus on and recount personal experiences and feelings.

Examinations of girls' blogs have shown that girls predominantly post about their everyday experiences: "For the most part, the girls appear to be reporting about their day in a way that constructs their experiences in a pleasing manner. They tend to talk about hanging out with friends, going to parties, having sleepovers, goofing around in class and other 'fun' experiences" (Bortree, 2005, p. 38). In Cadle's (2005) study, she found that Daily Log posts were most prevalent, in which girls reflected on the events of the day; however, for some girls, the writing was less reflexive and more factual. For example, one of the blogs she examined contained a high number of what she called School Updates, which, unlike Daily Log posts, tended to contain lists of activities "forming a kind of accomplishment tally that acts as a score sheet which gives the writer some idea where she stands in the at times demanding academic world" (p. 122). This style of writing is more closely associated with the journal than the diary if we consider traditional gender stereotypes with respect to personal forms of writing.

Much popular and academic writing continues to ignore or devalue blogs used as spaces for girls to write about themselves and their lives. This is in keeping with the historical differentiation of personal writing along gender lines: forms of personal writing are not all considered equal, with a distinction being drawn between the stereotypically male journal form and the female diary form. Gannett (1994) describes this distinction, where journals are seen as places to record experiences and collect information and diaries are considered places to record personal experiences in a more reflexive way: the former considered masculine, while the latter considered more feminine. These are, of course, cultural distinctions and do not necessarily reflect the actual function of personal writing. These views have, however, had implications for how personal writing and writing by women is perceived.

Despite girls' blending of both feminine (diary-style) and masculine (journal-style) writing in their blogs, Bortree (2005) found differences in girls' and boys' blog writing, which suggests that girls' blogs are more closely aligned with the feminine diary form. Bortree (2005) determined that even though for both girls and boys, "the content of the posts primarily included talk about what happened during the day, who the teens had hung out with, what they had done over the weekend, what they were planning to do over the weekend, what their family members were doing and what they were worried or upset about," girls' blog posts were more often used to "share intimate details about themselves, including feelings of vulnerability and affection" (p. 30). Thus, many girls appear to treat their blogs much like a paper diary, at least with respect to their writing style and content.

As argued by Gannett (1994), "women have been socialized to see their diary keeping as less important, as belonging only to the private sphere and to the realm of emotion rather than that of the intellect" (p. 149). The lack of value placed on girls' personal writing in the form of blogs suggests that this trend continues. As Cadle (2005) has succinctly stated, women's writing, 'infusing "too much" personal detail or connections', is often judged to be 'not rigorous or "significant" enough' (p. 51). This continuing stereotype results in a devaluing of girls' writing and lack of popular and academic consideration of the importance of girls' blogs.

While it is clear that blogs are in many ways similar to paper diaries and journals, there are important distinctions between the two. There is little research published thus far on the motivations of girls to author blogs; however, it has been suggested that "considering the historical affinity between women and diaries and the newer digital remediation of that form, adolescent girls should find personal weblogs to be a comfortable rather than a threatening space" (Cadle, 2005, p. 4). What is imperative to note here is not only the parallel drawn between the diary and the blog as stereotypically feminine forms, but also the stress that blogs are a new form of the paper diary, which incorporates the characteristics of digital media.

Herring (2004) goes so far as to argue that, for adolescents, "blogging is just the modern analog of keeping a personal journal" (p. 33), however, researchers have not yet fully explored the role of blogging as an expressive outlet or as a replacement of the traditional paper diary or journal. One clear difference between a paper diary and an online one is the "public" nature of the blog, which I will explore in detail in the following sections.

Shifting the Boundaries of Public and Private

It is important to recognize the significance of blogs as public spaces where adolescents can express their identity to others. With respect to blogs, this expression of self includes not only the thoughts and feelings expressed in the text, but also the use of style and form elements to demonstrate aspects of one's identity. For example, Bortree (2005) found that "blog designs included a sidebar that was used as a place for self-expression. In addition to providing links to friends [. . .] the teens on Blogspot provided links to their favorite bands and favorite web sites" (p. 30). One girl in Cadle's (2005) study was more interested in the visual aspects of blogs, so while she posted less often than others, her visual template and elements changed frequently as she learned about blog design. According to Cadle's (2005) research, this girl "consciously uses visual rhetoric to both persuade others and to define self," for example, by designing an icon communicating her support for then U.S. presidential candidate John Kerry (p. 111). Visual and textual elements of blogs such as these, are used by girls to communicate their personality and interests to others, drawing from the fact that, unlike a paper diary, blogs are public spaces open to a broad range of readers.

As Lowe and Williams (2004) put it, "to use blogs merely as a tool for private journaling is to privilege our understanding of journals as private writing spaces without considering the benefits of weblogs as public writing." It is significant that a blog author can potentially share their writing with any interested reader on the Internet. In a cultural and social context in which young people, particularly girls, are heavily monitored, the public nature of blogs becomes salient (see Boyd's discussion of networked publics in this volume).

As Miller and Shepherd (2004) have stated, "the diary raises the question about audience that has intrigued us from the beginning. Is the diary a personal or a public genre? Does it have an audience beyond the writer?" When the diary takes the form of a weblog, the answer appears to be affirmative:

> Even as they serve to clarify and validate the self, blogs are also intended to be read. Maintaining traffic and link statistics seems important to bloggers, and many provide readers the opportunity to provide feedback either by posting comments directly on the blog or through email. (Miller & Shepherd, 2004)

These and other characteristics particular to the blog add another dimension to girls' participation in this phenomenon. In addition to blogs being useful spaces to express oneself and to write about daily experiences, they are also public spaces, attractive to girls because they can use them to communicate with their friends, manage friendships, and build communities.

In Bortree's (2005) study, many girls said they kept a blog in order to "keep in touch with family or friends," revealing that they read their friends' blogs and vice versa (p. 33). With respect to maintaining and managing friendships through blogs, girls often link to their friends' blogs and remove those links as means of communicating levels of closeness and friendship (p. 33). Friendship is also built through posting about their lives and feelings, bringing friends closer together. Bortree found that girls felt writing blogs was "a way to get to know another person's thoughts without having to talk about it . . . One girl said, 'it makes it easier to communicate. We would probably not discuss our problems as much if we didn't blog'" (p. 33). Thus, in this respect the public nature of the blog, its easy accessibility to others through the internet, plays an important role for girls in terms of communicating with their friends.

In addition to building and managing individual friendships, girls use blogs as a means for building a sense of community. As Cadle (2005) states:

> The beauty of personal weblog writing . . . [is that] it can act as a repository for the shifting conception of self so necessary for growth in the adolescent. It can also through its concentration on introspection,

reflection, and support from other young women through the comments feature, create the sort of "women helping women" environment feminists heartily support. (p. 56)

According to one of the girls in Cadle's study, "the most fun aspect of blogging is leaving and receiving comments. I love to know when other people are actually reading my journal, and what they think about it" (p. 137). Another girl said "meeting people is the best thing. You get positive responses from your posts, and people are there to help you when you need it" (p. 137). As these examples illustrate, girls consider the public nature of blogs to be important, indicating that blogs, while they may be similar to paper diaries in writing style, provide very different opportunities for girls—ones in which they can engage in visual and textual communication with an outside audience of their peers. These readers may also include strangers however, which suggests an even more public nature to blogs. Thus, while girls appear to primarily focus on using their blogs to communicate with people they already know (treating it as a more or less private space of friendship), blogs are in fact open to much broader accessibility, suggesting that the space is much more public than private.

By virtue of their location on the internet, blogs complicate and challenge our usual notions about what is public and what is private. As Wynn and Katz (1997) argue, "we view the Internet as public. But its illusion of privacy presents a boundary problem" (p. 307). Blogs in particular are often seen as spaces where public and private information are combined and boundaries are blurred: "Because of the varied nature of the weblog, from personal journal to political soapbox, and because of the very public nature of the weblog as online text, the public and the private often overlap and conflict within the blogosphere" (Gurak et al., 2004). This blurring of boundaries has profound implications when we consider girls' participation in blog authoring and the incorporation of technology into their lives more generally. As Cadle (2005) has suggested, "today's adolescent girls, not all, but those who choose to, let technology flow from their fingertips like a force of nature. The division between the so-called natural world and the equally artificially-defined and separated technological world falls away as if it never existed" (p. 53). This raises important questions for how we think about public and private space, as well as where blogs fit into the public/private continuum.

A New Public Sphere?

Because they are on the internet and any person online could conceivably read them, blogs are commonly considered public spaces. A number of writers have argued that blogs may represent a new public sphere in the spirit of Habermas' notion of bourgeois public spheres of the nineteenth century. According to Habermas' theory, a public sphere is "simultaneously about the quality or form of rational-critical discourse and the quantity of, or openness to, popular participation" (Calhoun, 1993, p. 4). Applying Habermas' conception to blogs, Mortensen and Walker (2002) claim that blogs represent a new public sphere in that they allow private individuals to express themselves in a public arena.

Scholars and bloggers have commented on the potential of blogs to constitute a public sphere according to Habermas' criteria; however, many have also countered such claims. While some have argued that blogs incorporate elements of rational–critical discourse, such as the ability to comment on blog posts or the practice of discussing issues over multiple blogs (Jacobs, 2003, e.g.), others believe that blogs are actually more confined and restricted spaces since they usually do not attract large audiences or aim to engage others to comment or discuss issues (Herring et al., 2004; Roberts-Miller, 2004). This latter characteristic is reflected in adolescent girls' blogs where personal writing and maintenance of existing friendships are central, rather than any explicit desire to engage strangers in rational–critical discourse about political or social issues. Thus, considering girls' blogs from the perspective of public sphere theory fails to acknowledge the realities of girls' uses of these spaces, and further encourages a devaluing of girls' personal writing and friendship maintenance, since such uses do not help to build a new public sphere. More subtle forms of civic engagement may be inherent and unrecognized in girls' blogs. Girls may use satire or political humor. Their engagement with the public sphere may be unrecognized if it is being measured by the standards of a middle-aged, middle-class male scholar.

The Blog Audience and the Constitution of Publics

It should be clear from the preceding discussion that girls' blogs are not only about writing one's personal feelings and listing the events of the day. In addition to this, they are spaces in which girls interact with their friends and build community, while at the same time fashioning a particular presentation of themselves through color, graphics, internet links, and text. Thus, we must consider the dual nature of blogs as spaces of both a private and public nature. These girls are not only posting their thoughts and feelings on the web for their friends, they are also aware of the potential for a broader audience of readers.

The tendency in blog research has thus far been focused heavily on whether and how blogs fulfill their potential for creating a new public sphere, resulting in a preoccupation with popular A-list blogs (those focused on broad and inclusive discussion of issues) and less attention being paid to the many blogs that are more personal in nature and often smaller with respect to audience. This approach to blogs in terms of their relationship to the idea of a public sphere, while useful for examining certain parts of the blog universe, perpetuates the trend of devaluing personal writing through a continued overlooking of more personal blogs, such as those by adolescent girls. A different approach to girls' blogs is clearly needed. As I argue, one potential option is to draw upon Warner's (2002) conceptualization of publics, particularly the role of texts in constituting audiences of readers.

According to Warner, a public is something that "comes into being only in relation to texts and their circulation" (p. 66). Warner's conceptualization of a public, consists of a number of elements that are discernible in blogs: a public (i) is self-organized, (ii) exists by virtue of being addressed, (iii) is both personal and impersonal, and (iv) is a relation among strangers (pp. 67–76). As a means of addressing others, the blog allows its author to reach an audience beyond that which would normally be available, as previously discussed. Despite the fact that adolescent girls' journal-type blogs may not, in fact, be read by large numbers of people, they do provide the possibility of such reading by strangers and, therefore, the ability to create a public of readers.

Blogs also display Warner's third feature of a public, namely, the simultaneously personal and impersonal address. It has been argued that this feature is especially characteristic of the internet. Wynn and Katz (1997) found an "ambiguity of social boundaries" during an analysis of internet home pages:

> Some home page creators appear to perceive a more private world of readers than is in fact the case . . . . Yet how much social understanding do the creators of pages have, and how accordingly do they mediate their self-expression to account for the possibilities of a limitless audience? (p. 319)

This is a question that remains important in relation to blogs and their authors: Huffaker (2004) discovered that many adolescent bloggers reveal personal information about themselves in their blog without regard for who might see it, acting as if only themselves or their friends would ever read it. However, others, such as Bradley (2005), have found that girls who author blogs are becoming increasingly aware of their potential public audience and are learning to protect themselves and their identities accordingly (pp. 65–66).

In fact, recent studies of girls and their blogs have shown that at least some girls are aware of the potential their blogs have for a broad audience of readers, which includes strangers. A common challenge these girls face when authoring a blog is how to manage a dual audience of friends and strangers: "As the girls use this new medium to construct themselves and their relationships, they encounter challenges, most commonly the challenge of presenting self in a way that builds intimacy with friends while appealing to a larger group of teenage acquaintances who may be reading the same blog" (Bortree, 2005, p. 25). Bortree found that girls who recognized this potential for a larger audience would have "stopped writing a post because it was not interesting" or have "directed readers (assuming these are not close friends) to skip a post because they may not find it interesting due to the intimate or personal nature of the post" (p. 34). Another way girls manage and control the audience for their blogs is to abandon their blog completely and start a new one, or to only allow invited people to read posts. In Cadle's (2005) study, for example, one girl combined these strategies and "abandoned her original weblog and moved on to another weblog with a new username" after "telling all who wished to migrate to the new space to go there and ask to be added" (p. 117). As further evidence that girls are aware of the potential for strangers to read their blogs, many girls who have blogs read those of other people they do not know. In Bortree's (2005) study, for example, one girl "tried to read blogs of teenagers who live in other parts of the world that she wished to visit" (p. 35).

These examples point out that, as Mortensen and Walker (2002) argue, the challenge for blog authors is to establish a balance of writing for themselves, their friends, and strangers: "Blogs exist right on this border between what's private and what's public, and often we see that they disappear deep into the private sphere and reveal far too much information about the writer. When a blog is good, it contains a tension between the two spheres" (p. 257). This tension is one that needs to be examined closely as adolescent girls continue to use blogs as means of communication and as spaces for personal writing.

In light of the preceding discussions about publics (readers) and public spheres, it should be evident that the argument that blogs represent a new public sphere is not particularly applicable in the context of examining girls' blogs. What is more useful is Warner's notion of constituting publics of readers. By applying Warner's concept of publics to adolescent girls' blogs, we draw attention to the way in which blogs represent a kind of public address and how blog writing is for both the author herself, and for others who may potentially read the blog—both friends and strangers. This perspective brings to light a number of important questions about girls and blogs that require further research.

Conclusion: Future Research Directions

Why, when many agree that adolescent girls author a large number of blogs, has so little been written about their participation in this new cultural development? Herring et al. (2004) argue that part of the problem is that writing by adolescent girls is generally not valued in society and therefore is not of much interest to internet researchers (although there are notable exceptions). This compounds the devaluing of girls' blogs due to their association with personal writing and the paper diary, as discussed earlier.

In addition to being a reflection of traditional beliefs about the secondary place of female authors, young authors, and personal writing, the neglect of girls' blogging may also be a reflection of the ways in which blogs are being conceptualized. The tendency has been to emphasize the role of blogs in political discourse and the culture of journalism, as well as the potential for community-building around issues or distributing one's writing. This has resulted in an overemphasis on A-list blogs, predominantly written by older males, and a disregard for adolescent girls' journal-style blogs despite this group's increasing presence as bloggers. I have argued here that in order to fully appreciate girls' blogging it is necessary to take a different approach, one that focuses on the potential for blogs to constitute publics of readers. By focusing on the constitution of publics we are drawn to ask questions pertaining to audience and motivation rather than effectiveness of communication or popularity.

This shift in focus puts at the center of analysis the intersections of gender, writing, childhood, and notions of public and private. It encourages us to explore the ways girls are using blogs for documenting their lives and for communicating with friends and strangers, as well as to question what the participation of girls as bloggers might mean with respect to what is deemed appropriate in public spaces, particularly for young people. Adolescent girls' blogs provide one entry point for examining how the activities of girls are renegotiating boundaries: the boundaries of their lives, their relationships, and of public/private space. Given the opportunities that blogs offer girls, to write and share personal experiences and opinions with a potential public of readers, their importance in the lives of girls needs to be addressed and better understood. As I have argued in this chapter, it is important that we reposition ourselves and our approach to blogs such that we are able to directly address adolescent girls' experiences and activities as blog authors, instead of, once again, leaving them out.

Note

1. The original use of the term is most often attributed to Jorn Barger who published the *robot wisdom weblog* (www.robotwisdom.com) (Blood, 2000; Grossman et al., 2004; Kahney, 2000).

References

Blood, R. (2000). Weblogs: A history and perspective. *Rebecca's pocket.* Retrieved December 3, 2004, from http://www.rebeccablood.net/essays/weblog_history. html.

Bortree, D.S. (2005). Presentation of self on the web: An ethnographic study of teenage girls' weblogs. *Education, Communication & Information, 5*(1), 25–39.

Bradley, K. (2005). Internet lives: Social context and moral domain in adolescent development. *New Directions for Youth Development, 108,* 57–76.

Brooks, K., Nichols, C., & Priebe, S. (2004). Remediation, genre, and motivation: Key concepts for teaching with weblogs. In L. Gurak, S. Antonijevic, L. Johnson, C. Ratliff, & J. Reyman (eds.), *Into the blogosphere: Rhetoric, community, and culture of weblogs.* Retrieved December 2, 2004, from http://blog.lib.umn.edu/blogosphere/.

Cadle, L. (2005). A public view of private writing: Personal weblogs and adolescent girls. PhD thesis. Bowling Green State University.

Calhoun, C. (1993). Introduction: Habermas and the public sphere. In C. Calhoun (ed.), *Habermas and the public sphere,* pp. 1–48. Cambridge: MIT Press.

Carl, C.R. (2003). Bloggers and their blogs: A depiction of the users and usage of weblogs on the World Wide Web. Master's thesis, Georgetown University. Retrieved December 4, 2004, from http://cct.georgetown.edu/thesis/ChristineCarl.pdf.

Drejer, T. (September 2, 2003). Blog on. *PC Magazine.* Retrieved November 17, 2004, from http://www.pcmag.com/article2/0,1759,1217255,00.asp.

Gannett, C. (1994). *Gender and the journal: Diaries and academic discourse.* Albany: SUNY.

Grossman, L., Hamilton, A., Buechner, M., & Whitaker, L. (June 21, 2004). Meet Joe Blog. *Time Magazine, 163*(25).

Gurak, L., Antonijevic, S., Johnson, L., Ratliff, C., & Reyman, J. (2004). Introduction: Weblogs, rhetoric, community, and culture. In Gurak et al. (eds.), *Into the blogosphere.*

Henning, J. (2003). The blogging iceberg: Of 4.12 million hosted weblogs, most little seen, quickly abandoned. Perseus Development Corp. Retrieved November 29, 2004, from http://www.perseus.com/blogsurvey/.

Herring, S.C. (2004). Slouching toward the ordinary: Current trends in computer-mediated communication. *New Media & Society, 6*(1), 26–36.

Herring, S.C., Kouper, I., Paolillo, J.C., Scheidt, L.A., Tyworth, M., Welsch, P., Wright, E., & Yu, N. (2005). Conversations in the blogosphere: An analysis "from the bottom up." *Proceedings of the Thirty-Eighth Hawaii International Conference on System Sciences.* Los Alamitos: IEEE Press. Retrieved August 4, 2006, from http://csdl2.computer.org/comp/proceedings/hicss/2005/2268/04/22680107b.pdf

Herring, S.C., Kouper, I., Scheidt, L.A., & Wright, E.L. (2004). Women and children last: The discursive construction of weblogs. In Gurak et al. (eds.), *Into the blogosphere.*

Herring, S.C., Scheidt, L.A., Bonus, S., & Wright, E. (2004). Bridging the gap: A genre analysis of weblogs. Paper presented at the Hawaii International Conference on Systems Science, Waikoloa Village, Hawaii, January 5–8, 2004. Retrieved December 4, 2004, from http://www.ics.uci.edu/~jpd/classes/ics234cw04/herring.pdf.

Huffaker, D. (2004). Gender similarities and differences in online identity and language use among teenage bloggers. Master's thesis, Georgetown University.

Jacobs, J. (2003). Communication over exposure: The rise of blogs as a product of cybervoyeurism. Paper presented at the 2003 Australian and New Zealand Communication Association Conference, Brisbane, Australia, July 9–11, 2003.

Jensen, M. (September/October 2003). Emerging alternatives: A brief history of weblogs. *Columbia Journalism Review,* 5. Retrieved March 27, 2007, from http://www.cjr.org/issues/2003/5/blog-jensen.asp.

Kahney, L. (February 23, 2000). The Web the way it was. *Wired News.* Retrieved November 14, 2004, from http://www.wired.com/news/culture/0,1284,34006,00.html.

Lenhart, A. & Fox, S. (2006). *Bloggers: A portrait of the internet's new storytellers.* Washington, DC: PEW Internet & American Life Project.

Lenhart, A. & Madden, M. (2005). *Teen content creators and consumers.* Washington, DC: PEW Internet & American Life Project.

Lowe, C. & Williams, T. (2004). Moving to the public: Weblogs in the writing classroom. In Gurak et al. (eds.), *Into the blogosphere.*

Miller, C.R. & Shepherd, D. (2004). Blogging as social action: A genre analysis of the weblog. In Gurak et al. (eds.), *Into the blogosphere.*

Mortensen, T. & Walker, J. (2002). Blogging thoughts: Personal publication as an online research tool. In A. Morrison (ed.), *Researching ICTs in Context,* pp. 249–279. Oslo, Norway: InterMedia. Retrieved December 4, 2004, from http://www.intermedia.uio.no/konferanser/skikt-02/docs/Researching_ICTs_in_context-Ch11-Mortensen-Walker.pdf.

Roberts-Miller, T. (2004). Parody blogging and the call of the real. In Gurak et al. (eds.), *Into the blogosphere.*

Scheidt, L.A. (2006). Adolescent diary weblogs and the unseen audience. In D. Buckingham & R. Willett (eds.), *Digital generations: Children, young people and new media.* London: Lawrence Erlbaum. Retrieved August 3, 2006, from http://loisscheidt.com/linked/2006/Adolescent_Diary_Weblogs_and_the_ Unseen_Audience.pdf.

Stern, S.R. (1999). Adolescent girls' expression on web home pages: Spirited, sombre and self-conscious sites. *Convergence, 5*(4), 22–41.

Warner, M. (2002). *Publics and counterpublics*. New York: Zone Books.

Wynn, E. & Katz, J.E. (1997). Hyperbole over cyberspace: Self-presentation and social boundaries in Internet home pages and discourse. *The Information Society, 13*(4), 297–327.

CHAPTER SEVEN

Consuming Fashion and Producing Meaning through Online Paper Dolls

Rebekah Willett

Dani's Paper Doll Outfit

The design in figure 7.1 shows a fairly shapeless (and headless) cartoon model, displaying a top with a plunging neckline and a matching low-riding skirt; the top is marked with the "fcuk" label, and "you" appears as a label on the skirt. The message, "fcuk you," replicates slogans available on T-shirts from the popular clothing company, French Connection UK (FCUK). The design was produced by Dani, a twelve-year-old girl, in the context of a study of online fashion and identity. This fcuk you outfit epitomizes positions of the girls in a study I conducted—the clothing design is original, stylish, and technically quite advanced, expressing skill, creativity, and originality: the outfit is sleek, black, and sexy, expressing the fantasy play with future versions of the self; and the message (fuck you) is teen-speak, expressing confidence, independence, disregard for authority, and belonging to the group of teens who speak that language. In line with this interpretation, Rocamora's (2004) study suggests that teen girls wear "cheeky logo T-shirts" to make social statements (unlike a reading of the T-shirts that would place the wearers as victims of an industry that sexualizes girls and women). One could also interpret Dani's use of the label FCUK as a marker of the "tribe" she wishes to belong to (Sahlins, 1976). She is a member of the large tribe, "young teens," but belongs to a particular teen girlhood tribe—a tribe

Figure 7.1 Dani's paper doll outfit.

that knows "cool" labels, expresses itself through clothing, and is ready to play with sexy images. Here Dani's outfit also fulfils an aspirational function (Cook, 2004), orienting her toward future objects and practices, which Russell and Tyler (2005) describe as "position[ing] young girls in terms of a precocious sexuality, and in this respect, as both the subjects and objects of consumption" (p. 229).

As this brief introduction demonstrates, girls and young women occupy a complicated space—they are often in positions whereby they are gaining independence within their family in social and financial matters, giving them more choice in what they wear, who they see, and what leisure activities they pursue. Teenage girls are at a point in their lives when defining and performing their subject positions becomes complicated by choices as they become subject to discourses not only around children, but also around women. Girls are treading a fine line between being seen as victims of media and fashion industries, which position them as too sexualized too early, and being agents of "girl power"—confident, opinionated, and about to embrace their entrance to womanhood.

This chapter examines an attempt to engage girls in discussions about some of these competing discourses. The focus on digital fashion stems from research on girls' participation in a very popular online activity— dressing up online fashion figures on doll maker or "paper doll websites." Users can choose from hundreds of clothing items to dress the curvaceous online dolls, and they can also alter the dolls' hair, eyes, and skin color. These simple drop and drag activities were used by a large majority of the girls I studied across three research sites. The popularity of dressing up dolls, particularly the types of dolls found online, speaks to a continuation in girls' culture of doll-play, reflected in traditional dress-up activities using Barbie and more recent fashion dolls, such as Bratz. Attention to and experimentation with clothing style is also a prominent discourse in teen magazines. Finally, the design of avatars for a variety of digital activities, from *The Sims* to digital board games, is commonplace in girl culture. The focus on online dress-up, therefore, draws on these girls' experiences from a young age and also connects with activities that are part of their popular culture.

Dollmaker Designs

The study on which this chapter is based focuses on twenty-six girls aged twelve–thirteen as they both consume and produce dollmaker websites. Through visual data and interviews, the girls in the study position themselves in complicated ways—as innocent children, as scornful teenagers, as confident individuals, and as knowledgeable and savvy young women—and they seamlessly shift from one position to another as they appropriate and respond to surrounding discourses. Popular debates about girls as either subjects of negative effects of media images or as active agents who are employing media and fashion as cultural resources are both problematic. These critical positions overlook the complexity and internal tensions in girls' actual experiences. This chapter will explore how girls can be conscious and critical of the ways they are being positioned, yet also take pleasure in those positions, raising questions for researchers and educators.

Background: Children, Media, and the Female Body

Looking first at discursive practices that define children, a frequent, popular argument is that children are growing up faster than in previous generations (Elkhind, 1981; Winn, 1984). This is based on the premise that children's exposure to media has caused the "disappearance of childhood," as Postman argued in his book of that title in 1983. According to these authors, there has been a blurring, or even erasure of the boundary between childhood and adulthood partly due to children's media exposure to material that was previously kept from children, and partly to the increasing lack of relaxed free-play time (e.g., children are on adult-type schedules). The argument is that in contrast to previous generations of children, today's children are rushed into adult roles before they are ready, either psychologically or physically. As Buckingham (2000) concludes, these writers "explicitly draw on one of the most seductive post-Romantic *fantasies* of childhood: the notion of a pre-industrial Golden Age, an idyllic Garden of Eden in which children could play freely, untainted by corruption" (p. 35, original emphasis).

This "innocent child" discourse impacts on discussions about young teen clothing and media consumption. Moreover, the discursive field is further complicated by concerns about the sexualization of girls. Whilst girls are portrayed in the innocent child discourse as asexual (Gittins, 1998), there is also a paradoxical fear that they are at risk of sexual abuse. Drawing on psychoanalytic theory, Walkerdine (1997) explains that underlying the spoken fears of sexual abuse there is an unconscious fear of adults' own sexual desires for young girls. In this theory, adults are both drawn to the images of the attractive and seductive girl, and at the same time try to cover them up. Walkerdine writes, "This is not about a few perverts, but about the complex construction of the highly contradictory gaze at little girls, one which places them as at once threatening and sustaining rationality, little virgins that might be whores, to be protected yet to be constantly alluring" (p. 171). Girls, therefore, are subject to these contradictory discourses, which position them as both sexual and asexual, threatening and innocent.

Young teen girls are not only subject to discourses around children, as adolescents they are also positioned by discourses around women. Chernin (1994) analyzed what she terms "the tyranny of slenderness," which is created by men's desire for slender, nonthreatening women. Focusing on women with eating disorders, Chernin describes the oppression of women who feel they need to be small, quiet, and submissive in order to gain men's approval. Similarly, Wolf (1991) analyzes what she terms the "beauty myth," which pervades women's media saturated lives. According to Wolf, women are bombarded by unrealistic images of beauty through various media forms such as advertisements, movies, and music videos portraying stereotypically slender models with perfect skin and hair. The myth is reinforced by diet, cosmetic and plastic surgery industries that capitalize on women's inevitable insecurities, which are created by the beauty myth. This view of women as victims of media images is also reflected in writing about adolescent girls. Pipher (2002) speaks of American society as a "girl-poisoning culture" that threatens girls' developing identities by obsessing over aesthetic appearances. Instead of stabilizing and developing their individual identities as they move toward womanhood, girls conform to the idea that appearance is everything, and repress expressions of individuality.

These and other studies, which connect body dissatisfaction with images in the media, fall broadly under the media effects tradition (see also Harrison & Cantor, 1997; Hofschire & Greenberg, 2002; Myers & Biocca, 1992). Coming from mainstream sociology and behaviorist psychology, effects researchers take as their starting point the idea that media cause particular behaviors in their audience (see Barker & Petley, 1997, for an overview and critique of the "media effects" debate). This research implicitly assumes that children are passive and uncritical readers of media texts and as a result the texts are viewed as being "all powerful." In contrast, "active audience" research is based on the theory that the meaning of texts is constructed by the viewer, resulting in varying interpretations of any given text. Audiences in this role are able to resist dominant ideologies, reject meanings or messages from texts, enjoy a text without being affected by some implicit negative ideology, and use texts for their own purposes. However, as Buckingham (1993) argues, this approach simplifies readings of media by describing viewers as wholly autonomous, able to reflect and act upon their own needs and desires.

In feminist media studies, adopting a poststructuralist view has created a move to recognize the different, often contradictory ways of engaging with media texts. Studies on women and soap operas, for example, describe two modes of engagement: one is a critical mode in which the viewers are detached and express comments about the constructed nature of the shows; and the other is more involved and personal, where viewers identify with particular characters and narratives (Hobson, 1990; Katz & Liebes, 1990; Seiter et al., 1989). However, as

Van Zoonen (1994) describes, these studies, which indicate how house-wives relate to soap operas, take the category "woman" for granted and therefore fail to recognize "the way gender and the reception of popular culture are related," that is, the studies "reconstruct dominant gender discourse rather than analyse its dynamics" (p. 123). Van Zoonen calls for a more complex theoretical stance than the simplistic models employed by effects and active audience research. Similarly, McRobbie (1991) criticizes content analyzed of teen magazines and calls for accounts from readers and magazine publishers in order to gain a better understanding of girls' interactions with these media texts.

This feminist–poststructuralist stance can provide a useful framework for analyzing the complexity of interactions between girls and media texts. From this view, girls and women are neither dupes to all powerful media, nor are they always actively resisting the hegemonic discourses present in popular media. There is a tension here when analyzing structure and agency in girls' lives. Although there are dominant discourses that "invite" (or structure) a particular reading of a text, alternative readings are possible (e.g., girls have agency to resist dominant readings). However, the number of different readings is not endless—the discursive field offers a limited menu of options available to viewers. At the same time as viewers are choosing their positions or actively reading media texts, they are also being positioned by the surrounding discourses. By taking account of this tension between structure and agency, the study described in the remainder of the chapter will provide a nuanced description of the ways girls interact with discourses around media, fashion, and body image.

The Study

In order to engage with girls in discussion about their online fashion activities, I organized workshops in which girls designed their own fashion webpages. The workshops were conducted at a specialist ICT (Information and Communications Technology) center connected to a school in inner-city London. The group of girls recruited for the workshop were representative of the population of the school, which is ethnically diverse (about 75 percent of the pupils on roll are from minority ethnic groups, the largest being African Caribbean followed by Bangladeshi). The students came from a range of socioeconomic backgrounds, although the majority were from families with limited economic resources. The school arranged for the girls to be taken off their regular timetable to take part in the two workshops, spanning five days. We engaged in a series of activities, which alternated between planning and drawing with pencils and paper and then working on computers, using the software program Flash for designing. The girls worked in groups to produce a page of figures, clothing, and accessories for a drop and drag website (http://www.sens.eu.com/cc/cyberdolls_v2.html). All the girls' names used in this chapter are pseudonyms.

Using participant media production is becoming increasingly popular within media and cultural studies methodologies (see Bloustein, 1998; deBlock & Sefton-Green, 2004; Goldman-Segal, 1998). In the case of this study, I used media production as a way of gaining access to girls' understanding of their own media consumption practices. I hoped that through production, the girls would reveal their knowledge and ideas about media and fashion. In the workshops, the girls focused specifically on designing drop and drag fashion pages, similar to the websites they used. Through their designs the girls had to make choices about body shape, clothing styles, the range of clothing on offer, and specific cuts of clothing (necklines and skirt hemlines, e.g.). To help read the visuals I conducted semi-structured interviews to discuss design processes, fashion choices, and awareness of adult anxieties toward fashion and various dress-up activities. This chapter includes data primarily collected from these interviews.

As part of the analysis, I examined the girls' discourse in transcripts of the interviews, looking for patterns, commonalities, and differences. I color-coded themes that seemed most relevant to my research questions, looking at how girls make sense of dollmaker, what discourses they draw on in their discussion of dollmaker and fashion, and how they discuss body image in relation to these activities. The three themes that I will cover in this chapter are "modality," "good parenting," and "personal attributes." These themes relate broadly to the theoretical stance I am taking—they highlight the different ways girls' position themselves in opposition to powerful media structures; yet at the same time the girls' conversations are full of contradiction, and there are many instances that indicate media structures are powerful elements in their lives. The sections that follow discuss each of the themes, analyzing how girls are both positioned by and through the discursive practices surrounding them.

Modality

During the workshops, the girls designed a sales pitch for a fashion website. They discussed potential audiences for their site, and issues surrounding body shape emerged as part of those discussions. Most of the groups were careful to include clothes "for bigger people" as well as for "slim people." In conversations with the girls, the topic of media effects arose, and we discussed how playing with fashion webpages and dolls or reading magazines might affect how they feel about themselves. The girls had a variety of responses to this topic, centering on factors that affect the way media are read.

The study participants argued that they do not compare themselves to images on dollmaker sites ("but they're cartoons," explained Dalia) or to plastic dolls such as Barbie, which are clearly not real. The girls were suggesting that modality, that is, the truth claims made by a text, affects how a text is read. As Dalia described, "like if you look at Bratz they've got a really small body and like some big heads on it." The girls seemed perplexed that adults would consider play with disproportionate plastic breasts as affecting them: one girl exclaimed, "my boobs are normal!" The girls' reflection on dolls' modality supports Driscoll's (2002) ideas about the "multiplicity of Barbie": "[Barbie] is woman/not-woman and human/not-human, a game that can seem to denaturalize gender despite the anxieties of interested parties" (p. 97). The girls did not think adults would consider play with fashion dolls or dollmaker websites as risky and instead would see it as they do, as only a game—though one group considered that the possibility of becoming overly concerned with clothes might put a financial strain on their family.

With dollmaker and doll play, the girls indicate that the weak modality of the articles they are playing with limits their impact. In other words, because the dolls are so entirely unrealistic, they are unlikely to affect girls' self-esteem or body image. On the other hand, one group of girls indicated that body dissatisfaction might occur when looking at teen magazines:

> *Valerie:* "it's mostly when you start seeing idols or celebrities in particular that you want to turn yourself like that"
> *Grace:* "ya you wanna be like them" . . .
> *Valerie:* "unless they see an actual body they won't try and make themselves like them"

Resources with strong modality, therefore, are seen to have greater effect than those with weak modality. The girls argue that a simple cause-effect model is inadequate to explain their experiences with media, and that effects are more complex and at least partially determined by modality.

Looking past the effects argument, if the girls are saying that dolls and dollmaker images are not real and therefore do not affect them, one might ask, what is their interest in them and how are they relating to them? The girls' interactions with dollmaker can be described as play.

They construct outfits together, show each other their finished outfits, try on outrageous outfits and "have a laugh." Dalia describes the pleasure in this play: "Like, you can make them weird or make them really nice like they're going to a party." This play is partly about fantasizing about their future bodies. Numeyra said, "I just like the hairstyles, and I just go, 'Oh, I wish I had long hair,' or something." When I asked the girls if dressing up on dollmaker would make you then go and want to wear that sort of outfit, Jade said, "No, you would just think oh what would I look like if I wore that." These fantasy texts are similar to the double-page spreads or posters of celebrities that girls might view in teen magazines and pin-up in their bedrooms. McRobbie (1991) argues that fantasy materials offer spaces for girls to move away from childhood into adolescence (p. 184). Similarly, Walkerdine (1997) looks at girls' fantasies as spaces in which they play with and insert themselves into various discursive practices, such as those around womanhood, and therefore fantasies "become discursive and material in the social world" (p. 188). Finally, relating to digital images, Davies (2004) and Thomas (2004) describe how girls experiment with avatars, fantasizing and performing different femininities. Thomas concludes "they 'play' with the image and the text they use to present themselves in very particular ways to explore their fantasies of desire" (p. 376).

Questions arising from the girls' play with the dolls concern the role of fantasy in children's and teen's lives. If one argues that children and teens need spaces to rehearse and revel in different roles (gorgeous, curvaceous, or muscle-bound teenager) then we need to know more about what is happening in those spaces. Does fantasy satisfy curiosity regarding other possible identities, enable exploration of alternative roles, increase or decrease desire for particular roles? What is happening to identity: are we, as subjects, able to try on and then cast off different positions, and what is left behind when we do that? If the argument is made that it is better to have teens safely exploring fantasies by reading teen magazines or dressing up online dolls rather than dressing up themselves and going out into the real world, then parents, educators, and policy makers need to consider how to allow space for those fantasies. This is not to say that discourses embedded within those media should be accepted without critique. The challenge is how to allow teens to indulge in the fantasy but also encourage a critical awareness of, for example, oppressive discourses around female beauty. Again there are questions about how to engage in critical discussions with teens, but also more broadly about the ability to switch between seemingly conflicting positions. The next section will demonstrate the ease with which girls shift between various positions, starting with the position of a future parent.

Good Parenting

According to the interviews, the role of parents is a key factor in how girls read "the beauty myth." Several of the girls adopted the moral high ground criticizing parents who do not pay enough attention to how their daughters are dressed.

Jade: "there's some little girl who goes to some primary school I always see her and her mum's always putting her in these big high boots and short skirts and I'm like the girl's no more than six"

Mackenzie: "you can't make them [your children] be your twin"

In this excerpt, the girls reflect attitudes that will potentially inform their future roles as parents. Restricting what your child wears is one of the roles of a good parent, in these girls' opinions. We can see this type of argument as an indication that the girls see effects as mediated by a number of factors, so again the effects model is inadequate. It is also interesting to look at the discourses the girls are drawing on. Here discourses concerning childhood are being referred to (e.g., childhood innocence), but more specifically, the girls are using discourses that regulate childhood. In his analysis concerning the disappearance of childhood, Buckingham (2000) describes how adult definitions of childhood can not only repress and serve to control children but also produce particular behaviors. He writes, "[Adults] have defined the kinds of behaviour which are appropriate or suitable for children at different ages" (p. 12). A girl of "no more than six" is defined earlier as inappropriately dressed using this regulatory discourse.

Correct parenting is not only about how children are allowed to dress, it is also the key to how girls feel about their appearance, as Mackenzie describes:

it's probably about the way they talk to you . . . they should just sit you down and say "oh no matter what people say I think you're ok and there's nothing wrong with you," they shouldn't just say "oh don't be silly you're not ugly"

In this statement, Mackenzie is arguing that parents should not dismiss their children's anxieties by calling them "silly," but instead should "sit you down" and talk through concerns. Again, the girls are indicating that effects of the tyranny of slenderness are determined by a range of factors, and the way parents talk to children is a key factor. However, it is striking that these girls are using discourse that Walkerdine and Lucey (1989) assert serves to regulate mothers—providing readymade guilt trips for the mother who fails to raise a confident daughter. Walkerdine and Lucey describe how, particularly through talk, mothers are assigned a pedagogical role that psychologists and, more recently, the general public insist is crucial to their child's development. The girls in my study have used this discourse to assert that parents hold the key to their child's confidence; and in turn, confidence is a key to emotional stability.

Walkerdine and Lucey relate this regulatory discourse to social class, arguing that particular content and pedagogical structure in middle-class mothers' talk is seen to be essential to child development. There are questions, therefore, about how the girls, many of whom might not be considered middle-class, are using this discourse as well as a particular educational discourse around self-esteem. What is this middle-class discourse allowing or not allowing the girls to say? Furthermore, similar to when the girls are discussing body dissatisfaction and media images, we need to ask how much they are simply repeating particular discourses and how much they are actually engaging with them on a deeper level. Finally, although the girls take the moral high ground here, they also told me that they sometimes wear clothes to show off their figures. This raises some important questions regarding how girls are negotiating these conflicting positions.

Personal Attributes

As indicated in Mackenzie's description of correct parental talk, personal attributes are keys to resisting the beauty myth. These attributes include self-esteem, confidence, and individuality, as these girls describe:

> *Giovanna:* "Well, for me, to me I look at it . . . if you have good self-esteem then you shouldn't be worried. But then if you . . ."
> *Ashley:* " . . . If you don't, if you're not really happy with yourself, then you'll be one of those people who will force themselves to lose weight."
> *Giovanna:* "But then again, um, that thing brings the person out of you. Because what you wear tells a lot about you, that you feel comfortable about yourself or if you, um, just want to fit in, in a group, or . . . yeah."

The girls are not only highlighting the influence of parents on self-esteem, they are also connecting confidence with eating disorders and dress, and individuality with the ability to resist peer pressures. Clearly, girls' dress and body image is determined by many more factors than media. Looking closer at this excerpt, the girls are drawing in educational discourse around bullying and drugs. Educational discourse frames bullying as connected to confidence—for example, pupils are told that bullies pick on people's insecurities; and acting confident will dissuade bullies. Being confident and comfortable with oneself is also a message in drug education—pupils are told they need to be confident to follow what they think is right, to be themselves, and thereby to resist peer pressure to consume alcohol, tobacco, or other drugs.

Being comfortable with oneself was mentioned by many of the girls and seems to refer not only to a physical state but also an emotional feeling, as Giovanna indicates: "Because if you just copy someone else and don't feel comfortable, you're not really yourself." Again the girls are emphasizing the importance of feeling confident. This is echoed in a study on women's clothing choices, in which confidence is connected not only with choice of clothes but also with multifaceted feelings of comfort (Gillen, 2003). The girls indicated they would not feel comfortable in thongs and short skirts, and I am arguing that this feeling of discomfort is due in part to the discursive practices that position them as needing to express individuality and innocence.

An interesting element revealed in the earlier excerpts is the contradiction between expressing individuality and maintaining the sense of belonging in a group. According to Giovanna, if you feel confident, then you are able to resist "just want[ing] to fit into a group." The girls have highlighted another problem with the beauty myth—the notion that all girls are attempting to conform to one look. All the groups of girls said that developing an individual style was important, and they also saw it as a benefit of creating fashion designs and playing on dollmaker websites. Part of the fun of playing with dollmaker is "to create your own image" and "to express what kind of clothes you like." The girls are drawing on a particular discourse in which development of personal style is encouraged, for example, teen magazines suggesting personalizing wardrobes by searching in second-hand clothing shops (McRobbie, 1991). Although these girls use individuality as an argument to display their independence (from parents, crowds, or manipulative media), when I asked them where they would buy clothes if I gave them £100, every girl listed the same sports shop. The girls seem comfortable with these contradictions: expressing individual style and yet choosing similar clothing items from the same store. They argued that individual style can be expressed through wearing different trainers (sport shoes), which are indicative of the tribe to which one belongs (Sahlins, 1976). This is reminiscent of analyzed youth subcultures that show how material objects are used by young people as markers of identity, defining their specific social groups, and distinguishing class, race, and gender as well as age (Hebdige, 1979; Lury, 1996). And, as Widdicombe and Wooffitt (1995) describe, there is a tension around authenticity, between expressions of individuality and expressions of belonging to a particular subculture.

Conclusion

Using digital paper dolls as a site of discussion encouraged the girls in this study to examine relationships between clothing choices and discourses around individuality, self-confidence, and proper parenting. The girls argued that they make conscious decisions about what to wear. On the other hand, although the girls in the interviews stressed the importance of individual clothing style, their choices of clothes were all very similar. I am not arguing that girls are immune to powerful ideologies inscribed in the production of media aimed at girls, such as the constant bombardment of images of skinny or curvaceous women. The analysis highlights the importance of seeing teen girls as having "multiple subjectivities" (Davies, 1989), instead of fixed and unified identities implied in arguments about the tyranny of slenderness.

However, this begs the question, where does this leave girls? Griffin (2004) describes how girls are positioned in ambiguous and contradictory ways, which work "to render the girl herself as an impossible subject" (p. 42). Therefore, we need to consider how we can go beyond the passive/active debate and beyond a debate that ends up by saying, "it's both things and it's complex." Feminists are asking questions about the "undoing of feminism"; they question whether new generations of young women see a need for feminism (Griffin, 2004; McRobbie, 2004). In what seems a surprising turnaround from her influential work on teen girls as magazine readers, McRobbie has come out against notions of girl power, blaming these discourses on the absence of young activists today. She suggests, "So enthralled are young women by the seductive power of the media that critical faculties have been blunted. Female students, the very group who should be challenging these assumptions, are silent" (McRobbie, 2005).

The data described in this chapter shows that girls, as in McRobbie's earlier suggestions (1991), are familiar with "a range of narrative codes against which stories and fictions can be measured for their success or failure" (p. 143). They are rejecting particular narrative codes (around media effects, e.g.) and are buying into others (the pedagogical role of parents, e.g.). The challenge for researchers, therefore, is to examine how codes are being rejected, which codes are being accepted, and the questions these processes raise for any number of concerned parties including educators, parents, policy makers, and media industries. If students are critical of media representations of women but also take pleasure in them, as educators we need to find a way of engaging students in critical analysis that accepts these positions and also moves them on to look, for example, at ways ideologies are inscribed in the discourses students are using. If young people are able to take different positions that argue against the effects of media, this raises questions for parents and policy makers when considering media access and regulation. If girls are already reading against the grain of fashion media or if they use fashion media for important fantasy play, do we need to be concerned about the bombardment of skinny models? Do we need to restrict their access to curvaceous dolls or magazines that offer sexualized images of women? Finally, media industries are having to consider a different market for their texts. One might argue that media industries are already well-aware that codes are being read in ways that are different to previous generations' readings. However, industries also need to consider what new readings might entail, and what responsibilities they have in producing new readings.

References

Barker, M. & Petley, J. (eds.) (1997). *Ill effects: The media/violence debate*. London: Routledge.

deBlock, L. & Sefton Green, J. (2004). Refugee children in a virtual world: Intercultural online communication and community. In A. Brown & N. Davis (eds.), *World yearbook of education digital technology, communities and education*, pp. 196–210. London: Routledge.

Bloustein, G. (1998). "It's different to a mirror 'cos it talks to you": Teenage girls, video cameras and identity. In S. Howard (ed.), *Wired-Up: Young people and the electronic media*, pp. 115–133. London: UCL Press.

Buckingham, D. (1993). *Children talking television: The making of television literacy*. London: Falmer Press.

———. (2000). *After the death of childhood: Growing up in the age of electronic media*. Cambridge: Polity Press.

Chernin, K. (1994). *The obsession: Reflections on the tyranny of slenderness*. London: Harper Perennial.

Cook, D. (2004). *The commodification of childhood: The children's clothing industry and the rise of the child consumer*. Durham, NC: Duke UP.

Davies, B. (1989). *Frogs and snails and feminist tales: Preschool children and gender*. Sydney: Allen and Unwin.

Davies, J. (2004). Negotiating femininities online. *Gender and Education, 16*(1), 35–50.

Driscoll, C. (2002). *Girls: Feminine adolescence in popular culture and cultural theory*. New York: Columbia UP.

Elkhind, D. (1981). *The hurried child: Growing up too fast too soon.* Reading, MA: Addison Wesley.

Gillen, K. (2003). Choosing an image: Exploring women's images through the personal shopper. In A.Guy, E. Green, & M. Banim (eds.), *Through the wardrobe: Women's relationships with their clothes*, pp. 71–93. Oxford: Berg.

Gittins, D. (1998). *The child in question.* New York: St. Martin Press.

Goldman-Segal, R. (1998). *Points of viewing children's thinking: A digital ethnographer's journey.* Mahwah, NJ: Lawrence Erlbaum Associates.

Griffin, C. (2004). Good girls, bad girls: Anglocentrism and diversity in the constitution of contemporary girlhood. In A. Harris (ed.), *All about the girl: Culture, power and identity*, pp. 29–44. London: Routledge.

Harrison, K. & Cantor, J. (1997). The relationship between media consumption and eating disorders. *Journal of Communication, 47*(1), 40–67.

Hebdige, D. (1979). *Subculture: The meaning of style.* London: Methuen.

Hobson, D. (1990). Women, audiences and the workplace. In M.E. Brown (ed.), *Television and women's culture: The politics of the popular*, pp. 61–74. London: Sage.

Hofschire, L. & Greenberg, B. (2002). Media's impact on adolescents' body dissatisfaction. In J. Brown, J. Steele, & K. Walsh-Childers (eds.), *Sexual teens, sexual media: Investigating media's influence on adolescent sexuality*, pp. 125–149. London: Lawrence Erlbaum.

Katz, E. & Liebes, T. (1990). *The export of meaning: Cross-cultural readings of Dallas.* Oxford: Oxford University Press.

Lury, C. (1996). *Consumer culture.* Cambridge: Polity Press.

McRobbie, A. (1991). *Feminism and youth culture: From "Jackie" to "Just Seventeen."* Basingstoke: MacMillan.

———. (2004). Notes on postfeminism and popular culture: Bridget Jones and the new gender regime. In A. Harris (ed.), *All about the girl: Culture, power and identity*, pp. 3–14. London: Routledge.

———. (October 14, 2005). Cutting girls down to Victoria Beckham's size. *Times Higher Education Supplement.*

Myers, P.N. & Biocca, F.A. (1992). The elastic body image: The effect of television advertising and programming on body image distortions in young women. *Journal of Communicatio, 42*(3), 108–133.

Pipher, M. (2002). *Reviving Ophelia: Saving the selves of adolescent girls.* New York: Putnam Publishing Group.

Postman, N. (1983). *The disappearance of childhood.* London: W.H. Allen.

Rocamora, A. (2004). "You're a teenager and this stuff happens": Girlhood and cheeky slogan t-shirts. Paper given at Pluridisciplinary Perspectives on Child and Teen Consumption, Angouleme, France.

Russell, R. & Tyler, M. (2005). Branding and bricolage: Gender, consumption and transition. *Childhood, 12*(2), 221–237.

Sahlins, M. (1976). *Culture and practical reason.* London: University of Chicago Press.

Seiter, E., Borchers, E., Kreutzner, G., & Warth, E. (1989). Don't treat us like we're so stupid and naïve: Towards an ethnography of soap opera viewers. In E. Seiter, H. Borchers, G. Kreutzner, & E. Warth (eds.), *Remote control: Television, audiences and cultural power*, pp. 223–247. London: Routledge.

Thomas, A. (2004). Digital literacies of the Cybergirl. *E-learning*, *1*(3), 358–382.

Van Zoonen, L. (1994). *Feminist media studies*. London: Sage.

Walkerdine, V. (1997). *Daddy's girl: Young girls and popular culture*. London: MacMillan Press.

Walkerdine V. & Lucey, H. (1989). *Democracy in the kitchen: Regulating mothers and socialising daughters*. London: Virago.

Widdicombe, S. & Wooffitt, R. (1995). *The language of youth subcultures: Social identity in action*. Hemel Hempstead: Harvester Wheatsheaf.

Winn, M. (1984). *Children without childhood*. Harmondsworth: Penguin.

Wolf, N. (1991). *The beauty myth: How images of beauty are used against women*. London: Vintage.

CHAPTER EIGHT

Producing Gender in Digital Interactions: What Young People Set Out to Achieve through Computer Game Design

Caroline Pelletier

There has been much interest in the role that video games play in the process of socialization and the development of subjectivity in contemporary culture (see chapters one, two, and nine in this volume; Linderoth, 2005; Taylor, 2006; Walkerdine, 2004). My aim in this chapter is to capitalize on this emerging work about game play to analyze young people's game design activities. To do this, I examine how youth draw on their experiences with computer games to design their own games.

My focus is on the social functions that young people perform through game design, and more particularly on how design is deployed as a resource with which to construct a gendered subjectivity. The analysis highlights the processes by which games are used to establish social relations, and by extension, construct a sense of self. I argue that the ways in which games are played, interpreted, and designed are a function of the social relations within which they are located and which they make possible.

The data analyzed in this chapter emerged from a research project called "Making Games" conducted through a collaboration between media education researchers from the University of London and Immersive Education, a UK-based software company. Over three years, the partnership developed a production tool to enable young people to create computer games. We also researched strategies for introducing game design in English and Media classrooms, youth clubs, and the home. The rationale for teaching game design is that computer games are a significant cultural form and that young people should not only be able to play, talk, or read about them, but also construct their own.

Two types of data will be discussed here: a selection of drawings produced by young people as part of a grade eight (twelve–thirteen-year-olds) English, Media, and ICT course on computer games; and two games made by fourteen-year-old students in an after-school club. As I will discuss in detail later, comparing and analyzing these data suggests the ways in which game design is involved in the development of gendered subjectivities.

Girls Making Games

A number of research projects as well as local initiatives have sought to enable young people, particularly girls, to reap greater benefit from gaming technologies by giving them tools to design their own games (Denner & Campe, in press; Hughes in press; Kafai, 1996, 2000; see also CC4G 2006). Efforts to include girls in gaming are intended to counter concerns that game playing and design are predominantly male activities. It has been argued that knowledge of particular gaming technologies may provide an entry point into subsequent careers in science and technology. The fear is that the largely male demographic of game-players will dominate the field, leaving women behind to occupy less important positions in the key industries of the future (Cassell & Jenkins, 2000). In the wake of Gee's (2003) work on the pedagogical effectiveness of video games, apprehensiveness has also been expressed that girls may not be able to take full advantage of the anticipated boom in educational computer games (Kafai et al., in press).

It has proven difficult, however, to isolate what it is about game making as an activity that enables girls to learn, earn, or play more. This is, in part, because methods for analyzing how games become meaningful to people (how they shape what people do, think, and feel) have emerged only recently (Linderoth, 2005). In order to evaluate the potential benefits of young people making games, and particularly in regards to girls, researchers need frameworks to identify the meaning that this activity has to young people, its function in the development of thoughts and actions, and the role gender plays in this process (see chapter nine). The work of two theorists seems particularly relevant to developing such frameworks. Judith Butler (1993, 1997, 1999, 2004; with Laclau & Zizek, 2000) explores the processes by which gender assumes significance in social norms and relations. Gunther Kress (1997, 2003, 2005), together with others working on multimodality (e.g., Kress & van Leeuwen, 1996), develops methods for analyzing the production of meaning in relation to modes of representation and the individual's interest in a social context. In tandem, they provide conceptual tools with which to describe how gender is made significant in multimodal representations such as games. I will discuss the work of these theorists before suggesting how it can be used to analyze design work produced by young people.

Analytical Tools

Butler's work describes the means by which subjectivity is produced as an effect of representation. Traditionally, subjectivity is said to precede representation: when we speak, write, or draw, it is often understood that identity must first be in place prior to such an act. Butler argues that representation does not simply describe a state of affairs but brings it into being. Given that language (written, visual, musical, etc.) is not the property of the individual, but an intersubjective system that confers meaning by classifying and categorizing in particular ways, it follows that in representing the world, subjects draw on resources that precede them and that establish the terms by which it is possible to think and act. Using language is not, therefore, something that leaves the subject unaffected, but rather is precisely how the subject comes to know its own thoughts and beliefs. Since subjects continuously make representations, it follows that the constitution of subjectivity is a reiterative practice; subjectivity is never fully settled but always remade through representational practices. Butler calls this process "performativity."

The concept of performativity has implications for how gender is defined and researched. Rather than treat gender as a fixed and known variable, Butler argues that what is significant about gender is precisely the processes by which it is continuously produced and recognized. Gender can be conceptualized as a kind of doing, an incessant activity that is realized through representation. In this sense, people construct their own gender, but the terms by which they do so are socially made, and embedded in social norms and practices that give them meaning.

Like Butler, Kress defines representational resources as collective, social. The reason we can communicate is precisely because social conventions exist about how to formulate meaning. We select from available conventions of representation according to the interest we have in a state of affairs: "it is the interest [. . .] of the sign-maker which determines what is taken as criterial about an entity at the moment of its representation" (2005). The argument that representation is shaped by the interests of the social agent has two consequences. The first is that conventions are understood to be socially motivated, which means that individuals make choices about how to represent something according to the interest they have in it, including the intended audience and the desired effect upon them. The second is that conventions are defined in terms of processes of production rather than application. Kress' focus is on how conventions are adapted to a specific purpose, in line with the interests of the individual. This implies that conventions are never simply applied, but are continuously transformed, reshaped, modified. The (conventionalized) meaning of a word or image, for example, does not exist independently of instances of usage but is always reactualized or reasserted. It is Kress' concept of interest in meaning-making that overlaps with Butler's notion of performativity, as something that is carried out individually in order to achieve an effect whose meaning and value is defined within social terms. As a result, it is possible to analyze how individuals adapt social norms or conventions in processes of representation in line with their interest to achieve a particular subjectivity—and for the purposes of this chapter, a subjectivity defined in terms of gender.

Using the work of these two theorists, I will identify a rationale for girls' game-making. I will explore the implications of this analysis by examining two sets of data, a group of drawings, and games made by students.

Producing Gender through the Visual Image

The drawings presented here were produced by twelve–thirteen-year-old students as part of an English, Media, and ICT course on computer games. The course curriculum addressed how games can be analyzed as texts: how they tell stories; the business of games (including relationships between media companies, regulatory bodies, and distributors); and game culture, including the pleasures that players associated with games. As class homework in the third week of the course, students were asked to design a screenshot from a game they would like to make. They were given two design specifications: it had to fit within the role-playing genre and have a sci-fi setting. The conventions from each genre were reviewed in class by examining and classifying game screenshots as well as excerpts from sci-fi films.

I will focus on the screenshots (figures 8.1–8.6) produced by six students—three girls and three boys—selected from approximately twenty on the basis that they appear the most finished and polished. My analysis draws on *Reading images: The grammar of visual design*, in which Kress and van Leeuwen (1996) provide a framework to analyze visual data. Drawings can be interpreted in several ways; here I will provide what I believe to be the most convincing account. These images were produced in color, but they are reproduced here in black and white.

My interpretation of these drawings focuses on elements that appear to relate to the performative production of subjectivity. One of the most striking details is that the boys' representations reflect an almost identical moment: one game character shoots down a number of others. In Jak's drawing, this is achieved through the depiction of an "incoming missile" flying in from the left. In Tom's and Paul's drawings, the perspective and angle suggest that the player is doing the shooting, in the style, respectively, of a third- and a first-person shooter game. The girls' drawings do not feature this moment, and although reference is made to weapons and guns, they are not shown in use. I would argue, for example, that in Liz's screenshot, the female character is not aiming but displaying an available weapon (the male character seems unperturbed by having a gun pointed his way).

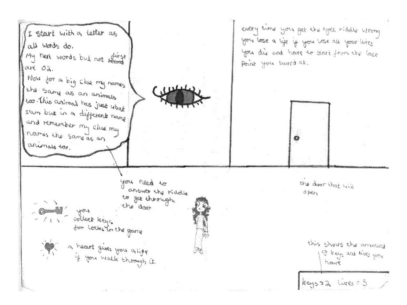

Figure 8.1 Kate's screenshot.

Figure 8.2 Liz's screenshot.

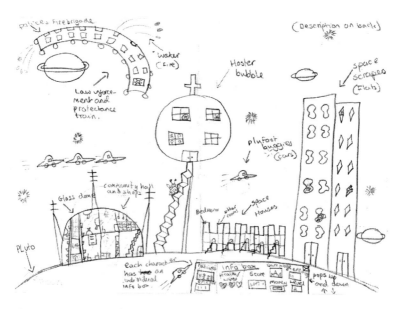

Figure 8.3 Janet's screenshot.

Figure 8.4 Jak's screenshot.

138

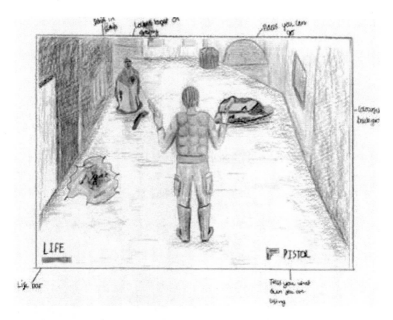

Figure 8.5 Tom's screenshot.

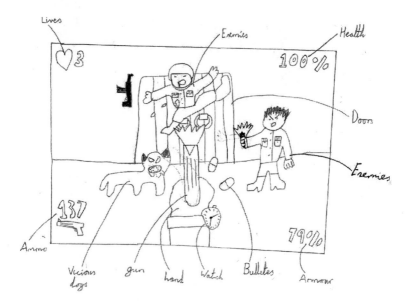

Figure 8.6 Paul's screenshot.

There are other striking differences between the drawings which can be interpreted more systematically. Unlike the boys' drawings, Kate's, Liz's, and Janet's drawings represent the potential experiences a player might encounter *throughout* the game, rather than actualizing a single moment within it. The images in these girls' drawing are labeled objectively, and items are displayed or posed rather than captured in movement; for example, in Janet's drawing, the lines behind the cars indicate movement but there is no clear vector indicating their direction or purposes in getting there. Similarly, the blank facial expression of Liz's and Kate's characters depicts them as items for contemplation rather than interaction. The viewer is positioned broadly at eye level and at a distance, which encourages objectification of the scene. This is further enhanced by the lack of a frame around the drawing; the representation is constructed as objective rather than as a subjective response.

Relations between the visual elements in the drawings are established primarily through writing. This has the effect of decontextualizing the items shown, making them generic, so that they become a "typical example" rather than connected to a particular moment in the game. For example, in Janet's drawing, she includes the fire engine but not the fire. Color is used primarily to differentiate rather than saturate the scene and the palette is relatively limited, removing the distractions that a vivid, visual spectacle might entail. Backgrounds are plain and the representation of depth reduced, with elements classified hierarchically across the page. In Liz's drawing, for example, the planets to be visited are at the top of the page, the avatars in their current status across the middle, and the buttons to be pressed at the bottom. The design principles underpinning these girls' drawings are similar to those used for the representation of analytical processes (Kress & van Leeuwen, 1996, p. 89). The screenshots are designed to present a static taxonomy of the whole game's essential attributes rather than represent a part of it in a life-like way.

Whereas the boys' drawings depict an image characteristic of a single genre (the shooter game, and in Jak's case, the strategy war game), the three girls combine elements from different game genres. Liz, for example, indicates that the actions in her game include shopping, jumping, bouncing, running, visiting, and shooting, among others. The forms of interaction characteristic of *The Sims* (Liz and Janet) and the puzzle genre (Kate) are combined with shooting, dying (Kate), "taking damage" (Janet), or "being injured" (Liz). Given that game genres and their visual characteristics had been reviewed in their class by studying screenshots, this medley of genre characteristics seems purposeful rather than a consequence of unfamiliarity. Indeed, the pick-and-mix approach demonstrates a certain pattern. Indicators of shooter genres are featured around the edges or on the back of drawings, rather than in the central space. In Janet's and Kate's case, they do not contribute to the drawings' symmetry, and in Liz's, the operational function of the gun is not included—it is not actually threatening anyone. This suggests two things. First, the girls' drawings are designed to present a conceptual representation of the essential features of games as a general category. The references to shooter games in Janet's and Kate's images serve to generalize a single representation; shooter games are often portrayed in popular media as representatives of games as a whole. This way of seeing objects is characteristic of the academic and scientific "viewpoint." In presenting the "general" attributes of games, the girls construct themselves as "good students," who understand the requirements of an academic (school-based) context. This finding supports Weber and Mitchell's (1995) analysis of gender in children's drawings in which they found that academic styles were much more prominent in girls' drawings than in those done by boys. Second, the girls make reference to shooter games but keep these to the margins of their drawings. Their interest may be double here. Whilst perceiving shooter games to be central to a representation of games in general, they do not wish to identify their own tastes with it.

A similar analysis can be carried out on the other three drawings. Whereas the representational structures in the girls' drawings are conceptual, depicting features as more or less stable and timeless, the representational structures in the boys' drawings are narrative: they serve to present an unfolding drama, foregrounding pleasure arising from sensation and visual spectacle.

The images in the boys' drawings are framed, constructing the scene as a subjective perspective and positioning the viewer as the player. This point of view, along with the representation of events, demand that the viewer/player engage with the scene actively rather than contemplate it dispassionately. The form of action required is established through vectors (shooting guns, a target symbol at the end of the line established by the avatar's gun) and perspective. The diagonals in Tom's drawing, for example, create strong directional thrusts that lead the eye straight upward. These imply a forward movement. Jak engages with the viewer by providing a visual spectacle rather than demanding direct action, but the image of the tank under attack and the use of vibrant color suggest his desire to arouse an emotional, subjective response.

The boys' drawings convey excitement and adventure and the color saturation in Jak's and Tom's images instantiate a hyperreal modality that Kress and van Leeuwen associate with fantasy (1996, p. 168). In Paul's drawing, the viewer's sensory appreciation is invited through the scaling of certain visual elements (notably the gun and its falling shells) as well as the representation of certain physical details, such as the dog's drool and the drops of blood spurting out of the enemies. This emphasis on the senses discourages more distant, dispassionate forms of engagement. In all three drawings, writing is kept outside of the frame and serves little explanatory purpose. Writing is thereby subjugated to the principles of a visual spectacle.

The Students' Design Strategies

The drawings reproduce certain popularly held notions about the distinctive pleasures of male and female gaming (Alloway & Gilbert, 1998; Graner-Ray 2002; Jenkins 2003). The boys' drawings focus on fast-paced, aggressive linear action carried out by exotically dressed and armed superheroes in fantasy settings, with the pleasures of gaming identified in terms of visual spectacle and sensory immersion. The girls' drawings suggest engagement with gaming at a more intellectual level, focusing on features such as exploration, "realistic" characters and settings, the development of relationships, reflective problem-solving, and conflict resolution without high levels of violence.

One could conclude that these drawings confirm well-established beliefs regarding differences between the gaming preferences of boys and girls. However, one should be suspicious of conclusions that appear to be "common-sense," particularly as they relate to stereotypes and ideologies about gender. Other data from the study introduce elements of doubt into such easy conclusions. In other situations over the length of the course, the students emphasized different aspects of games. In writing about historical strategy games, Jak placed value on their historical accuracy. In a questionnaire, Liz lists her favorite game as *Crazy Taxi*, although she excludes the racing genre from her drawing. As Carr shows in this volume, young people's preferences about games are not fixed and at different times, they emphasize different aspects of games to clarify why they like playing them. This argument clearly goes against certain assumptions about gendered gaming practices. Gaming is gendered, but the relationship between how people play, how they understand themselves as players, and how they present themselves as players to others is by no means predictable and stable over time.

These contradictions provoke important questions. What factors led students to make these particular kinds of representations in this context? Or as Kress would put it, what interest were they pursuing in choosing to design a screenshot in this particular way? The boys could have picked any moment from a shooter game, including scenes in which the avatar goes shopping or chats to other characters; such moments are not rare. Similarly, the girls could have chosen a shot from one genre they enjoyed (e.g., *The Sims*-type simulations) but they chose to combine genres, and made efforts to mix features characteristic of "realistic" simulations with shooter games. What might reasonably explain the students' motivations in making these choices?

I would argue that these drawings cannot be taken simply as indicators of how these students "see" games, but that this way of seeing games is intended to have an effect. What these representations performatively produce is the gender of their author. It is precisely because the producer and the viewer of these drawings identify the images as stereotypically "gendered" that they become effective statements of gender identity. What defines the shooter genre as masculine in popular representations of games is precisely the kind of scene that the boys depict. Similarly, the girls focus on characteristics that are often said, in popular media and in gaming websites and magazines, to be more "girl-friendly." However, the images are not representative or simple reflections of the games these students actually play and supposedly enjoy. Gender is therefore the effect, not the cause of these images. The students do not portray games in stereotypically gendered ways because they *are* boys and girls, but because they wish to produce and *identify* themselves as such.

To argue that students design their drawings to achieve a gendered identity is not to suggest they do so in a manipulative or deceptive way, and that they are hiding what they "really" like about games. How students interpret games, how they make meaning from them, is a social process, developed over time and in relation to social norms, including those relating to gendered behavior. Social norms about what boys and girls like are therefore not simply imposed on young people but one of the ways in which they come to know their own pleasures. The drawings these students produce demonstrate one way in which they come to understand themselves as players and designers. It is by constructing games as gendered that the students are able to construct themselves as gendered. It is precisely by drawing on popular stereotypes about games for boys and games for girls that young people come to recognize and assert their gender.

In this section, I have suggested that preparatory game design work enabled students to construct themselves as particular kinds of players and designers. In the next section, I will examine how students produced an identity through the process of making games.

Producing Gender through Game Design

The games discussed in the following paragraphs were made using software developed by *Immersive Education* over a three-year period in partnership with researchers, teachers, and students. Before analyzing a couple of games, I will outline how the software functions as a representational resource.

The game-authoring software consists of a number of readymade 3D assets, including locations (rooms and corridors), props, and characters. Designing a game means defining the rules by which assets interact with each other. For example, "if the player clicks on the door, the door opens." Emphasis is thereby placed on organizing relations between assets rather than producing the assets themselves. The number of assets is limited, although it is possible to import audio, written text, and 2D still images.

In order to improve the design of successive prototypes of the software, we ran after-school clubs in a couple of schools and worked intensively with small groups of students, making games. One of these clubs involved students from the same class we had worked with eighteen months previously. We invited twelve students to join. Over the first few weeks, some students dropped out, leaving us with approximately eight regular members. Only two of these were girls. I will discuss two games, one made by Alice and the other by Simon, to explore how gender-based considerations seem to have influenced their design.

Alice's Game

Alice began to design her game with two friends, who subsequently stopped coming to the club. The game is set up as a mystery for the player to resolve. It opens with the following message: "You have gone back in time to Lady Hosiepol's mansion. Your quest is to find the long lost scroll of Wasonant which holds Lady Hosiepol's deepest darkest secret." The author of the various written messages that appear in the game is not named, but their function is to provide explanations of objects and of the conditions under which the player is acting. For example, upon finding a dagger, the player can examine it to reveal the following written message: "Lady Hosiepol committed suicide with this very knife and now haunts this house . . . WATCH OUT!!!!" The message forewarns of danger but does not state what the threat might be, creating a level of suspense whilst also giving information that might be helpful to the player. A helper character is thereby evoked, who knows more than the player but not enough to tell them how to act. Playing the game, therefore, involves acting with the aid of a friendly presence. The implied in-game character and player character are positioned as being equally fearful of the dangers ahead, and one knows only a little more than the other.

Much of the game involves working out significant from insignificant objects (objects that delay or do not enhance the player's progress through the game). A series of apples left in a corridor are identified as being either healthy or unhealthy, with the player asked to "choose wisely." The reference to wisdom here is suggestive of a coming-of-age story in which the player learns how to act and behave appropriately within a particular environment.

Alice's game draws on a fictional narrative form often marketed to young women; the murder mystery featuring a young heroic detective, such as Nancy Drew. The story is unusual for a gaming format—it is psychological rather than action-based (the aim is to find out why a lady committed suicide). The genre of narrative that Alice draws on is one aimed at women; it is found across different media platforms rather than just in gaming. Alice goes to some length to evoke a helper character. The nature of this social relationship enacts familiar conventions about male and female relations—none of the boys had messages with a helpful, convivial tone in their games.

One could argue that Alice, through her choice of narrative genre and creation of mood, is constructing her player as female, and positions herself as a female designer. This process is not simply a consequence of Alice's experience of games—she was a keen game player, with a wide repertoire of gaming experiences to draw on. In selecting from this experience to inform her design work, Alice emphasizes features that define herself and her audience in terms of gender.

Simon's Game

In configuring his game (figures 8.7 and 8.8), Simon stated that he drew inspiration from one of his favorite games at the time, *Silent Hill*, which he liked because of its near-impossible puzzles. Following an opening message that simply tells the player they have been imprisoned by a maniac, Simon does not develop the storyline. Instead, he focuses on certain structural conventions of games. One of these is realized in the arrangement of weapons, which are situated spatially from small (a knife) to large (an exploding mine). This sequence indicates increasing firepower, following popular gaming conventions, which suggest an increasing level of difficulty. Another convention is reproduced in the creation of a training level at the start of the game. Here, the player is given instructions on what actions to perform—"click on this, use this here." However, the second level does not draw on the skills acquired in the training level. Simon displays two conflicting interests here: to bring together the "typical" components of a game (a training

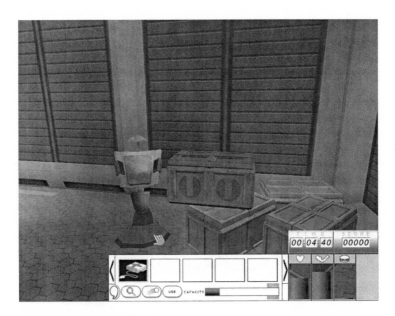

Figure 8.7   A screenshot from Simon's game in player mode.

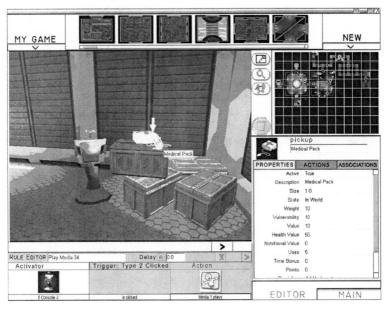

Figure 8.8   A screenshot from the same game in designer mode.

level, distinct from the rest of the game) and to create challenges that are fearsomely difficult, for which the player cannot be precisely trained. The basis on which Simon organizes his game positions him as a game fan, but in a gendered way. He emphasizes aspects that are often said to appeal to dedicated male gamers: the use of firepower, inclusion of fantasy-based action, and skills that can be acquired only through hours of practice and devoted attention. Simon could have drawn on any aspect of the *Silent Hill* games, including the highly developed narrative. This is de-emphasized in favor of the creation of fearsomely challenging puzzles. One cannot deduce from this that Simon is not interested in well-developed narrative or realistic characters; in fact, his list of favorite games is dominated by games with these two elements, unlike Alice's list. Rather, the basis on which Simon configures his game is designed to establish a particular social identity in the group—the knowledgeable, well-experienced gamer. This identity is also gendered. It is precisely because members of the group will recognize and acknowledge an interest in weapons and ludic design as "male" interests that Simon's game is effective as a statement of gendered identity. It is because such norms exist that they are drawn on by students to establish themselves as gendered.

Conclusions

Kress' argument that representation is shaped by the interest of the social agent makes it possible to explore the principles by which students select from their experience and knowledge of games in designing their own. In this chapter, I have made use of Butler's concept of performativity to show that one of these principles is the desire to produce a gendered subjectivity. Students draw and design games in a way that identifies them as belonging to a group; a group of players, fans, but also a group defined by gender.

This perhaps raises a question about why students put so much effort into signifying gender, to themselves and to others. Before answering this, I should state that in analyzing these data, I have focused on the production of gender rather than on other issues. The same data could be analyzed again to reveal other kinds of social affiliations, relating to fandom of certain texts or socioeconomic status (Pelletier, 2006). One of Butler's aims is to debunk the traditional view that gender is a more fundamental aspect of identity than anything else; indeed in another site of research, it seemed largely irrelevant as a consideration in students' approach to gaming (from their perspective), including game design (see chapter nine).

However, in the data analyzed here, I have focused on the production of gender as an aspect of identity. Classifying people into gender categories is a powerful social ritual; we make constant efforts to distinguish between boys and girls, women and men. This is clear in all aspects of social life, from public toilets to toys, including games. Games are often sold on the basis of a gendered target audience. The *Nintendo DS*, for example, comes in blue or pink versions. People create an identity for themselves by affiliating with one group of people and distancing themselves from another. Groups are distinguishable by the norms associated with them, which people generally try to abide by and fit in with. It follows that in seeking to achieve a social identity, situating oneself in relation to gender norms is usually necessary. The reason young people align themselves with gender norms, therefore, is that this offers a way of becoming intelligible to others.

Through their identification with gender norms, young people deny some of their experiences and overemphasize others. In this study, for example, girls and boys distinguished differently between game components (narrative versus action) claiming one as legitimate in opposition to the other. This cannot be taken as a simple reflection of their gendered interest in games. Rather, this representation is selected to produce an effect at a moment in time.

Defining gender as a continuous activity implies that it is never fully achieved—we put effort into constructing our gender identity precisely because it is in doubt. What counts as "masculine" or "feminine" changes over time and is a result of people's actions in negotiating and transforming social norms. If we accept that making meaning necessarily involves reshaping available social norms and their representational conventions, it follows that the value of young people making games can be understood in terms of reshaping game-based representational conventions, including conventions pertaining to gender. Alice and Simon drew on their knowledge of gaming conventions to make their own games—this is how their games are made playable. However, they do not simply maintain such (gender) norms but remake them. Designing a game means conforming to convention in order to be understood; but it also means appropriating and adapting convention to one's particular situation. This process inevitably transforms such conventions. The value of young people making games is that they are developing capacities as designers. They draw on established conventions, but are able through their position as game designers to reshape design patterns.

As more people, including girls, design games, norms about who designs and plays games are widened. It does not automatically follow that as a consequence, girls who make games in school or as a hobby are more likely to enter IT sectors or the games industry—there are undoubtedly larger barriers to this than girls' subjectivities. However, making game design more popular and widespread perhaps begins to denaturalize the situation and thereby makes the stakes, as well as the possible options, clearer.

Acknowledgments

This research is generously supported by the Paccit Link programme: http://www.paccit.gla.ac.uk/.

References

Alloway, N. & Gilbert, P. (1998). Videogame culture: Playing with masculinity, violence and pleasure. In S. Howard (ed.), *Wired-up: Young people and the electronic media*, pp. 95–114. London: UCL press.

Beavis, C. (2005). Pretty good for a girl: Gender, identity and computer games. In *Digra 2005 Conference Proceedings*, Retrieved August, 16, 2006, from http://www.gamesconference.org/digra2005/viewabstract.php?id = 368.

Butler, J. (1993). *Bodies that matter: On the discursive limits of sex*. London: Routledge.

Butler, J. (1997) *Excitable speech: A politics of the performative*. London: Routledge.

———. (1999). *Gender trouble: Feminism and the subversion of identity* (2nd ed.). London: Routledge.

———. (2004). *Undoing gender*. London: Routledge.

Butler, J., Laclau, E., & Zizek, S. (2000). *Contingency, hegemony, universality*. London: Verso.

Cassell, J. & Jenkins, H. (eds.) (2000). *From Barbie to Mortal Kombat: Gender and computer games*. Cambridge, MA: MIT press.

CC4G—Computer Club for Girls. Retrieved August 16, 2006, from http://www.cc4g.net/.

Denner, J. & Campe, S. (In press). What do girls want? What games made by girls can tell us. In Y. Kafai, C. Heeter, J. Denner, & J. Sun (eds.), *Beyond Barbie and Mortal Kombat: New perspectives on games, gender and computing*. Cambridge, MA: MIT press.

Gee, J.P. (2003). *What videogames have to teach us about learning and literacy*. New York: Palgrave.

Graner-Ray, S. (2002). But what if the player is female? In F.D. Laramee (ed.), *Game design perspectives*, pp. 304–309. Hingham, MA: Charles River Media.

Hughes, K. (In press). Design to promote agency and self-efficacy through educational games. In Y. Kafai, C. Heeter, J. Denner, & J. Sun (eds.), *Beyond Barbie and Mortal Kombat: New perspectives on games, gender and computing*. Cambridge, MA: MIT press.

Jenkins, H. (2003). From Barbie to Mortal Kombat: Further reflections. In A. Everett & J. T. Caldwell (eds.), *New media: Theories and practices of digitextuality*, pp. 243–253. New York: Routledge.

Kafai, Y. (1996). Gender differences in children's constructions of videogames. In P.M. Greenfield & R.R. Cocking (eds.), *Interacting with video*, pp. 39–66). Norwood, NJ: Ablex.

———. (2000). Video game designs by girls and boys: Variability and consistency of gender differences. In J. Cassell & H. Jenkins (eds.), *From Barbie to Mortal Kombat: Gender and computer games*, pp. 90–114. Cambridge, MA: MIT press.

Kafai Y., Heeter, C., Denner, J., & Sun, J. (Eds.) (In press). *Beyond Barbie and Mortal Kombat: New perspectives on games, gender and computing*. Cambridge, MA: MIT press.

Kress, G. (1997). *Before writing: Re-thinking the paths to literacy*. London: Routledge.

———. (2003). *Literacy in the new media age*. London: Routledge.

———. (2005). *Towards a semiotic theory of learning*. Unpublished manuscript.

Kress, G. & van Leeuwen, T. (1996). *Reading images: The grammar of visual design*. London: Routledge.

Linderoth, J. (2005). Animated game pieces. Avatars as roles, tools and props. In *Aesthetics of play online proceedings*. Retrieved August 16, 2006, from http://www.aestheticsofplay.org/linderoth.php.

Pelletier, C. (2006). Making meaning with games. Paper given at the IT-Learn conference *From Games to Gaming*, May, University of Gothenberg, Sweden.

Taylor, T.L. (2006). *Play between worlds: Exploring online game culture*. Cambridge MA: MIT Press.

Walkerdine, V. (2004). Remember not to die: Young girls and video games. *Papers: exploration into children's literature, 14*(2), 28–37.

Weber, S. & Mitchell, C. (1995). *That's funny, you don't look like a teacher: Interrogating images and identity in popular culture*. London: Falmer Press.

CHAPTER NINE

Contexts, Pleasures, and Preferences: Girls Playing Computer Games

Diane Carr

Women and girls in the West have reputedly refused to embrace computer games with the same zeal as their male peers. Theorists from a range of disciplines have investigated the reasons behind these statistics (Bryce & Rutter, 2002; Cassell & Jenkins, 2000; Kerr 2003; Krotoski 2000; Schott & Horrell, 2000). One thing these diverse efforts share is an interest in girls and their gaming preferences.

In this chapter the question of girls and their preferences is discussed with reference to observations of a computer games club at a single-sex state school in South London. Play observations were combined with video documentation, interviews, and questionnaires in order to investigate these girls' gaming tastes. These observations suggest that when considering games, gender, and preference, it is productive to employ a holistic and mobile or dynamic account of tastes and inclination—one that implicitly incorporates existing work within media and cultural studies on active and media-literate audiences, and their "reading histories" (Bennett & Woollacott, 1987; Buckingham & Sefton-Green 1994). This is important, because what became apparent over the course of a school term is that gaming preferences are not static, nor do they emerge in a vacuum.

The problem with ascribing particular preferences directly or solely to player gender is that it implicitly divorces gaming tastes from the economic, social, and cultural forces that fuel and inform gaming practices. It is worth noting that here, again, the question of games and gender focuses on the feminine. Games and masculinity is a topic calling for investigation, but one that is outside of the scope of this particular piece of research. Generally speaking, digital game developers, publishers, retailers, and their high-profile marketing campaigns have addressed a male audience. One unsurprising result of this is that this sector of the market has swelled, while others have remained relatively untapped. There are signs that things are changing, and it is feasible that as games continue to shift out of the subcultural margins and into the mainstream, distinctions other than that of gender may become more pertinent, diversity will be further accommodated, and patterns of participation may alter.

It was certainly the case that for the nine thirteen-year-old girls in the gaming club, computer and video games were a routine part of their lives. They were all casual rather than hardcore gamers in that they played for a couple of hours a week, rather than hours per day (although there were signs that at least one of the players desired much greater levels of access). The girls talked with their friends about games, played at home and when they visited family, and sought out information online or in gaming magazines occasionally. When interviewed the club members referred to games as a regular, pleasurable yet otherwise unremarkable part of their younger childhood. One of the girls, in fact, was jubilant that her dad had just promised her a new Game Boy as a reward for good grades. We issued questionnaires to fifty-five of the girls' classmates, and found similar results. There were certainly varying degrees of access, but most played digital games of one sort or another on a fairly regular basis.

Of course there are multiple factors active in contemporary culture and in the lives of male and female players, impacting on how games are regarded, and how players position themselves in relation to gaming culture. In the play sessions observed during this research, elements including humor, music, the attractiveness of certain male avatars, or the appetite for all things Harry Potter were integral to the choices and preferences demonstrated. These thirteen-year-olds would discuss the merits of the different platforms, and particular games, not just as players, but as canny, proto-contenders in consumer culture. This discourse cannot be divorced from wider gaming culture (where it links with notions of cultish expertise), nor can it be entirely separated from considerations of gender, age, race, or class.

Play and Situated Preference

Most of the participants who joined the computer games club were volunteered by the school, and a few girls heard about the club through friends, and joined up. The group quickly settled at nine members, with a few regular spectator/visitors and an ever-expanding waiting list. Once the club was up and running it became necessary to limit entry in order to prevent overcrowding. The club ran on Tuesdays at lunchtime for the duration of a school term. There is no pretence in this discussion that this is a particularly natural situation. The focus here is on the constituents of preference in a particular situation, and the links between access, context, and preference—so the fact that this is an arranged rather than a "found" scenario is not felt to be an issue. One or two adults were generally present, and would occasionally help out with technical issues or even join in a games session, but they did not orchestrate player groupings. In this instance the author did not participate in actual game play but rather observed and video-documented the sessions.

At the start of the term, and again at the end, the girls completed questionnaires in which they were asked to list their favorite games. On both questionnaires the girls listed a wide variety of games and genres: fighting and racing games were mentioned repeatedly, games from the *Grand Theft Auto* series were popular, as were action adventure games and *The Sims*. In the context of this chapter, however, what is significant is that the girls listed a total of twenty-six games on the later questionnaire, and this included sixteen new games, nine of which they had played during the sessions. The girls' new favourites included named titles (*Midtown Madness 3, Jak and Daxter*), but also entirely new genres ("fighting games"). The initial preferences expressed on the first questionnaire presumably relate to games that the girls had previously accessed. The alterations shown in the later responses could reflect a number of variables—the girls being in a different mood, for instance. These shifts, however, also indicate that simply offering these users alternative games in a new context was sufficient to generate changes in their stated tastes. What this suggests is that when investigating gaming inclinations, the relationship between previous access and expressed preferences should not be overlooked.

Certain site specifics were implicated in the preferences demonstrated by these users. These included the layout of the room, as well as timing, territory, and hardware (e.g., who's turn it was, who got there first). Obviously the games supplied were also a factor in the girls' choices (see table 9.1), as was the particular type of play offered by different games, and the allure of popular trans-media franchises. We attempted to

Table 9.1 Games supplied during the term

Xbox	*Halo, Midtown Madness 3, Terminator 3, Dead or Alive 3, Buffy the Vampire Slayer*
PS2	*Jak and Daxter, Tomb Raider 4, Tony Hawk's Pro Skater 4, Abe's Oddysee, Oni, Primal, Soul Reaver 2, Time Splitters 2, XIII, Enter The Matrix*
PC	*Deus Ex, Dino Crisis, Lord of the Rings; The Fellowship of the Ring, Neverwinter Nights, Warcraft 3, Tomb Raider 2, Baldur's Gate, The Sims, Harry Potter and the Philosopher's Stone, Tony Hawk's Pro Skater 3, Black & White, Sid Meier's Civilization III, HalfLife, Harry Potter and the Prisoner of Azkaban*

supply a mixed bag of popular games, but with a limited budget we were reliant, to some degree, on the games that we had at hand. The games were piled on a table in the center of the room and the girls were free to help themselves. If a girl did not have a particular game in mind she might rifle through the available titles and pick out one based on its packaging, but if the game play did not appeal, it would soon be discarded.

While most of these games were picked and played at some point, certain games were picked with notable regularity. There was a Playstation 2, an Xbox, and six PCs in the room. The consoles were near the door, and offered two-player games. For these reasons the area around the consoles was the loudest and the most social part of the room and thus, *in this specific instance* the consoles were less conducive to private or contemplative gaming than the PCs. As an outcome, the most popular games on the consoles were the ones that offered instant gratification, pace, tricks, humor, dual-play, and turn taking, rather than games that were orientated toward narrative or that demanded sophisticated tactics. This meant that *Tony Hawk's Pro Skater 4* (a skateboarding game), *Midtown Madness 3* (a comical driving game), and *Dead or Alive 3* (a fighting game) were consistently selected, and played for longest on the consoles. The stunts, options, character selections, and special moves in these games were accessed in an experimental, playful manner. Skills acquisition at the consoles did occur, yet it did not look particularly systematic: one player stated that she liked *Midtown Madness* "because I crashed into everything," but another girl said that she enjoyed learning new tricks in *Tony Hawk's*, while the girls who liked *Dead or Alive 3* appreciated that there were "loads of new moves to learn." One player remarked that "this game was good cos they had really good graphics and I'm always winning." The girls were happy to compete in *Dead or Alive*—the players occasionally sang or danced when they won a round—but instances of coaching were also frequent.

The PCs, on the other hand, were placed in a quieter section of the room and as an apparent consequence different genres were preferred. Here the girls generally put on headphones to settle in for thirty minutes of solo gaming. Onlookers were tolerated but interruptions were not welcome and there was little or no turn-taking. Different games were tried out, but the most consistently popular were *The Sims*, the two *Harry Potter* games and the *Lord of the Rings* games. These action–adventure games reward a player's investment of time with characterization, sequential missions, or storytelling. The *Harry Potter* games are "fun because [they] are just like the movie/book and you get to learn the spells." *The Sims* offers incremental complexity and the chance to take control—as one player explained: "I could make their lives enjoyable or miserable."

So, the division of the room into noisier and quieter areas, and into sociable or more private zones, combined with the styles of play (instantaneous, or more contemplative) that various games offered. In short, the preferences demonstrated by the girls were shaped by the context of play, in combination with the styles of play that various games offer, *and* the player's awareness of such offers. In each instance, the ability of the girls to recognize and actualize the pleasures promised by different games was enabled by their being literate in the forms of play available, and the kinds of experiences potentially on offer.

Text and Representation

As facilitators we made a concerted effort to include as many female avatars as possible, so a reasonable proportion of the games we supplied featured female leads, and showed images of the heroine on their packaging. These included *Oni, Primal, Enter The Matrix, Dino Crisis, Tomb Raider IV*, and *Tomb Raider II* (while in the RPGs *Baldur's Gate* and *Neverwinter Nights* the player has the option to construct a female lead character). For some women players the manner in which female avatars are included, excluded, or depicted is certainly an issue (see www. womengamers.com for a discussion of "digital women"). These girls, however, showed no noticeable, additional interest in these games. In fact we were impressed by the degree of ambivalence they inspired. Perhaps this was because of the girls' age, or because they were in a primarily female environment, or because they were in public. Whatever the reason, this disinterestedness is enough to suggest that thirteen-year-old girls playing games at a single-sex school do not regard a female avatar as a particular bonus. When given the option to play as either a male or a female character, the girls would either show no preference and playfully switch between the options (as with *Dead or Alive 3*), or they might actually prefer to play with/as a male avatar despite having the option of a female—as was consistently the case with *Tony Hawk's Pro Skater 4*.

We distributed a questionnaire to fifty-five of the club members' fellow students (same year, same school) in order to contextualize our observations of the gaming sessions. It included questions relating to games, access, and tastes. For instance, the girls were asked, "If you could create a computer game or video game character, what would they be like?" Nearly 60 percent of those who answered this question did not specify a gender for their character at all—they instead listed nonspecific characteristics ("joyful," "funny," "loud, adventurous," and "independent") or included the choice of male or female. Around 25 percent of the respondents wanted to play with funny or attractive male characters ("strong, buff male, muscley," or "tall, strong and rich with good taste and style," "muscley, dark, good looking," "six pack, single plaits in hair"). The smaller remainder specified that they would create a female character. Interestingly, it was girls with the highest degree of access (e.g., girls with a games console at home that they considered "their own") who were the most likely to specify a gender for their avatar, plus they were slightly more likely to designate it male. In other words, the allocation of a particular gender or maleness to an avatar might not reflect the preference of a player, as much as it reflects that player's familiarity with console game conventions.

When asked to list the attributes of the best games at the gaming sessions, the girls gave the following responses: being in control (especially of *The Sims*), and having good music and graphics. A game should have choice and variety; it should be unpredictable. There should be action and a range of characters, and the possibility of interesting missions and tasks. Magic and adventure were listed as desirable. Plus, a game should be easy to learn, yet hard to play (but not *too* hard!). In order to demonstrate, of course, that there was anything particularly feminine about these preferences it would be necessary to contrast them with the preferences of these players' male peers (peers in terms of age, and also in terms of their being casual rather than hardcore gamers).

The presence of these desired characteristics, however, was no guarantee of popularity. Other factors still determine if a player will become aware of an unfamiliar game's offers and potentials, or not. For instance, none of the club members showed any interest in playing *Buffy The Vampire Slayer* until the second-last week of term, when a few of the girls arrived early and found the sessions' facilitators playing it on the Xbox. What they saw of *Buffy*'s game play and combat was sufficient to spark their interest. Then, by passing around the controls, calling out instructions to each other, and shrieking at the "scary bits," the girls managed to convert it into a rowdy and sociable group activity. Thus several factors were complicit in their late predilection for *Buffy*. For instance, the game only became interesting after the girls had seen others engrossed by it, and, after a term with *Tony Hawk's* and *Dead or Alive 3*, the girls had become adept at generating their own preferred form of group play.

We had also supplied a number of role-playing-games for the PCs including *Baldur's Gate* and *Neverwinter Nights*. Computer RPGs feature rules and play-styles adapted from earlier social, table-top games such as *Dungeons and Dragons*. These games involve creating a central character, using spells and potions, and exploring a vast fantasy world. As noted, the players stated a preference for variation in character, magic, missions, and adventuring, and yet none chose to play these games. The players had no prior experience with the genre, and this appears to have played a part in their disinterest. If the group had contained one RPG enthusiast it may have been enough to trigger curiosity in the others—just as watching others play had resulted in *Buffy* attaining last-minute popularity. In this case, however, these games were unfamiliar and as a result they simply failed to register with these users.

This suggests that while preferences are open to alteration, there needs to be a motivating catalyst or transitional support (or "scaffolding") when players are confronted by a complex and unfamiliar genre. Such a catalyst might be social, but it is also possible that it could be textual, or trans-textual: had these RPGs been set in "Harry Potter world," for instance, it is likely that the girls would have at least tried them, regardless of their unfamiliarity with the genre.

Conclusion

So, what computer games do girls like? The answer is that it depends. Socialization may well play its part, yet our gaming preferences will also depend on where we are, what we know, who we know, what we've tried, and what we've grown tired of. Distinctions in taste between male and female players reflect patterns in games access and consumption that spring from (very) gendered cultural and social practices (Carr, 2006). As this suggests, accounts of gaming preference need to be situated within a framework that incorporates reference to players' previous access to games and existing gaming knowledge. Gaming preferences need to be conceptualized within a paradigm that can accommodate mobility, increment, learning, and alteration.

Different people will accumulate particular gaming skills, knowledge, and frames of reference, according to the patterns of access and peer culture they encounter—and these accumulations will pool as predispositions, and manifest as preferences. Familiarity and competence feed into a player's experiences of gaming, partly determining the pleasures that he or she will expect, recognize, and access, and thereby impact on preferences that might be expressed as a result. Preferences are an assemblage, made up of past access and positive experiences, and are subject to situation and context. The constituents of preference (such as access) are shaped by gender and, as a result, gaming preferences manifest along gendered lines. It is not difficult to generate data that will indicate that gendered tastes exist, but it is short-sighted to divorce such preferences from the various practices that form them. To attribute gaming tastes directly, solely, or primarily to an individual subjects' gender is to risk underestimating the complexities of both subjectivity and preference.

On a final note, it is certainly possible that various factors bolstered the club members' enthusiastic engagement with games during the computer-gaming sessions described in this chapter. It could be argued that we created something of an artificial environment, an anomalous "bubble" where it was the norm that girls and women enjoy playing and talking about computer games. However, it is also true that outside of any such bubble, the relationship of girls (or boys, women, or men) to computer games is just as constructed.

Acknowledgments

This chapter was first published as a conference paper in *Changing Views: Worlds in Play, Selected papers of the 2005 Digital Games Research Association's 2nd International Conference*, edited by S. de Castell and J.Jenson. The conference paper itself was abridged from a longer article then under consideration, and later accepted for publication in the journal *Simulation and Gaming* (eds., D. Myers and J. Colwell, December 2005, vol. 36, issue 4). This research was undertaken with the support of the Eduserv Foundation. I would like to thank my colleague Caroline Pelletier, who was the primary facilitator of these gaming sessions.

References

Bennett T. & Woollacott, J. (1987). *Bond and beyond: The political career of a popular hero*. New York: Routledge.

Bryce, J. & Rutter, J. (2002). Killing like a girl: Gendered gaming and girl gamers' visability. Paper presented at the Computer Games and Digital Culture Conferences, Tampere, Finland.

Buckingham, D. & Sefton-Green, J. (1994). *Cultural studies goes to school: Reading and teaching popular media*. London: Taylor and Francis.

Carr, D. (2006). Games and gender. In D. Buckingham & G. Schott (eds.), *Computer games: Text, narrative and play*, pp. 162–178. Cambridge: Polity.

Cassell, J. & Jenkins, H. (2000). *From Barbie to Mortal Combat: Gender and computer games*. Cambridge, MA: MIT Press.

Kerr, A. (2003). Women just want to have fun: A study of adult female players of digital games. Paper presented at the Level Up: Digital Games Research Conference, Utrecht.

Krotoski, A. (2004). *Chicks and joysticks: An exploration of women and gaming*. Entertainment and Leisure Software Publishers Association (ELSPA).

Schott, G. & Horrell, K. (2000). Girl gamers and their relationship with the gaming culture. *Convergence, 6*, 36–53.

Games Cited

Baldur's Gate (1998) Bio Ware Corp., Black Isle Studios/Interplay
Black and White (2001) Lionhead Studios, EA Games
Buffy the Vampire Slayer (2002) The Collective Inc., Electronic Arts
Dance Dance Revolution (2001) Konami, Konami
Dead or Alive 3 (2002) Team Ninja, Tecmo Ltd.
Deus Ex (2000) Ion Storm, Eidos Interactive
Dino Crisis (2000) Capcom, Capcom
Dungeons and Dragons (1974) Gygax and Arneson, TSR Hobbies Inc.
Enter the Matrix (2003) Shiny Entertainment, Atari Inc.
Grand Theft Auto III (2001) DMA, Rockstar Games
Half-Life (1998) Valve Software, Sierra On-line Inc
Halo (2001) Bungie Software, Microsoft
Harry Potter and the Philosopher's Stone (2001) KnowWonder, EA Games
Harry Potter and the Prisoner of Azkaban (2004) EA UK, EA Games
Jak and Daxter: The Precursor Legacy (2001) Naughty Dog, Inc. SCEA Inc.
Lord of the Rings, The Fellowship of the Rings (2002) Surreal Software Inc., Black Label Games
Midtown Madness 3 (2003) Digital Illusions CE AB, Microsoft Game Studios
Neverwinter Nights (2002) Bio Ware Corp., Atari Interactive, Inc.
Oddworld Abe's Oddyssee (1997) Oddworld Inhabitants, GT Interactive Software
Oni (2001) Rockstar Canada, Rockstar Games
Primal (2003) SCEE Cambridge, SCEA
Sid Meier's Civilization III (2001) Firaxis Games, Infogrames Interactive Inc.
Soul Reaver 2 (2001) Crystal Dynamics Inc., Eidos Interactive
Terminator 3: The Redemption (2004) Paradigm Entertainment Inc., Atari Inc.
The Sims (2000) Maxis, Electronic Arts
Time Splitters 2 (2002) Free Radical Design, Eidos Interactive
Tomb Raider II (1997) Core Design Ltd., Eidos Interactive

Tomb Raider IV, The Last Revelation (1999) Core Design Interactive, Eidos Interactive

Tony Hawk's Pro Skater 3 (2002) (for PC) Gearbox Software, Activision 02

Tony Hawk's Pro Skater 4 (2002) Vicarious Visions, Activision 02

WarCraft 3 (2003) Blizzard Entertainment, Blizzard Entertainment

WWF SmackDown (2000) Yuke's Co Ltd, THQ Inc.

XIII (2003) Ubisoft Montreal, Ubisoft Entertainment

CHAPTER TEN

Adolescent Girls' Expression on Web Home Pages: Spirited, Somber, and Self-Conscious Sites

Susannah R. Stern

Introduction

A predominant theme evident in many recent discussions of American girlhood is that self-expression is critical for girls' healthy development (see Brown & Gilligan, 1992; Furger, 1998; Phillips, 1998; Pipher, 1994; Taylor, Gilligan, & Sullivan, 1995). Girls appear to benefit from access to "safe spaces" where they feel comfortable expressing both who they are and who they wish to become (Furger,1998). Historically, how-ever, sites for girls' self-expression have been sparse (Pipher, 1994; Taylor, Gilligan, & Sullivan, 1995). Adolescence, in particular, marks a time period during which girls often struggle to find arenas where they may speak their minds without threat of damaging relationships. Adolescent girls[1] (see Lerner, 1993) learn from friends, media, and personal experience that speaking up can get them in trouble with teach-ers, worry their parents, and endanger their friendships (Orenstein, 1994; Phillips, 1998; Pipher, 1994). Many censor themselves to navigate more safely through a society that expects certain culturally defined and gender-appropriate behaviors (Pastor, McCormick, & Fine, 1996; Phillips, 1998). The process of self-silencing and subsequent missed opportunities for self-validation can become cyclical, driving girls further "underground" (Taylor, Gilligan, & Sullivan, 1995).

Despite concern over the shortage of spaces for girls to comfortably speak their minds, little research has examined the potential of a burgeoning technological enterprise—the internet—to furnish new forums for girls' self expression. The WWW, in particular, allows those with access and expertise to construct personal home pages to present their thoughts to a geographically removed, anonymous, yet potentially global public.

Of the myriad of home pages that now inhabit the web, hundreds (and perhaps thousands) were created by adolescent girls who blend text, images, and sounds to present themselves to a real yet faceless audience. Although boys outnumber girls online, the growing number of girls' home pages lends credibility to the notion that the web may present a new and much needed forum for girls' "safe" self-expression[2] (see Stern, 1998). Furger (1998), who talked with girls about why they liked going online, supports this proposition. She discovered that girls foremostly enjoyed the freedom to say whatever they wanted without fear of judgment or harassment.

It appears that the web provides an unparalleled opportunity to view how girls willingly present themselves in a public forum[3] (see Abbott, 1998). Currently, however, little is known about the actual composition of girls' home pages. The exploratory study described in this chapter examined adolescent girls' web pages to begin mapping out the kinds of expression exhibited.

Home Pages As Self-Presentation

Web personal home-page authors have begun to receive greater attention as their number—estimated at well over half a million—steadily climbs (Personal Home Page Institute, n.d.). Of the growing handful of researchers who study personal home-page authorship, most seem to concur that authors strategically select the information they present on their home pages to construct a public persona. Miller (1995), for example, analyzed home pages in terms of Goffman's theories of self-presentation. He concluded that "[T]he people producing homepages are drawing on their knowledge and experience of verbal and paper presentations of self to help them to construct their electronic presentations." Erickson (1996) suggested that rather than using their home pages to merely "publish information," authors use their pages to construct identity. Erickson (1996) explained, "A personal home page is a carefully constructed portrayal of a person." Similarly, Wynn and Katz (1997) proposed that personal home pages "are essentially people's self-created windows on themselves and as such are a construction of self offered to the random viewer." Chandler and Roberts-Young (1998) conducted email interviews with adolescent authors, concluding that home pages serve specific functions for adolescents as they construct their social identities. For example, the public nature of home pages encourages more thoughtful self-evaluation and self-presentation than other forms of expression, thereby heightening chances for feedback that may validate developing identities (Chandler & Roberts-Young, 1998).

Altogether, these studies suggest that home pages are usefully regarded as constructed self-presentations. The notion that mediated creations are deliberately constructed has earlier been applied to advertisements (Goffman, 1979), news productions (Gans, 1979), photo albums (Walker & Moulton, 1989), and zines (Greene & Taormino, 1997), among other creations. Mediated presentations oblige their creators to make choices about what to include and omit, and how to present and re-present information. Such decisions signal creators' attitudes about what is more or less important to them (Wynn & Katz, 1997). Girls who design home pages likewise make decisions that affect how their page will look and what their audience will learn about them. Chandler and Robert-Young (1998) noted that "creating a personal home page can be seen as building a virtual identity insofar as it flags topics, stances and people regarded by the author as significant."

Thus, in this study, girls' home pages were ultimately regarded as texts that reflect in some way the selves girls think they are, the selves they wish to become, and most likely, the selves they wish others to see. Such self-presentations are constrained not only by girls' individual resources and personal histories, but also by their subject position within our culture (in terms of gender, race, age, class, and so on). Conclusions for this study were drawn from the home pages themselves, based wholly on the selves the girls portrayed online.

Studying Girls' Sites

A qualitative, descriptive analysis of the content was conducted to identify stylistic and substantive themes of adolescent girls' home pages. Many researchers have endorsed the use of qualitative analysis to enrich studies of material culture (Altheide, 1996; Ball & Smith, 1992; Berger, 1991). Qualitative analysis seemed particularly appropriate because this study was exploratory in nature and a general understanding of girls' home pages was sought, rather than quantitative summaries of extant content. Qualitative analysis also allows for more description, as well as analysis of latent, rather than solely manifest content (Ball & Smith, 1992) and permits significant themes to emerge (Altheide, 1996).

The sample was drawn from a constructed universe of adolescent girls' home pages, since the actual universe of home pages on the web is ever changing and unknowable. This constructed universe was created in November 1998 by conducting key word searches[4] in prominent web search engines[5] and following appropriate links. Only those home pages that were authored by girls between the ages of twelve and seventeen were gathered. Thus, home pages were eligible for inclusion in the study only if they explicitly or implicitly identified both gender and age of their author. (An "implicit" reference to gender, e.g., might include a picture of the author of the site; an implicit reference to age might be a reference to the eighth grade prom.)

Because the number of gathered sites was deemed too large for in-depth qualitative analysis, a random purposeful sampling technique was used to draw a sample of ten pages. The first ten randomly drawn sites that were deemed "information-rich" were included in the sample (Patton, 1990). Information-rich cases were defined as those that contained original writing or art (i.e., a self-description, original poem, scanned drawing, etc.) and included at least one link (to another page within their site or to another website altogether).

It is important to note the kind of girls whose sites were likely to be included in the sample. Because the web is currently inaccessible to the majority of Americans of all ages, it is clear that adolescent girls with internet access comprise a very small segment of the adolescent teenage population. The most basic requirement, access to a computer, makes it difficult for almost one-third of all American teens to maintain web home pages, and one-third of those with computers are also hindered because they lack an internet connection (Turow, 1999). Not surprisingly, teens with internet access at home are usually privileged socioeconomically. A 1997 study found that teens from families that earned more than US$50,000 per year were much more likely than those from middle- or low-income families to have computers and internet access at home (National Science Foundation, 1997). A 1999 study by the Annenberg Public Policy Centre concluded that parents' experience with the web outside the home was the primary predictor of an online connection in a household (Turow, 1999). Income disparities also tend to correlate highly with race, suggesting that girls who create home pages are most likely white.

Altogether, we can assume that the girls who create homepages are of, at least currently, an elite group. Their unique cultural standing implicates not only the ways they choose to express themselves on their home pages, but also what they choose to discuss.

Data were collected from the adolescent girls' home pages following a basic protocol (Altheide, 1996, p. 26). The protocol included both formal (color, organization, etc.) and substantive features (content, form, etc.). This protocol was developed based on pilot work on adolescent girls' home pages, as well as analyses of other visual media (Gerber, 1979; Goffman, 1979).

Data analysis began by describing the home pages based on data collected. At this early stage, analysis remained at the surface level, answering the following question: what is apparent (substantively and formally)? A descriptive summary sheet for each home page was then compiled. Next, summary sheets and original data were reread multiple times. The constant comparison method was also employed to help organize and reorganize data according to dimensions that emerged as distinctive and significant (Strauss & Corbin, 1994).

Distinguishing among Girls' Sites

The most distinguishable dimension among and between adolescent girls' home pages was tone. "Tone" is used to refer to the various components of girls' pages (such as word choice, site organization, color, images, and the actual content) that work together to exude an overall demeanor. Among the small sample studied, three types of tones were identified.

The most common tone among the girls' sites was one of excitement and optimism. Sites with this type of tone are called *spirited* to convey their buoyancy and cheerfulness. Girls who created these types of pages constructed their public persona as self-confident and generally pleased with life. In direct contrast were sites that will be referred to as *somber*. Creators of somber sites presented an online self that appeared disillusioned with life, angry with friends and family, and gravely introspective. They portrayed themselves as dark and brooding, as well as articulate and witty. Last were sites whose tone oscillated between spirited and somber. Girls who authored *self-conscious* sites, as they have been named, presented themselves as unconfident and unsure how much they should share online. They combined happy images and thoughts on the same page as depressing pictures and writings, qualifying their words and discrediting themselves repeatedly.

The contrasting tones of the sites help illuminate the differing ways girls appear to use the web to express themselves. Some construct themselves as those who use the web primarily for self-description and self-glorification (spirited sites). Others portray themselves as those who consider their home pages as asylum from a difficult and hostile world, as a place to say the things they would never—or could never—say in real life (somber sites). And still others present themselves as cautious home-page authors, confused over whether to discuss the contradictions they encounter between their real experiences and inner thoughts (self-conscious sites). Their self-presentations imply that they are eager to speak, but nervous about revealing too much.

Spirited Sites

Five of the girls in this study [Devon (Tutak, n.d.), Lauren (Lauren, n.d.), Kelly (Kelly, n.d.), Danielle (Coffey, n.d.), and Babygirl (Babygirl, n.d.)] constructed spirited sites. These girls organized their pages somewhat haphazardly, almost in a stream-of-consciousness manner. Rather than linking to a new page for new topics, these girls added onto their original page much like run-on sentences. Pastel colors dominated these pages, as well as images of cuddly animals, bubbly hearts, and dainty flowers. The girls portrayed themselves as eager to show off their technical skills, urging viewers to sign their guest-books to tell them what is best about their pages.

Although the spirited sites focused on specific topics or people, they all contained a hodgepodge of unrelated information. "Babygirl" devoted most of her page to Keanu Reeves and Mike Vitar, two alternative rock band members (although Reeves is now an international movie star, she only referred to him in light of his band). But Babygirl also included much information about herself, her friends, poetry she likes and has authored, and stories about a professional baseball player she once met. Similarly, Lauren, a high-school sophomore from Wisconsin, created her site for the "not-so-serious musician." But in addition to discussing her experiences in the marching band and linking to music sites, Lauren also shared "ALMOST 300 redneck jokes!," "1994's most bizarre suicide!," and "nifty quotes!" Devon's opening page displayed a collage of trendy images including the Muppets, *South Park* characters, the musical *Rent*, an open book, the Pink Panther, a camera, the sun, and a butterfly. The montage of information exhibited on their home pages demonstrates the complexity of girls whose interests extend even beyond their own predefined focus.

Exclamation points covered spirited sites, as well as extreme words such as "love," "best," "favorite," and "hate." Typical comments included those such as Danielle's: "I HATE the [sic] Macareana" and "I LUV *new* clothes." Kelly, thirteen and from Seattle, created "I like" and "My Gripes" pages on which she documented her liking for "Good hair days," "My mom's [sic] lasagna," and "The GREEN BAY PACKERS," as well as her displeasure with "Mean People," "Being New," and "The Smell of Cows in the Summer."

All of the girls in this category provided explicit demographic information about themselves. It is surprising how much data they offered and interesting that they provided statistics as though they were filling out a survey, rather than freely constructing their own autobiography. Kelly wrote:

> [M]y name is Kelly and I am 13 years old. I moved in January to the pacific northwest [sic], near Seattle. When school starts again I will be a freshman at Kamiak High School. (Go Knights!) . . . My family is pretty small. I have 3 sisters: Katie, Tracy and Lindsay. (24, 23, and 8 years old.) The oldest one is married. I live with both my mom and dad. (I am forbidden to tell their ages.) I don't have any pets right now, but we will be getting a kitten in September . . .

Rather than organizing their personal information into prose like Kelly, Devon and Lauren incorporated tidbits into various parts of their page, and Babygirl and Danielle simply listed their demographic statistics, ranging from name and age to zodiac sign and favorite books.

Interestingly, Babygirl provided such details as her birthplace, birthday, high school, family structure, and ethnicity (Filipino), but never revealed her true name. This is even more surprising considering that she posted a large photograph of herself in the middle of her home page.

The girls who constructed spirited sites also frequently listed their favorite media stars, TV programs, and films. Television shows such as *Ally McBeal* and *Dawson's Creek* were among those most frequently mentioned, as well as movie stars such as Leonardo DiCaprio. Music seemed especially important to these girls; many of the girls listed their entire CD collections as well as their favorite songs. Teenage girls' attention to music has been well-documented (see Christensen & Roberts, 1998; Hendren & Strasburger, 1993; Strasburger & Comstock, 1998).

Overall, spirited site authors presented themselves as very pleased with their lives, their friends and families, and their place in the world. They also portrayed themselves as comfortable sharing their achievements on the web. Danielle relayed how she placed second at the WHRO Great Computer Challenge, Kelly wrote of "A"s on her report card, and Lauren explained, "In case you don't know me, I am a sophomore at Geneva High School. I'm involved in softball, Marching Band, Thespians, Model United Nations, and Symphonic Band. (Yes, everybody, I made symphonic band. Yay! I play trombone far Marching Band and Flute for Symphonic Band. I play third base and outfield for softball." Devon, only a sophomore in high school, even offered the names of prestigious colleges she will apply to when she is a senior.

Although the tone of their sites was spirited, not all of the topics the girls chose to discuss were upbeat. Danielle, fourteen, described the events she thinks have shaped who she is. Among them, she included: "In April of this year (1997), my mom died of cancer. We (my dad and I) went up to New York for the funeral. I miss my mom very much, I'm writing this section in pink, because it was her favourite colour. I know if she was alive, she'd like it!" Danielle's effort to turn a piece of her web page into a tribute to her mother seems characteristic of the type of girls who created spirited sites.

Overall, spirited site authors portrayed their world as a mostly happy place, in which adversity can be overcome and the future is bright. Perhaps the girls who create spirited sites aimed to present themselves as the "perfect" girls about whom Brown and Gilligan (1992) speak. Perfect girls are "nice and kind," and they "silence" themselves rather than speak their true feelings, which they come to consider "stupid," "selfish," "rude," or just plain irrelevant (Orenstein, 1994, p. 37). On the other hand, perhaps the girls who create spirited sites were, indeed, navigating relatively easily and happily through adolescence.

Somber Sites

Although only two sites in this study were classified as somber, they were among the most intriguing. Amanda, a fourteen-year-old girl from New Jersey, constructed one such site, (Hatfield, n.d.), and the other page was posted by Katie, a Fresno high-school student, who calls her page "Katherina's Euphoric Despair: A Rerun" (Cowles, n.d.). Both Amanda and Katie crafted well-organized, distraction-free pages. Their pages lacked the frills and clutter of spirited sites, with few images and links.

When describing themselves, Amanda and Katie often painted less-than-perfect pictures. Katie wrote "Hobbies: Experimenting (with everything), running around with my friends, writing, trying various drugs, reading, looking for something like a soulmate, smoking, munching on stuff, laughing, crying, learning, Figuring stuff out, writing more, receiving praise, receiving criticism, taking risks, working on my webpage."

Both in her list of hobbies and her numerous writings, Katie seemed to make a point of emphasizing the "bad" activities she enjoys, such as doing various drugs, getting stoned, and smoking. Both she and Amanda were more likely to use profanity online than the other girls, and their words were sharper and more hostile.

"Katherina's Euphoric Despair," a graphic-less page with blue text running down the middle, began by listing the titles of twenty-three poems Katie has written. Each title was linked to its own page, where nothing but the text of the poem stood on a white background. Her poetry was intense, her vocabulary sophisticated. Most of her poems seemed angry and disappointed. In a poem entitled "life in the 7/11/ tarma goes to heaven" (Cowles, n.d.), Katie wrote:

> wowie
> zowie
> the world flipped me off again
> I grabbed its finger and jabbed it down my throat
> full of hatin'
> shit of satan
> stumbled to my crapwall restroom
> vomited up purified blue love on yellow newspaper
> disguisable
> unrecognizable
> opened the magnetic door in the liquor section
> and was blown back into the candy bar aisle
> liquefied
> the sweetness died
> put some gas in my parents' shit car
> tried to peel out but got wheels weely stuckish
> pushed down the street
> ya peece of sheet
> back to the store for a fiftycent flyswatter
> to kill these goddamn butterflies
> love and beauty
> kiss my booty

Katie discussed darker, more complex, and dangerous issues than the girls who created other types of sites. Her word choices were packed with bitterness and frustration, and the content was more risky. She addressed topics that are culturally inappropriate to discuss in real life, particularly for adolescent girls.

Sexual exploration and its disappointments seemed a common theme in many of Katie's poems. The first verse of "Kamikaze psych" (Cowles, n.d.) began:

> I knew a boy who lied into her eyes
> As he slipped into her pants
> And told her she was pretty as he nailed her to the headboard
> And when the sun rose
> This boy, vampirelike, ran off to his distant coffin

Where he lies still
And left the tangled corpse of a girl upon the bed

Although it was difficult to know how autobiographical Katie's poems
were, they nevertheless illustrated the types of issues and concerns that
she pondered, or at least those she wanted her audience to *think* she pondered. Another poem described an intense, dark, and rarely discussed
experience:

sul.lied.
on a solemn evening (bluer and brighter than most),
as the shadow of an ash tree fell through the window,
it was you and me—
up the wall and across the ceiling
you were crying over matters of self-image, but
   am I not worthy?
when you returned from your jog around the block
and we'd surrounded ourselves with incense ambiance,
it was in your words—
   "I'm not even in deep yet."
you were mumbling about the hypocrisy of innocence, but
   am I not pure?
after I began wondering why the colors hadn't returned,
but before I felt the nauseating soreness of desire,
it was you and me—
   up the wall and across the ceiling.
(suddenly, with a violent jolt, I gasped—
   held my breath, closed my eyes—
and purged the last drop of white sugar out of my body.
   I could not speak.
      I waited for something more.)
through the hours of screaming and tying and endless nonpleasure,
when no part of me could go any further,
it was in your words—
   "I'm not even in deep yet."
You said I was unjustified when I bitched about life, but
   Am I not alive?
Yes! He screamed.
Yes.
Yes!
(Cowles, n.d.)

The full text of Katie's poem is included not only because it is powerful, but also because it is strikingly unfamiliar. Only rarely do we (girls,

women, people in general) read such personal writings. Reading the poetry of those we do not personally know has heretofore been limited to published or broadcast works. Considering the particular paucity of writing published by adolescent girls, the web presents an extraordinary opportunity for girls to speak out. Girls like Katie seem to be taking advantage of the web's potential for easy and "safe" self-disclosure. Perhaps because Katie does not know and cannot see her audience or their reactions, she feels less vulnerable when presenting her art. On the other hand, perhaps feeling anonymous renders Katie more comfortable with creating an identity entirely different from her real self.

Amanda was cognizant of the freedom the internet granted her to speak openly and safely. She wrote:

> In real life I'm deathly shy. Getting me to talk is an almost impossible thing. My teachers try. It doesn't work. I'm extremely sensitive although you wouldn't guess if [sic] unless you knew me well . . .
>
> On the Internet, I make impish sarcastic and witty comments, joke about trolls, and scream at people who annoy me. This keeps me sane. I'm really not either person but they both work for me at the moment.

Because the voice Amanda used on her web page was articulate, sophisticated, and sharp-edged, it is hard to imagine her as the "deathly shy" girl she considers herself in "real life." In an October 1998 journal entry she wrote, "I wanted a quote for today. All day, I've had this in my head. 'You're so damn poetic? Go fuck a tree.' I never curse in real life. But I wanted to say that to someone all day. But there was no good context to fit it into. I probably wouldn't have been able to say it anyway."

Amanda recognized the autonomy the web granted her to explore and/or create her personality without fear of repercussion. Amanda could be impudent and obnoxious on the internet, yet, she explained, her real-life teachers must struggle to engage her in simple conversation. For girls like Amanda and Katie, the appeal of speaking in an easily accessed yet removed and anonymous forum like the web seems to transcend the inhibition manifest in their real lives.

Amanda modified her site approximately every two days during the fall of 1998. Only fourteen, Amanda seems both mature and reflective. She made fun of the sites I refer to as "spirited." She wrote:

> I'm 14 years old and in the 9th grade. My birthday is August 21. Mark your calendars. I live in a small town in New Jersey that's all of 5 minutes from New York (state.) My favorite shows are The X-Files and Buffy the Vampire Slayer and a bunch of cartoons. (Rugrats, Daria, Sailor Moon,

etc . . .) My favorite movies are Good Will Hunting and Star Wars and
One True Thing. *Was that superficial enough for you?* (Italics added)

To Amanda, real information seemed better suited to journal entries,
rather than lists of general statistics. On her site, Amanda posted over
thirty journal entries, each of which reveals small nuggets of information
about her real life. In one entry, Amanda divulged her family life by
describing a frustrating encounter at a restaurant. She annotated:

Anyway, with the house in shambles, we had to go out for dinner and we
wound up at Boston Chicken . . . So anyway, we go there, and this lady
says to me, Oh, I'm so glad your father gets out. I know a quadrlapedic
(sp? I can't spell. It's quite annoying) and he never gets out . . . I get
annoyed. (wait a minute. I guess you could use some background. My dad
has distonia and he's in a wheelchair. That's why I live in an apartment, it's
a special thing for handicapped people and my mom has cp and she was
[*sic*] no use of her right hand. but anyway, dystonia causes muscle spasms
and a lot of other crap.) I mean, why couldn't she have told him that? He
can talk. He's not deaf. He's kinda hard to understand, but I can translate.
And what right did she have to assume that I know a lot about other
diseases like that of my dad's. Even though I do.

Amanda also frequently documented her frustration with her friends
and social life. She portrayed herself as one who cannot depend on her
friends, yet who desperately wants them in her life. For example, in one
journal entry, she wrote: "Debra . . . really pisses me off. She's fucking
inconsiderate. I try so hard to be her friend. I wait for her to walk to
lunch. I tell her what the homework is. I lend her pens and pencils . . .
I try. She does nothing." Despite her confession that she is really a
quiet person, Amanda lashed out on the web when she was angry or
frustrated.

Amanda expressed hostility toward many of her peers at school, as
well. In a mid-October journal entry, she described how two girls from
her Spanish class looked at her and told each other how ugly they
thought she was. In her journal, Amanda responded, "What the hell is
her problem??? True, I'm ugly. But the rest isn't. And they say it just
about right to my face. I hate those two. I'm so glad they won't be in class
tomorrow. 11th graders have testing. And they're in the 11th grade. I
hate them I hate them I hate them I hate them . . ." Noticeable both in
this comment and many others, Amanda had the tendency to put herself
down ("True, I'm ugly"). She often expressed feelings of incompetence
both socially and academically. Amanda asked her audience, "Am I the

only freak?" and harshly criticized her schoolwork. ("My art project is pure crap. It's a contrast painting and it's disgusting. Why do I suddenly suck at art?")

Ironically, Amanda was the most technically impressive girl I had ever encountered on the web. She had posted more than thirty-five home pages in the past two years. Though she documented the content and organization of each of these sites, she did not boast as girls who created *spirited* sites did. Also, unlike most other girls in this study, whose sites seem to be pasted together somewhat haphazardly, Amanda meticulously plans out each page before she begins to create it. She explained that she will publish a page on the web only when it is absolutely perfect. The easy readability and coherency of her site can be credited to her patience and diligence, as well as the amount of time she spends on the computer. Amanda implied that she has very few people that she can talk to in real life, and thus her computer—and ultimately, we, her readers—are her confidantes.

Overall, the somber tone of their sites appeared to derive from Katie and Amanda's portrayal of themselves as unable to speak openly in real life. Their self-presentations implied that they relegated their darker thoughts to the web—a forum that presents less immediate risk than real-life expression. Girls like Amanda and Katie presented themselves as willing to share themselves and their thoughts more intimately than any of the other girls, perhaps because their true thoughts would get them in trouble in the real world. Or, maybe what drove Amanda and Katie to present themselves as extraordinarily self-revealing on the web was the confirmation site visitors can give them that their presentations are normal, or at least respected. Katie's construction of herself as desirous of such self-validation can be seen in the final words on her homepage:

> So it gets kind of lonely sitting here in Fresno, and I get to thinking, "Gee, I wonder how many people visit my pages that never even bother to communicate with me!" So I'm telling you now, and I'll only tell you once: write to me! It's very simple. Just click this little thingy-doo (or one of the millions of the mail links all over my site) and type "Hey Katie, I loooove your page. I think you're such a goddess! Will you marry me? Pleeeeeeeease??"
>
> Well, I guess you don't have to say that. But say something nice. It would be lovely if you'd let me know what you think of my stuff, since I'm hoping to be a professional writer someday. But anyway . . . My point was, write to me. *I need pen pals. I need to know that there are other people like me out there! This is very important. I think.* (Italics added)

Self-Conscious Sites

Erin (Marissa, n.d.), Mel (Melissa, n.d.), and Raven (Raven, n.d.) created the third type of home pages, sites whose tone can best be described as "self-conscious." These sites looked in many ways like the spirited sites discussed earlier; they are adorned with bright colors, various musings, and elaborate images. But unlike spirited site creators, these girls de-emphasized their achievements and technical expertise. Rather, Erin, Mel, and Raven expressed skepticism with the world and their place in it.

Self-disparagement was common among all of the self-conscious sites. Mel introduced her *Writings* section by articulating, "These are just various things I have written. They may be good, or they may be horrible; I'm not claiming that I'm an accomplished author or anything!" Similarly, Raven ended her brief autobiographical section by saying, "There really isn't much to say about me. So I won't bore you any further . . ." Erin's apologetic though humorous manner was most dramatic. On her opening page, she wrote, "I'm sorry that you had to come across this page. Please don't send me nasty letters about how rancid my site is . . . I already know Ÿ_Ÿ Just back away slowly and in a few minutes you'll forget that this tragic experience ever took place."

Not only did Mel, Erin, and Raven put themselves down more than any of the other girls in this study, but they also admitted to abridging what they published on their web pages. In this way, they constructed themselves dramatically differently from the girls whose somber sites appeared to chronicle their every thought and feeling. Raven wrote, "Obviously, I won't devulge [*sic*] all my inner thoughts, because you never know when the words 'black mail' might creep into someone's mind while reading these entries. So I hope you enjoy, and welcome to my pitiful little world."

In a later entry, Raven explained how she might be able to speak more freely if she did not have to worry about her real friends' opinions:

> I've been going through other people's journals on the net. They're so depressing! I have to admit that I get really depressed, but I feel weird writing about it. Especiall [*sic*] when my friends and boyfriend read this. Sometimes I regret letting this page's address get in the hands of those who know me and could possibly sabotage my life with the information I have let the whole world read. But I have nothing to worry about because no one gives a shit about me anyway.

Raven's comments also illustrated a feeling commonly expressed among the girls that they don't receive enough attention. Erin provided another example in her poem "Friday Night" (Marissa, n.d.):

> Another Friday night
> I'm home washing my hair
> Herbal Essence never seems to do for me
> What it does for the chicks on TV.
> Maybe I need to be in some exotic location
> Like an airplane or a desert or a girl's dormitory.
> I lay on the floor
> I sit by the phone
> Did you think I was serious,
> When I told you to leave me alone?
> Another Friday night
> And nobody's there
> At least my hair smells nice
> But nobody's here to care

In addition to portraying themselves as emotionally neglected, these girls indicated a desire for "more from life." They presented themselves as those who feel they are missing out on something, that life could be better if they could only get away from their current lives or meet the "right guy." Raven professed, "Sometimes I wish I could just leave home and get started with my life. But I sill have a little more than 2 years to go. There is no way I can see the world while living under this house."

Love, too, was construed as a desirable diversion from their current reality. For instance, Erin prayed to God to "send me someone who would become a part of me." She explained how she tries to be patient as she waits for God to prepare her true love "just as you're preparing me, for that perfect time when we'll be ready for each other." Self-conscious sites were the only sites in this study that addressed love hopefully and excitedly.

Not all discussion about love was optimistic, however. Each of the girls presented herself as one who had encountered romantic difficulties, and poetry seems to be the preferred forum for discussing them. Mel calls one of her poems "Lurking Disaster" (Melissa, n.d.) and concludes it thus:

> every flutter your stomach perceives
> like excitement or happiness is knocking
> is actually warning
> that love cannot come without devastation

Despite their implied fascination with love, the girls portrayed themselves as wary and fearful of its power. In a February journal entry, Raven detailed a dream she had about her boyfriend:

> My boyfriend and I were driving home . . . and we have to go across a bridge, but it's a really strange bridge . . . The next thing I know we're at some restaurant [sic] and my boyfriend is telling me that we have to go now, because the bus is leaving and we have to follow it . . . I say no, and he just leaves me there. I can't go home on the bus, and we're in the middle of nowhere and I can't call my parents to pick me up.

She firmly concluded that this dream symbolized her "fear of abandonment" [sic].

Second only to love was the girls' implied preoccupation with depression and death. Mel posted a poem written by an anonymous author that details a tragic drunk-driving accident. Raven displayed a poem she wrote about a girl who takes a walk at night "to get away from home" and gets beaten up and killed. Erin also published her own despondent poem, "The Mirror" (Marissa, n.d.):

> Just like my reflection in the mirror
> Life is filled with ugliness and despair
> I respond by looking away in disgust
> Just like I respond to my reflection in the mirror
>
> Life
> Like drinking Coke at room temperature
> Or taking a long drink of the dregs that settle
> At the bottom of my coffee cup
> 'Till not even the dregs are left.
> That's life.

Overall, the girls who created self-conscious sites presented themselves as confused about who they are, what they want to say, and whether the web is the right place to speak out. Visually, their pages were cheerful and perky, but their words betrayed the colors and images.

Their acknowledged reluctance to speak too freely and their simultaneously professed desire to spill their thoughts onto the page makes their sites unsettling and less coherent. They portray themselves as more concerned about what their readers will think than any of the other girls, as Raven demonstrated at the end of one of her journal entries: "Well, I better stop now. This is getting quite long, and I don't want to bore anyone who might be reading it."

The girls who created self-conscious sites, more than any of the others, constructed themselves as deep in the throes of identity construction.

They portrayed themselves as consciously struggling to determine who they are and how they should present themselves. They suggested that they were conscious of their ability to construct their own persona, online as well as in real life, but unconfident about which self-portrayal would be best. Mel, Erin, and Raven seemed unsure whether what they have to say is important or worthwhile, but their home pages may have enabled them to at least experiment with different identities more that they might otherwise have considered possible.

Discussion

This study suggests that adolescent girls who post homepages are, indeed, using the web as a safe space to speak. However, it appears that the girls do not all use their home pages to construct the same type of self or to use the home page for the same purposes. Girls who create spirited sites construct themselves as openly proud and optimistic, while self-conscious site creators portray themselves as concurrently doubtful and hopeful. Girls who posted somber sites presented themselves as willing to share dark and unfeminine topics that are rarely addressed in real life.

Were one to take the girls' home pages at face value, somber site creators seem to be using the web to its greatest potential. They present themselves as eager to disclose thoughts and ideas they feel unable to utter in real life. They indicate that they consider their web pages as venting stations, to get off their chests the dark and unlady-like feelings that engulf them. They also suggest that they use their sites as sounding boards, as places where they can receive feedback from faceless comrades and critics regarding their creativity and insight. Alternatively, perhaps these girls are actively constructing a fictitious persona—addressing topics they know "push the envelope," not because they are real preoccupations, but rather because they would like for their audience to think so. Either way, the girls build their pages so the self-reflection and explication seem dominant, and they imply that they find comfort in the risk-free environment the web provides.

Girls who create spirited sites present themselves as web users who view their home pages as tools for self-validation or to portray themselves in the best light possible according to cultural expectations of "good girls." They list their interests, personal statistics, and accomplishments to verify their self-worth. These girls present themselves as less inwardly self-reflective, and focus more on presenting an interesting, dynamic self to their audience. The range of images and writings they display may, in fact, reflect their uncertainty about who they would like to "be" online.

The girls who create self-conscious sites, on the other hand, openly present themselves as self-doubting and insecure. They suggest that the web is not necessarily the low-risk space that spirited and somber site authors imply they perceive. The web can be accessed by those who can—and very well may—use their personal information against them. Self-conscious site authors suggest that they allow the inhibition they feel in real life to infiltrate their online personae. In fact, they seem quite conscious of their own ability to shape their virtual identity.

Conclusion

Ultimately, it is clear that adolescent girls are speaking on the web—speaking in ways and words that are infrequently heard. This small, exploratory study indicates that home pages provide girls with greater opportunity to openly express thoughts, interests, and to create a public identity. It seems likely that for some girls, the internet presents the "safe company" they need to "speak their experience" and "say what is true" (Taylor, Gilligan, & Sullivan, 1995, p. 69). It also seems to grant some girls the freedom to "develop their sense of possibility, and to experience themselves as active agents in their own lives" (Phillips, 1998, p. 86).

More research is needed to better understand the role the web can play in girls' lives. This study was unable to account for developmental, psychological, racial, or other characteristics that undoubtedly influence the ways in which girls speak. The study was also unable to address girls' motivations for home-page decisions. Also, due to the nature of the web, this study and others like it faced unique challenges. Home pages are not stable documents. They may be modified, expanded, abridged, and even deleted. Not only does this present an obstacle for analysis (in the difficult decision over whether to analyze sites online or in a downloaded or printed format), but it also complicates the potential for other researchers and interested audiences to visit the "same" home page that was analyzed in a published report. Ultimately, however, future research is encouraged in the hope that any potential the web may hold for granting girls a louder voice will soon be shared by many more girls across the globe as internet technology becomes more affordable, accessible, and relevant.

Taylor, Gilligan, and Sullivan (1995) remark in their book *Between Voice and Silence* how ours is "a landscape that is strangely silent—where girls for the most part are not heard in public, or if heard are generally spoken about in the third person" (p. 1). Perhaps the girls in this study are the first signs that the landscape slowly is changing.

Notes

1. "Adolescent girls," in the present research, will refer to girls between the ages of twelve (when menarche, on average, commences) and eighteen (when most girls earn greater freedom and autonomy from institutions such as family and school). Operationalizations of "adolescence" vary tremendously; the present range (twelve–eighteen) likely captures the inner boundaries of most age-defined interpretations.

2. Discussions of safety in the context of the web inevitably conjure up images of online stalkers and questionable content. However, when I use the word "safe" in this chapter, I am referring to girls' belief that they are free to speak without fear of endangering themselves, their relationships, or their "realities." For example, many girls' explain on their web pages how they would be embarrassed or scared if their "real" friends knew about their sites.

3. Most research that has examined home pages has addressed predominantly male populations.

4. Key words included: "girl home pages," "high school and girl," "teen girl." These terms elicited the one hundred sites included in the constructed universe.

5. Search engines included: Yahoo (http://web.yahoo.com/), Excite (http://web.excite.com/), and Alta Vista (http://web.altavista.com/).

References

Abbott, C. (1998). Making connections : Young people and the internet. In J. Sefton-Green (ed.), *Digital diversions: Youth culture in the age of multimedia*, pp. 84–105. London: UCL Press.

Altheide, D. (1996). *Qualitative media analysis*. Thousand Oaks, CA: Sage.

Babygirl's funky dreamland. (n.d). Retrieved October 10, 1998, from http://web.geocities.com/Hollywood/Hills/6452/.

Ball, M. & Smith, G. (1992). *Analysing visual data*. Thousand Oaks, CA: Sage.

Berger, A. (1991). *Media analysis techniques*. Thousand Oaks, CA: Sage.

Brown, L. & Gilligan, C. (1992). *Meeting at the crossroads : Women's psychological development*. Cambridge, MA: Harvard University Press.

Chandler, D. & Roberts-Young, D. (1998). *The construction of identity in the personal homepages of adolescents*. Retrieved July 21, 1999, from http://web.aber.ac.uk/~dgc/strasbourg.html.

Christensen, P. & Roberts, D. (1998). *It's not only rock and roll: Popular music in the lives of adolescents*. Cresskill, NJ: Hampton Press.

Coffey, D. (n.d.). *Danielle's favourite things*. Retrieved October 3, 1998, from http://webwhimzees.com/danielle/.

Cowles, K. (n.d.). *Katherina's eurphoric despair: A rerun*. Retrieved November 11, 1998, from http://members.aol.com/tonightbc/euphoria.html.

———. (n.d.). *Life in the 7/11/tarma goes to heaven*. Retrieved November 20, 1998, from http://members.aol.com/tonightbc/heaven.htm.

Cowles, K. (n.d.). *Kamikaze psych.* Retrieved November 20, 1998, from http://members.aol.com/tonightbc/kamikaze.htm.

———. (n.d.). *Sul.lied.* Retrieved November 20, 1998, from http://members.aol.com/tonightbc/sullied.htm.

Erickson, T. (1996). *Communications of the ACM.* Retrieved July 21, 1999, from http://web.pliant.org/personal/Tom_Erickson/SocialHypertext.html.

Furger, R. (1998). *Does Jane compute? Preserving our daughter's place in the cyber revolution.* New York: Warner Books.

Gans, H. (1979). *Deciding what's news.* New York: Random House.

Goffman, E. (1979). Gender advertisements. *Studies in the Anthropology of Visual Communication, 3*(2), 69–134.

Greene, K. & Taormino, T. (eds.) (1997). *A girls guide to taking over the world.* New York: St. Martin's Griffin.

Hatfield, A. (n.d.). *Wintergirl.* Retrieved October 4, 1998, from http://members.xoom.com/wintergirl/.

Hendren, R. & Strasburger, V. (1993). Rock music and videos. In V. Strasburger and G. Comstock (eds.), *Adolescent medicine: State of the art reviews,* pp. 577–588. Philadelphia: Hanley and Belfus.

Kelly's Kingdom. (n.d.). Retrieved November 11, 1998, from http://web.geocities.com/EnhancedForest/5665.

Lauren's world on the web. (n.d.). Retrieved October 15, 1998, from http://web.angelfire.com/oh/Cleocatra/index.html .

Lerner, R. (1993). *Early adolescence.* Hillsdale, NJ: Lawrence Erlbaum.

Marissa, E. (n.d.). *Nadir of despair.* Retrieved November 20, 1998, from http://web.geocities.com/SoHo/Coffeehouse/7989/.

———. (n.d.). *Friday night.* Retrieved November 20, 1998, from http://web.garden.net/users/atrain/

———. (n.d.). *The mirror.* Retrieved November 20, 1998, from http://web.geocities.com/SoHo/Coffeehouse/7989/poetry.htm.

Melissa. (n.d.). *Mel's corner.* Retrieved November 23, 1998, from http://web.angelfire.com/ny/mell.

———. (n.d.). *Lurking disaster.* Retrieved November 20, 1998, from http://web.angelfire.com/ny/mell/disastor.html.

Miller, H. (June 1995). *The presentation of self in Electronic Life: Goffman on the internet.* Paper presented at Embodied Knowledge and Virtual Space Conference, Goldsmiths College, University of London. Retrieved July 21, 1999, from http://web.ntu.ac.uk/soc/psych/miller/goffman/htm.

National Science Foundation. (1997). *U.S. Teens and Technology.* Retrieved July 27, 1999, from http://web.nsf.gov/od/lpa/nstw/teenov.htm.

Orenstein, P. (1994). *SchoolGirls: Young women, self-esteem, and the confidence gap.* Atlanta, GA: Longstreet Press.

Pastor, J., McCormick, J., & Fine, M. (1996). Makin' homes: An urban girls thing. In B. Ledbeater & N. Way, (ed.), *Urban girls: Resisting stereotypes, creating identities,* pp. 15–34. New York: New York University Press.

Patton, M. (1990). *Qualitative evaluation and research methods* (2nd ed.). Newbury Park, CA: Sage.

Personal Home Page Institute. *The First World Wide Web Personal Home Page Survey.* Retrieved July 21, 1999, from http://web.asc.upenn.edu/USR/sbuten/phpi.htm.

Phillips, L. (1998). *The girls report: What we know and need to know about growing up female.* New York: The National Council for Research on Women.

Pipher, M. (1994). *Reviving Ophelia: Saving the selves of adolescent girls.* New York: Ballentine Books.

Raven. (n.d.). *Insanity.* Retrieved November 20, 1998, from http://web.garden.net/users/atrain/.

Stern, S. (1998). *Using media to create media.* Unpublished.

Strasburger, V. & Comstock, G. (eds.). *Adolescent medicine: State of the art reviews.* Philadelphia: Hanley and Belfus.

Strauss, A. & Corbin, J. (1994). Grounded theory methodology: An overview. In N. Denzin & Y. Lincoln (eds.), *Handbook of qualitative research,* pp. 273–285. Thousand Oaks, CA: Sage.

Taylor, J., Gilligan, C., and Sullivan, A. (1995). *Between voice and silence: Women and girls, race and relationship.* Cambridge, MA: Harvard University Press.

Turow, J. (1999). *The internet and the family: The view from parents, the view from the press.* Philadelphia: The Annenberg Public Policy Center of the University of Pennsylvania.

Tutak, D. (n.d.). *Devon Tutak's homepage.* Retrieved October 10, 1998, from http://members.aol.com/BdwyBby/Devon.html.

Walker, A. & Moulton, R. (1989). Photo albums: Images of time and reflection of self. *Qualitative Sociology, 12*(2), 297–327.

Wynn, E. Katz, J. (1997). Hyperbole over cyberspace: Self-presentation and social boundaries in internet home pages and discourse. *The Information Society, 13,* 318.

CHAPTER ELEVEN

Playing At and With Popular Teen Culture on "Girl" Websites: The Case of Alice

Jacqueline Reid-Walsh

"When I Type 'Judge' I Get a Mansion"

One aim of the Digital Girls Research Project has been to develop methodologies for analyzing different aspects of the virtual domain that girls encounter when surfing the web. A large part of this highly commercialized realm is the corporate website that draws on a company's market research to produce a sophisticated product. Sites targeting children are unlike the "virtual brochure" sites targeting adults as potential investors or buyers where the so-called interactivity may be limited to a virtual turn of the page or an email request for information (Downes & McMillan, 2000, pp. 173–174). In contrast, corporate sites aimed at children pitch their products through elaborate interactive design features that evoke or reproduce the world of children's play and games, touting their products, whether they be fashion dolls, action figures, computer games, construction toys, and so on, as an integral part of the play. These websites are fairly sophisticated forms of advertising; ones that researchers and other adults may view as a means to further seduce or enmesh the child into the interlocked commercialized world of play. As Stephen Kline, Nick Dyer Witheford, and Greig de Peuter (2003) point out in *Digital Play*, technology can act as a "middle sphere" linking marketing and culture (pp. 51–53). Children, however, may view these sites differently. From their perspectives, these sites are not only sources of (commercial) information, but also, and even mainly, spaces for free online play. Aware of and accustomed to being targeted by advertisers, young users accept the commercial imperative as the norm (Mitchell & Reid-Walsh, 2002). These contradictory aspects and opposing perspectives need to be kept in mind when performing any analysis, to respect both the insight and interests of the young user and the experience and knowledge of the adult researcher. That is what I try to do in this chapter, which draws in part on a case study I conducted of a ten-year-old girl named "Alice."

Introducing Alice

Alice is the youngest of three children, the "baby" of her family, and is the younger sister of my daughter's best friend from high school. Two of her favorite things are ice cream and the color pink. On a hot Montreal summer day, Alice arrived at my home wearing red capris and a blue t-shirt decorated with a decal of a mouse. She gave me a crayon drawing that looked similar to the "Paws park" page we subsequently visited on the *Polly Pocket* website. We had organized a two-hour play session prior to going swimming at the local pool across the park with her sister and my daughter. We used my computer, which is at the end of the living room in a home office area I share with my daughter.

My analysis of the time I spent with Alice has a double focus. It is girl-centered in that it is grounded in a summary of a participant observation session with Alice—building on her comments, which were qualified by rare interjections from her sister. Because we chatted as she showed me her favorite websites and play strategies, the research is equally adult-centered, reflecting my observations and interpretations of her site choice and mouse use. Alice's relation to the internet is limited in that she has no active email account nor has she engaged in website construction. Her connectivity time is also limited for she uses a family computer. She has high-speed access but needs to share the computer with other members of the family—particularly a teenage brother and sister.

Combining Alice's behavior, preferences, and views with theoretical rubrics drawn from media analysis (e.g., Burn & Parker, 2003), girlhood studies (e.g., Mitchell & Reid-Walsh, 2005), and play theory (e.g., Barker, n.d.; Benjamin, in Buck-Morss, 1998; Caillois, 1961; Cassell & Jenkins, 1998), I will examine the interactive design of select commercial websites directed toward "tween" girls. Alice's preferences and comments will be interwoven throughout the analysis.

Tween Websites as Visual Culture

The commercial websites under discussion here are quite different from the so-called educational sites targeting teens, for example, the PBS site (http://mynptv.org/kids/tweens/), which is a largely word-based, stand-alone site. Researchers often approach educational sites as texts combining written language, design, and links, for example, see Andrew Burn and David Parker in their chapter "Chocolate Politics" in *Analyzing Media Texts* (2003). By contrast, commercial sites that are intended for play seem to be mainly visual, using both static and moving images, as well as auditory text in their multimedia design. Traditional text design analysis alone is thus not suitable. Consequently, the approach I take in this chapter combines an adaptation of reader response theory from Wolfgang Iser (1974) with ideas about interactive design and user applications from Janet Murray (1997) and Sally Macmillan (2002). Murray's classic discussion of interactivity in *Hamlet on the Holodeck* (1997) is especially useful because she approaches interactivity in terms of user control and participation (MacMillan, 2002, pp. 164, 173) and because she distinguishes between agency and activity. As examples of activity, Murray mentions board games where the user throws dice, turns a dial or moves counters, and in a digital environment, when the user clicks a mouse or moves a joystick. In both cases, the player's actions achieve an effect but these actions are not chosen by the player nor are they related to the player's intentions. By contrast, agency occurs in a game such as chess where the player's actions are autonomous, selected from a wide range of choices, and determine the course of events. Agency goes beyond participation and activity to include aesthetic pleasure (Murray, 1997).

Virtual Dolls' Websites and
Web-Sphere Analysis

Consideration of the content and design of the interactive features of commercial websites reveals that they are often directed toward a specific age-group. Consider, for example, three websites owned by Mattel: *Polly Pocket*, *Barbie*, and *My Scene*. The *Polly Pocket* site visually, aurally, and graphically evokes a miniaturized, domestic and garden world of young girls, featuring sticker albums, play sets, dollhouses, pets, and a cartoon-like representation of a prepubescent white girl. The interactivity on this site is limited to a few choices on a menu or to a visual game such as "spot which items are out of place" in a middle-class, suburban kitchen (http://pollypocket.everythinggirl.com/home.aspx Polly Pocket).

The *Barbie* site also uses the design metaphor of a house and garden with attendant activities. In this site, despite the wide range of available activities, in the doll dressing games, for example, the limits of the design (or "affordances") of the menus not only limits the choice to a prescribed set but forestalls possibilities of unconventional play in that the choices of mixing and matching items of clothing are set within strict limits of a "Barbie look"; (http://barbie.everythinggirl.com/activities/ fashion/).[1] In contrast to the two sites just described, which are mainly "white cultural spaces" (Barbie having multicultural friends) offering limited choices, *My Scene* features images and avatars that represent multicultural teenage bodies and links to a broader trendy teen world of fashion, music, celebrities, and so on. There is a wider choice of activities that require more elaborate software for the computer (http:// myscene.everythinggirl.com/home.aspx0).

These "virtual dolls" sites speak to girls of many ages, targeting age-groups from five or six years old up to teenagers. They begin with *Polly Pocket* for the youngest child and progress through *Barbie, My Scene*, and *Bratz*, culminating in sites such as *Flava*, which appeal to older girls. All the sites except for Bratz and Flava are owned by Mattel and grouped under an umbrella site called "everythinggirl.com." The banner at the top of the *Barbie* page signals an attempt to create not only a "microworld" of Barbie, as is the case with the CD ROM (Cassell & Jenkins, 1998, p. 58), but also a strategy to colonize commercialized girlhood in a virtual domain across a developmental spectrum from young girls to tweens.[2] At the top of the Barbie page one can click and link to all the other Mattel commercial doll sites. These links appear to invite the user to follow a certain "reading path" in the context of the visual design of the Barbie microworld (Kress & van Leeuwen, cited in Burn & Parker, 2003). In terms of their interactive design features, all the sites seem carefully constructed to appeal to girls, or as a Marxist analyst would put it, to "interpellate" girls to a particular subject position, namely, that of trendy consumer (Kline, Witheford, & de Peuter, 2003, p. 53).[3] A question thus arises when observing girls play as to whether they seem to accept, reject, or adapt this position on their own terms.

I asked Alice to evaluate the appeal of the site's top banner, which links users to all the other Mattel sites. She retorted that she ignores the banner, preferring to use her own approach to site usage. Since she has memorized a number of different site URLs, she not only disregards the links built into the site, but also jumps from site to site as part of her play, blithely leaping from product to product and company to company. The sites that Alice led me to crossed a fairly wide age-range, and included sites meant for both older and younger girls. Sites designed for younger girls had not yet lost their appeal for Alice, nor did she consider them in opposition to one another: *Polly Pocket* is not relegated to the dust heap nor is *Barbie* opposed to *Bratz*. Rather, Alice moves freely within and among all these sites. One could deduce that the sites provide a range of alternatives with different positive and negative features—a trans-site menu perhaps, tailored to Alice's interests. She seems to view the entire range of sites as places to visit—and the navigating within and among sites is complex digital play.

To respect the complexity of Alice's online activity, we cannot limit ourselves to "reading" each site as a discrete unity, even if it is part of a hyperlinked set. Each site she visited needs to be considered part of a play-organized cluster of popular culture girl websites that are not necessarily linked to one another in their construction. To do this, I am adapting one aspect of web-sphere analysis that Schneider and Foot (2004) describe as identifying websites related to the object or theme of the sphere, and expanding it to apply a more useful cluster approach: one that is based on similar themes or topics within a wider constellation of girl-focused sites.[4] In the case of Alice, for example, the context for analyzing the tween doll sites is the range of sites devoted to popular dolls and to other girls' culture, no matter the implied age of the girl player.

Girls' Websites and Play Realms

Polly Pocket for Fun

Alice demonstrated the cross-age appeal of *Polly Pocket* during her use of the performing girl-band option drawn in comic-book style (http:// pollypocket.everythinggirl.com/park/band/band.asp). She noted, while politely turning the sound off for me, that the song rapidly becomes irritating. I asked if she thought this site was for little girls and she said "probably" but that nonetheless she likes to go there for fun too. Her favorite place is "Paws Park" where she plays with different moving animals and birds that look like the stickers young children love to collect and stick into albums. The implied off-line play activity of the site recalls that of play sets for young children with a board, a design of a background scene, and accompanied by plastic or felt cut-out images that can be moved around (http://pollypocket.everythinggirl.com/ garden/pets/pets.asp). In some ways the site resembles the drawing with animals and trees in a stylized cut-out or sticker style that Alice gave me when she arrived, suggesting how a website aesthetic may influence her drawing on paper. She remarked that in her physical world she has no pet because of allergies in the family. It appears that this type of play allows her to interact with virtual animals to compensate for restrictions on this kind of play in reality.

Barbie, the Favorite Website

Alice's favorite website is the *Barbie* site. When I asked her how she discovered it, she said that her mother (having reviewed various girl sites for her) introduced her to the Barbie site when she was seven. She stated that she likes Barbie and owns some dolls but doesn't know how many. Her older sister said Alice has inherited a lot of her dolls. I asked her why she liked the Barbie site and she said it has "fun games" and "things to play." She swiftly showed me the section called "Magic Dreams'" which is a kind of fairy-tale narrative in cartoon form. Although there are instructions that pop up when you first visit the section, Alice remarked, without demonstrating how, that after a while you can ignore them and just play (http://barbie.everythinggirl.com/activities/magic/). The next section of the *Barbie* website we visited is called "Happy Families," which looks like a sticker play set.[5] Here, Alice said "it is like looking after a child but on a computer"—it is a baby-sitting game; you click on objects and they move. Based on this interest, I asked Alice if she liked looking after digital animals like *Neopets*. She responded that she did, skipped immediately to the *Neopet* site and directly found the games. However, she expressed some frustration with the site, as *Neopets* is a club that the user is asked to join, and Alice has no access to email and cannot therefore participate with the site on this level.

Cruising the Bratz Site

In discussion with Alice about the *Bratz* website, I relayed my own frustration with attempting to navigate the site—I continually ended up in areas you had to sign up for (give your email address and name) before you could play.[6] Alice immediately circumvented these to go to the Slumber Party section, clicked on a computer icon in the party room, and went to a quiz, called M.A.S.H. (Alice called it a game, but its format is like a quiz). I asked what the acronym stood for and she translated: Mansion, Apartment or Attic, Sewer or Shed, or House. To play, you fill in the blanks of a quiz providing information about your dream job or career, then you click to submit it and presto! You receive a statement about where you will live. While loosely based on a young girl's fortune-telling game played on paper (Krista Walsh, personal communication) the digital version is a parody of quiz questions (http://www.bratzpack.com/index2.asp). Alice told me a story about a friend of hers who answered the quiz and ended up in a sewer, but said that she herself could not get that result: having typed "judge" as one of her career choices, she ended up in a mansion! In the large Slumber Party section, which is designed to allow horizontal movement, Alice likes to go round and round the space quickly by moving her mouse in rapid circles. Similarly, in another section of the site called "the Mall" she likes to move her visual perspective on the stores in the mall horizontally by rapidly moving the mouse so that she cruises the mall in a dizzying fashion (http://www.bratzpack.com/index2.asp). The cruising activity is accompanied by disco music that reinforces the kinetic effect.[7]

Reflecting back on my time observing and talking to Alice, I was reminded of the insights of several other researchers in the field who link the appeal of virtual play with "real" play. For example, in "Paws Park" on the *Pocket Polly* site, the appeal for the user seems to be one of virtually going alone to a park and playing. Henry Jenkins has talked about how much computer game play resembles traditional boys' play in forts and tree houses (cited in Cassell & Jenkins, 1998). He notes that cultural geographers believe that "children's ability to explore and modify their environments plays a large role in their growing sense of mastery, freedom and self-confidence," and that computer games may help to address this need (p. 268). After comparing most video and computer games to the genre of boys' adventure stories, Jenkins turns to the genre of girls stories: "Traditional girls books, such as *The Secret Garden*, do encourage some forms of spatial exploration, an exploration of the hidden passages of unfamiliar houses or the rediscovery and cultivation of a deserted rose garden" (p. 280). He then discusses the now defunct *Purple Moon* computer games designed with and for girls:

> Purple Moon removes the walls around the garden, turning it into a woodlands. Producer Brenda Laurel has emphasized girls' fascination with secrets, a fascination that readily translates into a puzzle game structure, though Secret Paths pushes further than existing games to give these "secrets" social and psychological resonance. Based on her focus group interviews, Laurel initially sought to design a "magic garden," a series of "romanticized natural environments" responsive to "girls' highly touted nurturing desires, their fondness for animals." She wanted to create a place "where girls could explore, meet and take care of creatures, design and grow magical or fantastical plants." (Personal correspondence, 1997.) What she found was that the girls did not feel magical animals would need their nurturing and in fact, many of the girls wanted the animals to mother them. The girls in Laurel's study, however, were drawn to the idea of the secret garden or hidden forest as a "girl's only" place for solitude and introspection. (pp. 281–282)

By seeking out the park as a place to play on the *Polly Pocket* website, it seems that Alice may be engaging in play similar to the girls' play described earlier. She is interacting with an idealized version of what she would like to do in the real world—seek out a green space with animal companions—an activity with no overseeing guardian such as a sister or mother.

The baby-sitting game at the *Barbie* site reveals another virtual space that mimics conventional imaginary play. Users interact with activities that revolve around daily domestic life, a virtual version of the kind of play noted by Iona and Peter Opie in *Children's games in street and playground* (1969). That Alice participates in this site by pretending to be baby-sitter in a virtual household while she is still considered the baby of her family could indicate her desire for future competence—to act like a mature girl not the baby. Similarly, through her interaction with the *Bratz* site, by repeatedly playing a game based on economics and winning the "financial stakes game" through her choice of judge as an imagined future career, Alice is pretending to possess a solid economic future. This is the opposite of the present financial situation of her family. In this way these games of "pretend" can be seen as wish fulfillment. At the same time, the *Bratz* game is a crude but funny parody of capitalism and our obsession with home ownership. By returning repeatedly to this game, in her present position of economic and age-based disenfranchisement and winning, Alice could be indicating her desire to invert or even subvert adult capitalist mores engaging in individual "power play" similar to actions noted by John Fiske (1993) with disenfranchised individuals engaging with media play. On the other hand, this type of play is simply fulfilling the premise or mandate implied by the name and appearance of the doll—to behave in a socially inappropriate way—and since the enactor is a child not an adult, she is behaving like a brat.

Play Theory, Mouse Use, and the Kinetic Sense

Part of the appeal of the *Bratz* site as opposed to the other girls' websites may be the way the construction of the site enables a certain type of engagement with motion. Like the virtual Barbie and Polly Pocket dolls, the virtual Bratz dolls seem to exist in a self-contained urban world of domestic and commercial interiors such as bedrooms, kitchens, playrooms, and mall. The large room where the Bratz dolls are situated and the mall they visit can be visualized by users in different ways. By moving the mouse, the player can move across the interior landscape and the panning action achieves a panoramic view, which in itself can be exhilarating for the viewer (*pace* Benjamin, in Buck–Morss, 1998). Moreover, the speed of the panning action can be adjusted by the way the user moves the mouse. This aspect of the interactive design of the *Bratz* website thereby affords the user a different option than those offered on other sites. Since the "Slumber Party" and "Mall" sections have horizontally placed arrows on the entrance page that enable viewing at different speeds, it is possible, as Alice capably demonstrated, to whirl around the expanded room and, similarly, to rush through the mall. The appeal of this kind of play recalls the child's fascination with whirling or spinning, something also noted and evoked by both poets of childhood, such as Walter de la Mare, and scholars such as Iona and Peter Opie in their discussion of children's games on the playground (1969, p. 273).

In *Man, Play, and Games* (1958, 1969), play theorist Roger Caillois developed a complex structural approach to human play that speaks to the importance of motion. He categorizes play into four main types existing on a continuum from *paidia*, which he sees as the "power of improvisation and joy" and "gambolling," to the other extreme of *ludus* or "the invention of the rules of game" (pp. 27–29). His four mains types seize on the sensation of vertigo as the last of his fourfold divisions of play: *agôn* (competition), *alea* (chance), *mimicry* (simulation), and *ilinx* (vertigo). For this last, he includes children's "swinging" and "whirling" as prime examples. Julian Barker in "An investigation of play studies" adapts Caillois' ideas to both physical and digital realms and includes the activity of "rolling down hills" under the category stimulation or *ilinx* while noting that at theme parks *ilinx* is defined as "activities that distort sensory stability" (http://www.julianbarker.org/work/text/invesigating%20play%20studies%20and%20art/investplaystudsmall.htm).

Caillois' anatomy of play and games could be overlaid onto many of the activities Alice engaged in, both on and off-line; however, I am particularly interested in linking this to a feature of computer-mediated play—the use of the mouse or touch pad for moving the cursor. I question what the precise "use value" of the technology is from the child's point of view (Brown, 1998). As well, I am interested in how the virtual environment enables a type of kinetic engagement when playing with a website that could be compared to Andrew Darley's (2000) notion of "vicarious kinesthesia" in computer game play: "The impression of controlling events that are taking place in the present through moving the joy stick or mouse" (p. 157). I use the term "vicarious kinetics" to refer to the pleasure of the fast-clicking mouse and the perception of a "virtual dizziness" or vertigo of physical play that can be achieved by the user. This sensation of speed remains firmly under the control of the mouse in the girl's hand. In her *play with* tween popular culture, she not only controls what she sees through selection, but also directs the rate of movement. She *plays at* tween culture through her mastery of the degree of "whirl" in this complex, ephemeral microdomain of her own construction—a process she reinvents at each play session.

Conclusion: Cross-Media Play, Negotiating Design Limits, and Striving for Agency

Throughout the course of this study, I was struck by the comments of a number of researchers regarding digital play, or "cross-media" play, as they relate specifically to the practices and objects of play and their association with different ages of girlhood (Mackey, 2002). Ellen Seiter observes that the computer seems to function as a transitional object in the web play of small children, moving them from game-playing (such as collecting Barbie images) to perusing media-based fun activities (cited in Goldstein, Buckingham, & Brougere, 2004). David Buckingham and Julian Sefton-Green (2003) suggest, through their analysis of *Pokemon*, that within the multivarious aspects of the phenomenon, there are different kinds of appeal and different types of complexity that, while they may appeal to different ages groups, also encourages a "playing up or down" in age (p. 382). Rebekah Willet (2005) concurs, noting that girls may "read up" in age in their website use (see chapter seven in this volume). Her study of a group of tween girls in Britain demonstrates that they may disregard tween girls' sites completely, preferring to use the highly interactive website of a popular soap opera *The Eastenders* (2005). This phenomenon is comparable to extensive studies of girls "reading up" when they pore over adult magazines, romance novels, and watch soap operas (e.g., as observed in the groundbreaking work of Linda Christian-Smith 1990, and Gemma Moss, 1989).

Surprisingly, teenage girls also like to "read down." This can be seen, as Krista Walsh reveals, when older girls at a Catholic girls' school use the computer lab at lunchtime to play with *Barbie.com* (Krista Walsh, personal communication). This slightly subversive use of the computer lab when they have free time allows them to momentarily escape from school stress. Instead of doing homework, which is the intended use of the lab, they can play at being young girls again, revisit sites they liked when they were younger, and take a nostalgic trip down memory lane to a time when they were not under pressure.

As I described earlier, through her web play, Alice constructs her own set of sites that enable her to freely play at *being* different ages. It is important for a researcher not to pit the sites against each other; they should be seen as providing separate options for play. Each site has appealing features that entice her to return. From her perspective, the choice of sites is not limited by "implied age" (Iser, 1974) Indeed the *Polly Pocket* site is just as interesting and entertaining as the *Bratz* site. To this tween, the child culture of the park, the girl culture of the home, and the teen culture of the mall are all equally attractive. The alternative spaces that Alice uses to construct her imaginary realm draw equally on: idyllic, pastoral spaces, consistent with romantic conceptions of childhood; a domestic world of chores associated with responsible girlhood; a teen world promising the excitement of mixed gender associations at the mall; and a game that co-relates job to dwelling in an ironic fashion. I suggest that the sites appeal to Alice because they allow her, by her play, to momentarily create a virtual world that is expansive, not restrictive; whether this be in terms of age-stage developmental logic, or the difference of regulation between domestic spaces and outside spaces, or her implied, limited future work world (if her life trajectory follows that of her sister).

To conclude my analysis, I need to return to a question I posed near the beginning of the chapter concerning the design of commercial websites being carefully constructed to appeal to or "interpellate" girl users as consumers. The question to consider when reflecting on how Alice plays with girls' websites is whether she seems to accept, to reject, or to adapt this construction of herself as a powerless girl. Her position seems very weak in relation to both the issue of computer access in the family and to the hegemonic power of commercial girls' digital culture. She has limited access to the family computer, slow dial-up access, and an old browser system that does not allow her to store "favorites," or allow her an email address. Yet, as we have seen, Alice often negotiates or circumvents the constraints of website design in ingenious ways as she draws on her knowledge of play culture and web use. She compensates for temporal and physical limits on her computer use through her ability to memorize and reproduce a complete set of URLs. Her surfing play temporarily creates a miniature virtual world. Through her own selections and rate of movement, Alice plays with tween popular culture by controlling what she sees, for example, controlling the degree of "whirl" in a microdomain of her own construction.

As Colin Lankshear and Michele Knobel (2003) note, in regards to de Certeau's notions of tactics versus strategies, strategies refer to the art of the strong: producers who seek to define and regulate knowledge by defining the commercialized spaces we live in. Tactics refer to a practice of the weak: consumers who must maneuver within the constraining fields (p. 150). With respect to girls' websites and Alice's play patterns, I consider the design limits (or affordances) of the commercial sites to reflect producer strategies while Alice's play demonstrates a consumer's tactics to break through design constraints. Similarly, Alice's approach to play on the websites can be seen as a strategy to circumvent the limits of website design such as the *Barbie* website that forestalls unconventional play or the *Bratz* site that seems to encourage it. Looking at these play patterns through the lens of John Fiske's elaboration on de Certeau (1993), Alice's activities can be seen as an enacting of a combined "power play" on commodified and contained young femininity.

In terms of Janet Murray's (1997) ideas about the difference between activity and agency, whereby the latter enables a user to be autonomous, select a wide range of choices, and determine the course of a game (p. 128), ultimately I consider Alice to be seizing considerable agency in her play activities given the confines of the sites' limiting designs. Her pleasure seems less an aesthetic one than a thrill from the power of her whirling moves enabled by the mouse and her ability to construct her own microworld by ignoring the posted links and linking sites up as *she* chooses. In this way Alice can be seen to be modifying the constructed subject position of girl as presented on commercial girls' sites. She does not accept the position as given nor does she reject it completely. Rather, for the duration of her play she modifies the spatial design and temporal framework of the existing sites to momentarily construct her own virtual domain.

Notes

1. The *Barbie* website can be compared to the now defunct *Barbie Designer* CD ROM in terms of the dolls' shape, its mobility, and the activities associated with the play design process both virtually and in the physical realm. The site provides virtual paper doll play in that you can move one of several preselected and constructed garments onto a Barbie form. On the CD ROM, the choices are formed by a couple of simple menus that you click and choose. As with the website, there are four different dolls: one Barbie and three friends to choose from, three of which do not appear to be Caucasian. Due to the modest undergarments represented on the website dolls, the Barbie shape seems less attenuated at the waist than on the CD ROM. Indeed, this visual clue in the design of the CD reveals that the CD virtual doll is a virtual mannequin for the physical doll. Another interesting aspect of the CD ROM is that Barbie "walks" like a runway model posing her outfits. The ungainliness of her gait, bent knees on high heels eerily suggests that of the three-dimensional doll trying to walk—evoking the automaton dolls of the past in literature, dance, and in images (Jacqueline Reid-Walsh "Virtual Dolls" 2002).

2. One might add across income groups as well since mattel also owns *American Girl* dolls, an expensive, quality doll positioned as an anti-fashion doll which is not advertised on their banner.

3. Surveying this self-promotion by Mattel, it must be remembered that this commodified girl culture monopoly has not been achieved, for Bratz dolls are outselling Barbie and other Mattel products (La Flava, 2003).

4. This idea about constellation is adapted from Christopher Rollason's project "Walter Benjamin's Arcades Project and Contemporary Cultural Debate in the West" at http://www.wbenjamin.org/passageways.html#part8, in his discussion on section eight of Walter Benjamin's "theses on history."

5. Andrea Immell, curator of the Cotsen Children's literature collection at Princeton University, notes that the card game "Happy Families" was first popular in the eighteenth century (personal communication).

6. Subsequent to this play session in 2004, the Bratz doll has become more conventionally pretty (Barbified) and the look of the website has changed as well to become more conventional.

7. Now these pages are not accessible unless one joins a club that requires having an email address.

References

Barker, J. (n.d.). *An Investigation of play studies*. Retrieved July 11, 2004, from http://www.julianbarker.org/work/text/invesigating%20play%20studies%20 and%20art/investplaystudsmall.htm.

Brown, B. (1998). How to do things with things (A Toy Story). *Critical Inquiry*, *24*, 935–964.

Buck-Morss, S. (1998). *The dialectics of seeing: Walter Benjamin and the arcades project*. Cambridge, MA: MIT Press.

Buckingham, D. & Sefton-Green, J. (2003). "Gotta catch 'em all": Structure, agency and pedagogy in children's media culture. *Media, Culture and Society*, *25*, 379–399.

Burn, A. & Parker, D. (2003). *Analyzing media texts*. London: Continuum.

Caillois, R. (1958, 1961). *Man, play, and games* (M. Barash, trans.). New York: Crowell-Collier.

Cassell, J. & Jenkins, H. (Eds.) (1998). *From Barbie to Mortal Combat: Gender and computer games*. Cambridge MA: MIT Press.

Christian-Smith, L. (1990). *Becoming a woman through romance*: New York: Routledge.

Darley, A. (2000). *Visual digital culture: Surface play and spectacle in new media genres*. London: Routledge.

Downes, E. & McMillan, S.J. (2000). Defining interactivity: A qualitative identification of key dimensions. *New Media & Society*, *2*(2), 157–179.

Fiske, J. (1993). *Power plays power works*. London: Verso.

Goldstein, J., Buckingham, D., & Brougere, G. (Eds.) (2004). *Toys, games, and media*. Mahwah, NJ: Lawrence Erlbaum.

Iser, W. (1974). *The implied reader*. Baltimore: The Johns Hopkins Press.

Kline, S., Witheford, N.D., & de Peuter, G. (2003). *Digital play: The interaction of technology, culture and marketing*. Montreal: McGill-Queens Press.

La Flava, R. (October 26, 2003). "Underdressed and hot: Dolls moms don't love." *NYTimes.com*. Retrieved July 10, 2004, from http://www.stanford.edu/class/humbio169/Archives/Fall2003/readings/hot_dolls.03.10.26.html.

Lankshear, C. & Knobel, M. (2003). *New literacies: Changing knowledge and classroom learning*. Buckingham, UK: Open University Press.

Mackey, M. (2002). *Literacies across media: Playing the text*. London: Routlege Falmer.

Macmillan, S. (2002). Exploring models of interactivity from multiple research traditions, users, documents, and systems. In L.A. Lievrouw & S. Livingstone (eds.), *Handbook of new media: Social shaping and consequences of ICTs*, pp. 165–182. London: Sage.

Mitchell, C. & Reid-Walsh, J. (2002). *Researching children's popular culture: The cultural spaces of childhood*. London: Routledge.

———. (2005). *Seven going on seventeen: Tween studies in the culture of girlhood*. New York: Peter Lang.

Moss, G. (1989). *Un/popular fictions*. London: Virago.

Murray, J. (1997). *Hamlet on the Holodeck: The future of narrative in cyberspace*. New York: Free Press.

Opie, I. & Opie, P. (1969). *Children's games in street and playground*. Oxford: Clarendon.

Reid-Walsh, J. (August 2002). *Virtual dolls: From paper cut-out to digital design to simulated construction*. Presentation at the International Toy Research Association. Institute of Education, University of London, London, England.

Schneider, S. & Foot, K. (2004). "The Web as an object of study." *New Media & Society, 6*(1), 114–122.

Willett, R. (2005). Constructing the digital tween: Market Discourse and girls' interests. In C. Mitchell & J. Reid-Walsh (eds.), *Seven going on seventeen: Tween studies in the culture of girlhood*, pp. 278–293. New York: Peter Lang.

CHAPTER TWELVE

Girl Culture and Digital Technology in the Age of AIDS

Claudia Mitchell and
Jacqueline Reid-Walsh

In this chapter we focus on girls' magazine reading, examining both traditional hard copy and digital versions of popular magazines targeting girls. We investigate how magazines represent issues around female bodies and sexuality and how girls, through the process of reading traditional and digital texts, participate in the information culture that surrounds them. As Angela McRobbie (1999) observes in her essay on girls' magazines: "For over twenty years feminists have singled out girls' magazines and women's magazines as commercial sites of intensified femininity and hence rich fields of analysis and critique" (p. 46). Research on magazines aimed at the young teen market, like the work done on women's magazines more generally, has been extensive. Investigations into this subject range from McRobbie's work in the 1980s and early 1990s, where she offered a semiotic reading on the codes of romance found in these magazines, to Dawn Currie's straightforward content analysis of these texts and their readers. Currie's work (1999) and additional research demonstrate that readers of teen magazines are mainly young teens and preteens, no matter the inscribed textual age of the magazine (such as *Seventeen*).

In our previous work we have found teen girls' magazines to be rich sites for exploring the phenomenon of girls' bedroom culture (Mitchell & Reid-Walsh, 2002), and themes such as "back to school" (Weber & Mitchell, 1995), and "the prom" (Mitchell & Reid-Walsh, 1999;

Weber & Mitchell, 2000). We have also identified girls' magazines as "catalogues of desire" (Mitchell & Reid-Walsh, 1998). Our current interests follow new areas of inquiry that investigate tween and early adolescent culture and its relation to digital versions of popular girls' magazines such as *Seventeen, Cosmo girl, Teen vogue, Bliss,* and *YM* (the paper magazine is now defunct, but not the website).

This chapter draws on work from two separate research projects. The first, a three-year study (GAAP), focused on the health knowledge and behaviors of teenagers in Canada and South Africa and included a component on images within media and popular culture that address HIV and AIDS, condom use, and STDs (Larkin, Mitchell, & Reid-Walsh, 2001–2004). The second examined girls aged ten–fourteen, from Canada, the United Kingdom, and South Africa, and their everyday use of digital technology (Weber et al., 2003–2006). In the GAAP study we were particularly interested in the vulnerability of girls and young women to STDs and HIV infection, and within that context, explored a central question: "Where do young people get information about sexuality, STDs and AIDS?" The focus of this inquiry arises from the recognition that we need to know more about how young people understand their own sexuality, their vulnerability to HIV and related infections, and the particular risk factors for girls and young women in relation to these issues. In one component of the project on girls and digital technology, we have been looking specifically at the pedagogical possibilities of how and what girls are accessing online. In the second study of girls and digital technology we also examined information sources for girls, but focused our attention on the pedagogical possibilities for online forums as a means of distributing knowledge.

The tween age of girls (nine–twelve) represents, as we have explored elsewhere, an important demographic for exploring the simultaneous downward shift in marketing, moral panics, and the politics of innocence (Mitchell, Walsh, & Larkin, 2004), and the need for age desegregation in girlhood studies more generally (Mitchell & Reid-Walsh, 2005). We are particularly interested in the following questions: What kind of information related to sexuality do girls access when they click on the web version of a magazine, and how is it different from the information they receive from the paper magazine? What difference does the mode of delivery make? Are there possibilities for seeing the representation of sexuality on the internet as counter to how it is typically constructed by media as being a predatory danger zone for girls and young women (see, e.g., the work on cyber-stalking)? What can we learn about the ways in which information, which may be of a particularly personal nature, is embedded in popular texts?

Methodology

Our work for this project has been largely based on the textual analysis of popular magazines (online and paper) consumed by tweens and girls in early adolescence. This type of analysis draws on our previous work related to girls' websites where we have compared commercial sites for girls, adult-organized websites, and the private websites of girls (Mitchell & Reid-Walsh, 2002; Reid-Walsh & Mitchell, 2004). Here our general protocol was to look for specific information in ads, advice columns, quizzes or articles that dealt explicitly with HIV and AIDS, STDs, condom use, safe sex, negotiating sex, and feeling pressured to have sex. By limiting our textual analysis to articles, advice columns, and quizzes that make explicit reference to these issues, we recognize that this kind of analysis doesn't take into consideration the influence of implicit messages in such articles as "are you ready for love" (*Seventeen*, February 2002, p. 62) or "Quiz: Jealous?" (*Seventeen*, April 2002, p. 94), or the numerous ads that depict girls in ways that suggest that they are "ready for sex." In the long run, such messages may have a greater effect on girls' sense of agency and control (or lack thereof) in sexual relationships than pragmatic safe-sex advice. We also recognize that the messages that girls are receiving need to be contextualized in relation to the information and messages their male partners receive in popular culture texts. Here we note, for example, the work of Buckingham and Bragg (2004), which draws attention to the various porn sites that the boys in their study visited. While we looked at six or seven different magazines for girls, our focus in this chapter is on (the now defunct) *YM* and *Seventeen*, the latter being the most enduring magazine for girls and young women. In terms of time span, the bulk of our data was collected in 2001–2002 with a return (albeit less comprehensively) to the magazine and websites in 2005.

Close Readings

It is apparent, from scanning a random selection of these mainstream magazines, that information and advice about AIDS and STDs is inter-meshed with all the expected features of fashion, beauty, news about stars, and so on. In our general review, *Seventeen* magazine had the most references to sexuality and disease. We found the greatest number of references, in both magazines, in either the advice columns (e.g., "Condoms, yes or no?" in *YM* (ask anything) by Kristen Kemp, *YM*, February 2002, p. 22) or in regular question and answer columns. Examples here include articles such as "Sex and body" in *Seventeen* where Linda Marsa also encourages condom use (August 2001, p. 116) or a feature article about "The best sex ed ever" by Gayle Forman (February 2002, p. 78). The advice in the paper copy of the magazine is often hidden; there is no regular or predictable section that talks about sex and health. There is no consistency of information; instead, information is presented in intermittent feature articles in the "real life" section of the magazine, ranging from different types of advice columns ("Who knew" and "The best sex ed ever," February 2002 and "Torie talks," March 2002 to a feature story about a teen prostitute who had befriended a drug user dying of AIDS (April 2002).

Though the paper version is defunct, the online version of *YM* is still active and continues to utilize the intermeshed strategy that the hard copy employed. For instance the July website has a STD quiz embedded in its list of quizzes: http://www.ym.com/jsp/quiz/mar2604.jsp. These quizzes have an extended life beyond the death of the paper version, as all the YM quizzes are now online (access the STD quiz at: http://magazine-directory.com/YM.htm).

In contrast to the intermeshed strategies of *YM* magazine in the paper and online formats, *Seventeen* magazine provides a consistent source of information on sex-related issues through a feature called "sexsmarts." The July 2005 issue, for example, offers a quiz testing the reader's knowledge of STDs as well as their preparedness for having sex. While the sexsmarts feature is an intermittent characteristic of the paper version, it is a constant of the online version of *Seventeen*, and even the paper version of the magazine urges readers to visit the sexsmarts section on the magazine's website (http://www.seventeen.com) and to email the advice to a friend. The footnote to the sex home page gives a sense of the goals of the section (http://www.seventeen.com/sexbody/sexbody. sexsmarts.homepage.html) explaining, "We're here to provide you with information and resources on a range of sexual health issues, from decision making about sex, including how to say 'no,' to the real facts on HIV and other sexually transmitted diseases (STDs)" (*Seventeen Magazine Online*, 2003).

"Talking Sex": Interactive Dialogue on Paper, Online

The sexsmarts section offers girls the opportunity to participate in interactive quizzes on sexual health issues. For example, this is the preamble for "Getting to know yourself is a good thing" quiz—"Are you being pressured to have sex?":

> When it comes to sex and relationships, navigating the who's, when's, and why's can be pretty tricky stuff. Setting a pace you feel comfortable with

for all stages of physical intimacy, from hand-holding to kissing to intercourse itself, is easier to do when you're armed with some simple facts about sexual decision-making, and some simple strategies for good, honest communication. Take our quiz to find out how well prepared you are to talk about your comfort-level, and to make sure you get the respect you deserve.

Similarly, the "Sex and Body" section of *Seventeen Magazine Online* includes a question and answer facility. Girls can email their questions on issues of sex and the body to sexQA@seventeen.com. Answers to the most frequently asked questions: "Is the pill reliable?" and "Can I get an STD even if I didn't have sex?" are posted on the site.

On the one hand, as David Buckingham (personal communication) and others suggest, these quizzes are a way for the magazine to obtain statistics about the readership of the magazine. On the other hand, the site is unusual both for the purpose it serves in individually answering girls questions on sex and health and for its sponsorship, which is separate from the Hearst Corporation. The sexsmarts component of *Seventeen Magazine Online* is funded by the Kaiser Family Foundation (KFF),[1] a nonprofit health and sexuality based organization in the United States. KFF is also the principal funder of *loveLife*, the largest youth-focused HIV prevention campaign in South Africa, one that has, incidentally, drawn as much controversy (if not more) for its youth "coolness" as *Seventeen Magazine* has in North America. The *loveLife* campaign, which aims to promote sexual health and to motivate positive change in high-risk sexual behavior among young South Africans, was launched in September 1999. It specifically encourages "delayed initiation of sexual activities among teenagers, reduction of sex partners or abstinence among the already sexually active, and consistent condom use" (*loveLife*, 2002, p. 5). It combines a media education and awareness campaign with adolescent-friendly sexual health services, and community-level outreach and support programs. *LoveLife's* activities are implemented by the Health Systems Trust, Planned Parenthood Association of South Africa, and the Reproductive Health Research Unit of the University of the Witwatersrand in cooperation with a number of community-based, nongovernment organizations. Major funding is provided by the Henry J. Kaiser Family Foundation and the Bill and Melinda Gates Foundation. Additional funding is provided by the South African Government and the Nelson Mandela Foundation (*loveLife*, 2002, pp. 2, 5; *Kaiser Family Foundation Online*, 2003). Organized under the auspices of a national advisory board chaired by South African first lady Zanele Mbeki, *loveLife* combines an innovative multimedia

202 • Claudia Mitchell and Jacqueline Reid-Walsh

approach promoting behavior change among South African adolescents and a major countrywide effort to set up adolescent-friendly sexual health clinics, counseling and educational services and outreach programs. It includes the *loveLife* train, a poster campaign, a website and magazine, and even a specific group of peer educators called Groundbreakers (Lesko, 2005). The *loveLife* campaign is implemented by a consortium of leading South African nongovernmental organizations in partnership with the South African government's health ministry. Girls who visit the sexsmarts section of the *Seventeen* website then have the option of clicking onto one of the largest-scale youth, gender, sexuality, and AIDS campaigns in the world.

As we describe elsewhere (Mitchell, Reid-Walsh, & Pithouse, 2004), the *loveLife* website (http://www.lovelife.org.za/) is an online sexual health and relationship resource for teenagers. This interactive website aspires to "mirror the hip new lifestyle young people all over South Africa associate with the *loveLife* brand." Visitors to the site can access information on HIV/AIDS and related issues and find out about *loveLife*'s events and outreach programs. The site has three core menu options, each customized for a specific audience: young people, parents, and organizations. According to its producers, the website averages fifty thousand hits per month (*loveLife Online*, 2003). Questions and answers about sex and relationships are posted in the "Ask Gerald" section of the *loveLife* site (http:// www.lovelife.org.za/kids/lovenlife/lovenlif.php). For example:

Dabbling with Danger

"Hey, Gerald! I'm a 14 year old virgin. I met a 23 year old guy I really like. He says he loves me but that he doesn't want to get into trouble with my parents. He likes touching my face, hair, hands and other parts of my body, but I don't like it. I'd like to remain single, but it's hard. I'm so torn apart. What can I do?"

Gerald replies

"Hi there, girl! This situation must be terribly confusing for you. Let me be straight: this brother ain't in your league. The age gap is too wide and his needs are more advanced than yours. Although he is scared of your parents now, I sense that the 'heat of passion' might drive him to have sex with you at some point—in which case he will be guilty of statutory rape. The way he fondles your body definitely spells trouble for him. If you don't want him to go to jail, you'd better let this one fly! Over and out."

(*loveLife Online*, 2003)

The "Love Talk" (http://www.lovelife.org.za/kids/forum/index.php) section of the site consists of two discussion forums for teenagers. "Kids Forum" provides an opportunity for general discussion and the other forum is a space to talk about views on HIV testing:

is it fun to do an aids test
Author: samkelisiwe (—.dit.ac.za)
Date: 07–25–03 11:23

ive been wondering for a long time whether it fun to sit there in those benches in hospital and do a hiv test i fear a lot that maybe they will dissappoint me.pls have your say and encourage me to do it.

Re: is it fun to do an aids test
Author: Talk at lovelife (—.hst.org.za)
Date: 07–29–03 10:50

Hi
Taking an HIV test is an informed decision. A person might be thinking of taking a test and may have personal reasons for doing so. Before taking a test the person is counseled (i.e. pre-test counseling). This is a confidential process which allows you to question all doubts that you may have and to clarify issues about taking the test.

Re: is it fun to do an aids test
Author: Nompumelelo (—.dit.ac.za)
Date: 08–01–03 10:27

I think each and everyone has his or her choice to do the test.u are not forced to do the test so before taking a test u have to think b4 u do so.so don't delay to go for councelling too.

Re: is it fun to do an aids test
Author: olwethu (—.utr.ac.za)
Date: 08–01–03 19:47

I think the test depends on what the results are and what u will do if it turns out that u're positiv.
personally: i would neva do the test cuz 4 me it would mean the end of the world . . . i would commit suicide.
u probably thinking that im an idiot and u right. my only problem with HIV and stuff is phase 2 of the desease i.e. when u can't move even ur arms, losing hair, those blisters in the mouth, and so forth.
my point is, if i found out that im positive 2day 'd kill ma self 2moro so it's better when i dont know ma status.
i hope u get what i mean!!!!
olwethu signs out!!!!!!!

(*loveLife Online*, 2003)

Clearly, clicking on to this website provides South African youth with information that they would find difficult to obtain through the regular channels of life-skills programs at school or through traditional healers and health care workers in the community. Equally, clicking on to this website for North American girls who are the main readers of *Seventeen* also gives them access to more in-depth information than they would find in the magazine (paper or online).

Emerging Issues

In this section we explore a number of issues emerging from our comparative study of the paper and online versions of magazines:

Relaying Information to Readers

One aspect we need to investigate further is how the information about sexual health and AIDS education is relayed to the readers within the context of the magazine. On the one hand, one young informant, a *Seventeen* reader of long-time standing, has remarked to us about the paper version of *Seventeen*: "Seventeen is all sweet and good in its reporting of STDs. The issues are camouflaged between ads for make-up and fashion. Nothing alarming. We don't want to upset the readers or the sponsors!" On the other hand, this aspect of camouflage (as we are describing it) may be necessary, for youth are not the only readers of *Seventeen*; there are adult gatekeepers as well. For instance, "Communique: a pro-life update" at http://www.all.org/communique/cq980306.htm has the following newsnote:

> LONG ISLAND: The Long Island Hauppauge Middle School has pulled *Seventeen, Teen* and *YM* from their shelves, citing sexually-oriented material, reports *The New York Times*. The teachers' union may sue, arguing that students in grades six through eight have a right to see these magazines. The material included information on sexual activity, birth control pills and condom use. (Reading: "Girls Magazines Banned at N.Y. Middle School," *New York Times*, February 13, 1998)

In order to discuss this camouflaging, we use a combined method of textual analysis and reader/viewer theory to investigate the relative invisibility of sex information in the paper version, and to examine the relative prominence of AIDS education in the online version. Specifically, we adapt Wolfgang Iser's (1978) notion of the implied reader and combine it with Zohar Shavit's (1986) idea that many texts for children and youth are actually addressed to more than one reader—not only the young reader—but also an adult reader lurking in the background. We suggest that there may be at least two implied readers/viewers of the texts of *Seventeen*—a young person (girl) who is seeking information and an adult censor. The adult may have an interest in restricting the transmission of this information and therefore may employ a variety of gatekeeping functions ranging from choosing whether or not to provide the money to purchase the magazine or, as in the case referred to earlier, exorcising their power to remove magazines from school libraries.

Recognizing New Ways of Reading

A number of researchers of popular youth culture have studied how girls and young women read fashion magazines. For example, Paul Willis (1990), Angela McRobbie and Jennie Garber (1991), Linda Christian-Smith (1993), and Dawn Currie (1999) have all noted that girls do not read paper magazines in a straightforward manner as when reading a book but rather, read in a random and fragmentary way: dipping into the magazine, skipping over certain bits, and pouring over others. Indeed, it is very difficult to read a magazine as if it were a book: using the table of contents for an efficient approach. In print magazines, it is easier to just thumb through the pages until you find the article you are looking for. For example, if one is looking for AIDS-related pieces in the March 2002 issue of *Seventeen*, you will find that the table of contents is buried in the midst of a number of ads and only appears some fourteen pages into the magazine. In between the two parts of the table of contents are more ads for makeup and shampoo. The sections: fashion, beauty, boys, real life, access, and columns are clearly marked. It is interesting to observe that the AIDS education article is not in the "boys" section where one might expect to find it but instead can be found in the "real life" section. In the March 2002 issue, it is buried in an article called "Torie Talks: Post-Prom Sex" where the writer tells readers about sex as depicted on screen in films "with soft, forgiving lighting and no fumbling with condoms."

Embedding sexual content in print formats may serve several purposes. For example, the publisher may be influenced by research that suggests girls read magazines in a desultory fashion, and believe they can thereby better attract girls' attention by placing articles at random. By interlacing AIDS advice and sex education with the expected beauty, fashion, and dating features the publisher can be seen as encouraging individual responsibility for (future) heterosexual encounters. To a young viewer/reader the article's placement does not set it apart as something "dangerous" or illicit but as a part of an active heterosexuality that many of the readers may not have participated in yet. In this way, article placement can be seen as a pragmatic, "normalization" strategy seen in other youth media forms and consumed by young girls. For instance, a 2002 MTV television special entitled "Going on a date with Jennifer Lopez" (January 12, 2002) presented condoms as part of the regular "gear" one would need when preparing for an imaginary date (along with clothes-shopping, buying flowers, and booking a table in a restaurant). In a similar fashion, by inserting safe sex information into advice, and question and answer sections of magazines and by featuring the occasional real life sex story, magazines may be normalizing responsible sex and sexuality for girls rather than setting it apart from day-to-day life. Also, because sex information in paper magazines is not made obvious or highlighted as a monthly feature, it may prevent adult censors from immediately seizing on this content.

In contrast, the online version of *Seventeen* is both discrete and more accessible in its sections devoted to AIDS education and sexual health. It is also free; provided one has access to the technology and the internet whether at home, at school, or at a public library. One section of the *Seventeen* website is the "sex and body" page, http://www.seventeen.com/sexbody/index.html, which is one of nine options on a clearly marked list on the left-hand side of the page. There is also a "real life" section, as in the print version of the magazine. Two of the nine options, then, could be dealing with sexual health and providing AIDS information, although this is not advertised. Indeed, if one clicks on the page called "Sex & Body," there is a partial image of bikini-clad girls and advice about hair removal—mundane advice for the girl reader and perhaps nothing for a censor to worry about. There are four main sections: two Sexsmarts' segments, a question and answer section, and a link to the off-site www.gURL.com website. The Sexsmarts link changes month to month. On the whole, the website is much more advice-based than the paper magazine. The format is such that each is an equally accessible link and each is presented as another option to click on. The neutrality of the set of possible links can again be interpreted as a kind of positive normalizing strategy. In a manner similar to the paper version the embeddedness of advice normalizes the material, presenting sexuality as an ordinary aspect of teen behavior. The online version is additionally more interactive for a viewer due to the possibilities offered by the medium; a user can email questions to the editors.

As noted earlier, the bottom of the Sexsmarts page informs the reader that the site is the result of a partnership between *Seventeen* and the

Kaiser Family Foundation. Interestingly, when we first began to collect data from the *Seventeen* website in 2002, the information about the Kaiser Foundation was easily visible and accessible. When we returned to the site in 2005, only the more savvy user would manage to find this information, a point worth thinking about in the context of the policies of the Bush administration around abstinence (see also Levine, 2002) and in relation to Cindy Patton's (1995) writings about the politics of safe sex in the United States. It is worth noting that in the 2005 issue of *Seventeen*, there is a four-page article on the virtues of abstinence, which not only tries to convince readers to be abstinent through various quizzes and statistics ("53% of high school students are virgins, 70 % of sexually active teens say they had sex to try to make their relationship closer, and 92% of teenagers agree that being a virgin in high school is a good thing"), but also allies itself with the virginity movement ("one in eight teenagers has taken a virginity pledge") by advertising pictures of virginity bracelets ("I'll wait"). The article also directs readers to three websites: candiesfoundation.org, which carries a strong abstinence message ("to be sexy you don't have to have sex"), teenwire.com, which offers useful information to readers about STDs and HIV testing while promoting planned parenthood, and teenpregnancy.org, which suggests a strong abstinence message as well.

The maintenance of different magazine layouts in paper and digital formats, as with most commercial sites that are "spin-offs" of a product, reflects the publisher's desire to utilize formats that compliment each other, rather than compete. For example, the cover of the April 2005 paper *Seventeen Magazine* features a variety of jeans' styles, while the home page of the website for the same month headlines trench coats. At the same time, the relative lack of fashion images on the website and the domination of verbal text indicate that the website serves a supplemental purpose for the publisher, ensuring that readers will not prefer the "free" web magazine to the purchased paper version. At the same time, by the website being known simply as a supplement to the paper magazine, girls whose parents approve of their reading *Seventeen* may also seek it out with parental approval as a "safe" website for girls.

New Perspectives on Advice Literature

One way to interpret these sections in both the print and web-based versions of *Seventeen Magazine* is by examining how the genre of advice literature is being presented in a different way. Historically, advice literature for girls and young women has been a way to regulate their behavior around sexuality by urging conformity of conduct and appearance. At the same time, early advice literature helped formulate a middle-class, heterosexual feminine ideal that was presented as the standard for behavior against which all girls/young women were to be judged (Armstrong & Tennenhouse, 1987). The logic of advice literature on the whole can be interpreted as forming part of a training process in creating conventional femininity, a strategy that works through the technique of normalization. As Foucault (1977) relates, normalization demands that the rule be made to function as a minimal threshold, as an average to be respected or as an optimum toward which one must move. It measures in quantitative terms and hierarchizes, in terms of value, the abilities, the level, and the "nature" of individuals. It introduces, through this "value-giving" measure, the constraint to a conformity that must be achieved (p. 185).

The advice in *Seventeen* could perhaps then be interpreted as a means of constructing a "new" safe sex norm in heterosexual relationships. Instead of training or "constraining" girls to deny the presence of sexual relationships, the advice in *Seventeen* can be seen as trying to urge an automatic "norm" of self-protective education on the part of the girls and of safe sex practices when becoming sexually active. At the same time, the different modes for accessing information in the magazine—web and paper—can be seen as creating a type of safe and private space for the girls seeking out the information. The information is more readily available to a knowledgeable user, the access is free, and the relation between user/viewer and the web text may be different than with the paper version.

Discussion

In this chapter, where we have primarily focused on print and digital texts and not the readers or users, there are, of course, limitations to our analysis. Research by Buckingham and Bragg (2004) is particularly relevant for extending this work in that it represents an in-depth study of the views of young people about sex and the media, some of which may pertain specifically to how they use advice columns in magazines. In another recent pilot study carried out in an internet café in Nigeria with a group of girls between the ages of eleven–sixteen (see chapter thirteen in this volume), we saw firsthand how girl-dedicated cyber-spaces might operate through the eyes of first-time users who were looking specifically at sites linked to body and reproductive health. At the same time, it appears that some producers of popular texts are utilizing new forms to create safe spaces for girls to access "sex-ed" information. Young people in a Kaiser study released in December 2001 ("Generation Rx.com: How Young People Use the Internet for Health Information" at http://www.kff.org/content/2001/20011211a/) think that web-based versions of magazines function as safe spaces for accessing sex and health information. Due to the private nature of these spaces online magazines can be more overt in the presentation of sexual heath and AIDS information. The fact that the information is not immediately obvious or is embedded as in the print magazine enables girls who are expert "users" of magazines to extract information about sex as easily as coming across tips about bedroom décor. To enable this freedom of access girls need privacy, within the public or private spaces of libraries, living rooms, and bedrooms. If an adult comes along they can always turn the page or click on another link; they do not need to advertise what they are doing. In this way the "camouflage" effect can be seen as serving a protective function for the young reader, although their actions could be reconstituted on the desktop by doing a simple web "history" search.

As important as these issues are to girls in North America, we are even more concerned about access to information on HIV and AIDS prevention and sexuality in a country like South Africa where the HIV infection rate for girls and young women is between 20 and 30 percent. Here girls and young women are three or four times more likely than young men of the same age to be infected with AIDS, and, as Catherine Campbell (2003) has pointed out, there has been to date an overall failure in terms of AIDS prevention programming (e.g., Life Skills, peer education) for young people. Notwithstanding the fact that there is often a failure for these programs to take into consideration the significance of gender itself (Mitchell & Smith, 2001), there is an overall information overload that is described elsewhere as the "sick of AIDS" phenomenon (Mitchell & Smith, 2003). Many young people are literally "sick of AIDS" and even more, are sick of hearing about AIDS. We would go so far as to suggest that access to information through the internet may be an empowering, "taking action'" mode in and of itself for girls and young women. While the internet is clearly not the only channel to pursue within AIDS prevention programming the idea of the internet as social intervention remains a promising one.

While South Africa, in general, is much better off than most other African countries in terms of access to the internet (although as Wasserman, 2003, points out, internet cafes, at least in the urban areas of many African countries, are now quite common), it nonetheless brings its own digital divide along the lines of race, class, economics, and even language. At the same time, there are some points of convergence between access to digital technology, access to information about sexuality and AIDS, the need to empower girls, and indeed, a growing awareness that strategic alliances between the private and public sectors are required in relation to media studies more generally.[2] While we are not arguing that young adolescents should spend all of their time online, or that they should not also look to parents and teachers for appropriate information about sex, we are seeing that the answer to the longstanding question "where do you get your information about sex?" is likely to now include websites along with responses such as, "my friends" or "I just heard it." Reading the internet this way can open up a critical space for tween girls in the age of AIDS.

Acknowledgments

We gratefully acknowledge the Social Sciences and Humanities Research Council of Canada for its financial support. We also acknowledge the work of Nikki Kamur in preparing some of the analysis of magazines for this chapter. We thank Ran Tao for her assistance in preparing the manuscript.

Notes

1. On the KFF website (http://www.kff.org/), the foundation's work is described in this way:

   The Henry J. Kaiser Family Foundation is an independent philanthropy focusing on the major health care issues facing the nation. The Foundation is an independent voice and source of facts and analysis for policymakers, the media, the health care community, and the general public.

   KFF is an operating Foundation that develops and runs its own research and communications programs, often in partnership with outside organizations. Through our policy research and communications programs, and through contracts with outside partners, we work to provide reliable information in a health system in which the issues are increasingly complex and the nation faces difficult challenges and choices.

   Our work is focused in three main areas: Health Policy, Media and Public Education, and Health and Development in South Africa. (Kaiser Family Foundation Online, 2003)

2. Here we are referring to the newly formed South African Media Studies Initiative Task Team that includes SABC, the Department of Education, but also private sector interests. See www.gcis.gov.za/docs/portcom/govreport.pdf

References

Armstrong, N. & Tennenhouse, L. (Eds.) (1987). *The ideology of conduct; Essays on literature and the history of sexuality*. New York: Methuen.

Buckingham, D. Personal communication, June 2005.

Buckingham, D. & Bragg, S. (2004). *Young people, sex and the media: The facts of life?* Hampshire & New York: Macmillan Palgrave.

Campbell, C. (2003). *"Letting them Die."* Why HIV/AIDS intervention programmes fail. Cape Town: Double Storey.

Christian-Smith, L. (1993). *Texts of desire: Essays on fiction, femininity and schooling.* New York: Routledge.

Currie, D. (1999). *GirlTalk: Adolescent Magazines and their Readers.* Toronto: University of Toronto Press.

Forman, G. (February 2002). The best sex ed ever. *Seventeen,* 78.

Foucault, M. (1977). *Discipline and punish: The birth of the prison.* (A. Sheridan, trans.) New York: Pantheon.

gURL. Retrieved from www.gurl.com.

Iser, W. (1978). *The act of reading: A theory of aesthetic response.* Baltimore: Johns Hopkins.

Kaiser Family Foundation Online. (February 13, 2003). *New York Times.*

Kemp, K. (February 2002). Condoms, yes or no? *YM,* 22.

Larkin, J., Mitchell, C., & Reid-Walsh, J. (2002–2005). Gendering adolescence and AIDS prevention. Social Sciences and Humanities Research Council of Canada.

Levine, J. (2002). *Harmful to minors: The perils of protecting children from sex.* Minneapolis, London: University of Minnesota Press.

loveLife. (2002). *loveLife 2002: Report on activities and progress.* Retrieved September 8, 2003, from http://www.lovelife.org.za/corporate/research/loveLife_2002_report.pdf.

loveLife Online. (2003). Retrieved September 9, 2003, from http://www.lovelife.org.za/.

Marsa, L. (August 2001). Sex and body. *Seventeen,* 116.

McRobbie, A. (1991). *Feminism and youth culture: From "Jackie" to "Just Seventeen."* Cambridge, MA: Unwin Hyman.

———. (1999). More! New sexualities in girls' magazines and the women's magazines. In A. McRobbie (ed.), *In the culture society: Arts, fashion and popular music,* pp. 46–61. London & New York: Routledge.

McRobbie, A. & Garber, J. (1991). Girls and subcultures. In A. McRobbie (ed.), *Feminism and youth culture: From Jackie to Just Seventeen,* pp. 1–15. Cambridge, MA: Unwin Hyman; originally printed in S. Hall and T. Jefferson (Eds.) (1978). *Resistance through rituals: Youth subcultures in post war Britain.* London: Hutchison.

Mitchell, C. & Reid-Walsh, J. (1998). Mail-order memory work: Towards a methodology of uncovering the experiences of covering over. *Review of Education/Pedagogy/Cultural Studies, 20*(1), 57–75.

———. (1999). Nine going on *Seventeen.* American Educational Research Association. Montreal, Canada. April.

———. (2002). *Researching children's popular culture: Cultural spaces of childhood.* London & New York: Routledge Taylor and Francis.

Mitchell, C. & Reid-Walsh, J. (2005). *Seven going on seventeen: Tween studies in the culture of girlhood.* New York: Peter Lang Associates.

Mitchell, C., Reid-Walsh, J., & Pithouse, K. (2004). "And what are you reading, Miss? Oh, it is only a website." Digital technology as a South African teen's guide to HIV/AIDS. *Convergence, 10*(1), 191–202.

Mitchell, C. & Smith, A. (2001). Changing the picture: Youth, gender and HIV/AIDS prevention campaigns in South Africa. *Canadian Women's Studies Journal, 21*(2), 56–62.

———. (2003). Sick of AIDS: Literacy and the meaning of life for South African youth. *Sexuality, Culture and Health, 5*(6), 513–522.

Mitchell, C., Walsh, S., & Larkin, J. (2004). Visualizing the politics of innocence in the age of AIDS. *Sex Education, 3*(2), 159–172.

MTV Television Special. (January 12, 2002). *Going on a date with Jennifer Lopez.*

Reid-Walsh, J. & Mitchell, C. (2004). Girls' web sites—a virtual room of one's own. In A. Harris (ed.), *All about the girl: Culture, power and identity*, pp. 173–182. New York & London: Routledge.

Seventeen Magazine. Hearst Communications Inc., February 2002, April 2002, July 2005.

Seventeen Magazine Online. (2003a). Retrieved September 8, 2003, from http://www.seventeen.com/.

———.(2003b). http://www.seventeen.com/sexbody/sexbody.sexsmarts. homepage.html

Shavit, Z. (1986). *Poetics of children's literature.* Athens: University of Georgia Press.

Wasserman, H. (2003). Dial-up identity: South African languages in cyberspace. In H. Wasserman & S. Jacobs (eds.), *Shifting selves: Post apartheid essays on mass media, culture and identity*, pp. 79–95. Cape Town: Kwela.

Weber, S. & Mitchell, C. (2000). *Dress fitting.* A video documentary. www.iirc. mcgill.ca.

———. (1995). *That's funny, you don't look like a teacher: Interrogating images of identity in popular culture.* London & New York: Falmer Press.

Weber, S., Mitchell, C., Reid-Walsh, J., & Buckingham, D. (2003–2006). Digital girls: From play to policy,. Social Sciences and Humanities Research Council of Canada.

Willis, P. (1990). *Common culture: Symbolic work at play in the everyday culture of the young.* Milton Keynes: Open University.

YM. (July). http://www.ym.com/jsp/quiz/mar2604.jsp.

CHAPTER THIRTEEN

New Girl (and New Boy) at the Internet Café: Digital Divides/Digital Futures

Claudia Mitchell and Grace Sokoya

Imagine a scene of a computer keyboard full of hands. One might think of a typical image of a keyboard as having two hands (with both belonging to the same person), but in this image there are many pairs. In the scene we have in mind, thirty-nine primary school children are all visiting the local Spar Shop in Mandini, a small town several hours north of Durban, South Africa, where there are four computer terminals. They are logging on to UNICEF's Voices of Youth website. It is impossible to see which hands belong to whom, and the ideas on "what is violence against children" are coming from everywhere. This is what we term a *digital futures scene.*

In this chapter we are interested in digital futures like the scene just discussed, but we are also concerned about "digital divides" and the ways in which issues of gender, geography, language, and power affect children's internet access. We will examine two case studies that cross the digital divide in various ways. Drawn from a three-year study, these cases focus on young people's first visits to a cyber café in Africa. By honing in on this experience, we are interested in reframing current understandings of digital divides by looking at the complex interplay of inequalities of access—inequalities that are only sometimes about resources. The first case we will present involves a group of tween girls from an urban center in Nigeria, and focuses on a one-week period in which they were given free rein access to the internet and offered information retrieval instruction, particularly in relation to health and sexuality information on the net. The second case, from KwaZulu-Natal, involves a similar age range, this time with both boys and girls whose first exposure to the internet is at a small cyber café in a local convenience store—the Spar Shop— located in a rural area. There they participate in a UN sponsored chat room focusing on violence against children. Each of these cases offers rich data on what has come to be described as the digital divide, provoking complicated conversations and reflections.

Case One: Girls' Cyber Play at the Abeokuta Cyber Café

This case takes place in Abeokuta, the capital of Ogun-state, Nigeria, which is one of thirty-six states in the country. Ogun-state is one of eight states in the southwestern part of the country where the majority of the inhabitants belong to the Yoruba tribe. Modern communication technologies such as the internet and cell phones are now entering the public domain in Nigeria, although an Internetworld (2004) study indicated that the percentage of internet users in Nigeria out of the entire population was 4.2 percent, whereas 81 percent of Canadian children and youth have access to computers at home (Media Awareness Network, 2001). Like many urban settings in Nigeria, there are now many cyber cafés in the city where young people and adults make use of the internet for various purposes, in spite of the relatively low level of computer/internet literacy. Although the majority of schools in Abeokuta now offer computer science to students at primary and secondary school levels, these schools do not have enough computers to provide the children with adequate opportunities to master learnt computer skills. The cost of procuring personal computers and internet connectivity is not affordable for the majority of families.

We focused mainly on tweens and early teenage girls, although there were a couple of older girls who participated as well. As noted elsewhere in this volume (see chapter twelve), the tween age-group is a phase that had been studied extensively by feminist psychologists and literary scholars who claim that it is a critical time in terms of developing voice and agency (Brown & Gilligan, 1992; Cherland, 1994; Christian-Smith, 1990). The girls in our study ranged in age from ten to twenty years. The involvement of the older girls proved to be critical: they were able to provide support and encouragement for the younger ones, facilitating their participation. Additionally, the older participants offered retrospective accounts, reflecting on their own cyber-autobiographies about how their lives during preteen and early teenage were different from the current group who had an earlier access to the internet.

In setting up the study we had several objectives, ranging from assessing preteens and teenage girls' access to the internet to exploring how girls could use the internet to understand their own bodies and sexuality, and acquire information about STDs and HIV prevention—an area of work that we had already begun to explore with young people in South Africa (Mitchell, Reid-Walsh, & Pithouse, 2004). We also wanted to see just where their cyber-play would take them in terms of identifying the kinds of websites they would like to access. We worked intensively with the girls for a full week. This included booking enough internet terminals for the girls at a local internet café, and holding focus group sessions with the girls in Grace's home. The first focus group served to elicit data on girls' experiences of internet usage prior to visiting the internet café, while the second provided information on girls' experiences of internet usage discoveries during the study. A closing session on sexuality education was given, followed by an interactive "Questions and Answers" discussion during which participants were encouraged to be as free as possible in their queries. The girls were also encouraged to maintain a communication link with each other and the project coordinator via email after the completion of the study. Follow-up interviews were conducted with each of the girls.

Access to Computers and the Internet

Before the research project began, only five out of the twelve cyber-girls had previous internet experience. Since none of their home PCs is connected to the internet, the five girls were all patronizing the commercial cyber cafés. One of the other seven girls had a Yahoo email account but she could not operate it independently. The remaining six neither had internet experience nor email accounts. As one ten-year-old participant observes:

> We have a PC in our family, on which I usually play games, and do word processing for my parents. Before now, I have never visited the Internet. I have been hearing my sister saying she wants to browse and when she comes back, she will tell me she checked her mail, composed e-mails, chatted, and visited some websites. My prayer had been that I would have an e-mail address one day and an opportunity to visit the Internet. I see my inclusion in this project as an answer to my prayers.

From the girls' comments and observations during the first two days of the study, the cyber-girls in the younger age-group were using the internet mainly for the purposes of sending and receiving emails, sending e-greeting cards, and engaging in only occasional chatting because of the high costs. The younger girls had no favorite websites apart from "Yahoo," before the commencement of the study, while the older girls used Google and other educational sites for their literature searches. During the study, however, the cyber-girls learnt about more websites and had more opportunities and time to visit the internet.

All the girls enjoyed chatting on the internet. They claimed that instant messaging livens them up and prevents boredom. One of the girls notes: "I enjoy chatting with my friends on the internet a lot, because I live quite far away from my friends. Most of my time was spent chatting with some of my friends that I met on line. I even met a new friend on-line, and we chatted a lot." Another says: "I chatted and also I visited websites like www.greeting100.com, which was full of e-cards. I found the day so interesting because it was so lively." A thirteen-year-old also comments: "I chatted for the last two hours with my friend and I had a nice day meeting and chatting with people."

The girls were excited about their experiences and also with the rate at which they were able to learn new things within such a short period. As one participant comments:

I have never been on the Internet before the commencement of this project. I never knew anything about it, although my elder ones used to hint me about it. But now, I have gained a lot of information about it during the course of this project. I now know how to check mails, send mail, visit websites, and download data and information.

Gender

Factors responsible for the digital divide between boys and girls, as well as amongst different age-groups in a developing country such as Nigeria, are complex. Whereas girls in developed countries, for example, might be reproducing established gender stereotypes in their interactions with technology and the internet, they are still a privileged group when compared with their counterparts in developing countries who have limited access to the internet. While three of the girls had started visiting the cyber café earlier (i.e., at ages fourteen, twelve, and twelve, respectively), a year before the commencement of the study, the two twenty-year-old participants reported having their first internet experience at age eighteen, confirming that age is an added disadvantage for the younger girls. One of them recalled: "I became computer literate when I was sixteen years old, after my secondary education. I started visiting Internet at age 18, during my first year in the University. I got my first e-mail address then too." The older girls are also disadvantaged, because as they grow and mature, they are expected to take on additional responsibilities in the home, relieving their mothers of some of the many duties commonly associated with their gender roles. One of the older girls mentioned how boys enjoy more freedom, while girls are bogged down at home with domestic chores: "We girls have to cook at home. We assist our Mums in the kitchen. The boys are not bogged down with all these."

Findings of the study reveal that while the girls perceive themselves as capable of using the computer and the internet, their gender (and age, in the younger children) constitute a limiting factor. This scenario is representative of what might be happening in many developing countries, and shows a contrast between what constitutes a digital divide in a developed and developing context. Girls have limited opportunities and access to computers and the internet at home when compared with boys, although they have equal access to these facilities in the schools. These are some of the effects of the sociocultural constructions of gender and gender roles.

An additional feature of access and usage relates to the position of girls within Yoruba more generally. Boys are perceived to be able to cope with the intellectual and physical demands of technology education better than girls, while girls are encouraged to improve their home skills so that they may become more efficient in playing their socially accepted and traditional roles of caregiver, homemaker, and unpaid worker; anything to increase their marriageable value (Thas, 2003). Young girls within the age range of ten–fourteen in the study, however, have a dual disadvantage. The ages of children usually found in the cyber cafés starts from thirteen and above, more so, because the Yorubas are very protective of their children and rarely allow the very young ones to go out unaccompanied, especially the girls. For instance, an eleven-year-old girl comments:

I am the last born of my family and also the baby of the house. My brothers visit the internet more than I do. Our parent would not allow me to go out of the house un-accompanied. They say that I am too young to go out alone, and because I am a girl. More boys are therefore found in the cyber cafés because they enjoy more freedom.

Access

The level of computer literacy for Nigerian adults is relatively low. In addition, personal computers and internet connectivity is not affordable for the majority of families. Eleven out of the twelve cyber-girls had experience with the computer in their nursery, primary and secondary schools. Four of the nine families from which the cyber-girls were drawn had personal computers, to which five of the twelve girls had access. All the five girls in this category claim that they play games on their computers. None of the girls reported sibling rivalry in the use of the computers at home. Prior to the commencement of the study, only five out of the twelve cyber-girls had internet experience.

In the course of our project, we found that the factors influencing access to computers include level of computer literacy, culture, gender, age, and money. The socioeconomic status and computer literacy level are primary limiting factors for many parents. Even for those who have computers at home, the computers are not often connected to the internet in the majority of cases, due to the financial implications. In addition, the fact that children need to move out of their respective homes to access the internet limits the opportunities of the younger ones to develop skills learnt in school. Even outside the home, opportunities to access the internet are very limited. Participants observed that internet access is quite expensive because cyber cafés charge by the minute. The rate charged at the cyber cafés ranges between three and five Naira per minute. The rate is lower for "overnight browsing," ranging between four and five hundred Naira per night. Not many parents and children can afford the cost of the daytime and overnight browsing. School children usually save part of their daily meal allowances for browsing for a few minutes or hours as they can afford. As one of the older girls says:

> It is very costly to visit the internet on a regular basis. It therefore depends on how much time someone has to spend on the internet, and also by how you have in your pocket. I visit cyber café any time I have money and have important messages to send to friends and when I have assignment from school. Most of the time, we go for night browsing because it is cheaper.

As participants in our action-based research project, the cyber-girls had opportunities throughout the period of the study to visit the internet without having to pay from their purse.

Our findings concur with that of Thas (2003), who states that gender-related barriers to using technology include issues of infrastructure and access; issues of affordability; issues of time (women's triple burden of reproductive, productive, and community work) and mobility (limited access to transport and ability to leave the home), as well as issues of basic literacy.

Favorite Websites

Before coming to the internet café, none of the cyber-girls really had any favorite websites. Only the older girls mentioned that they used Yahoo and Google for literature searches. During the first two days of the study however, the younger cyber-girls aged nine–fourteen years were fond of visiting the Yahoo site to send emails and e-cards to their friends and relatives, as well as for the purpose of chatting online. These activities were practically all they did on the internet during the first three days of the study.

On the fourth day of the project however, new girl-centred websites were introduced to our participants. Some of these websites were discovered during a web-review we conducted before the study began, while others were chosen from among the favorite websites reported by the girls in chapter seven of this book (also a Digital Girls team project). Although the girls in our study were initially reluctant to suspend their "communication" activities in order to visit these new websites, they eventually became quite excited. Following is a brief description of several of their favorites:

www.bigfatbaby.com
The girls loved this site, which was also a favorite in the London study mentioned earlier. It has many funny pages, funny pictures, funny cards, jokes, and dance pages. The girls' reaction to the site is evident in the comments they made: Derin, an eleven-year-old, said: "It was fun for me because I went on dance pages, jokes pages and so on. I sent one of the dance pages to my sister and her friends." Thirteen-year-old Mosun: "The website I like best is 'bigfatbaby' because of the fun-pages funny pictures, jokes and funny cards. I really like this website because you can send the pages to friends."

www.goaskalice.columbia.edu
Go Ask Alice! is the health question and answer internet service produced by Alice!, Columbia University's Health Education Program—a division of Health Services at Columbia. *Go Ask Alice!* was established in 1993 at Columbia University's Health Education program, likely making it the first major internet health Q&A site. The mission of *Go Ask Alice!* is to increase access to, and use of, health information by providing factual, in-depth, straightforward, and nonjudgmental information to assist readers' decision-making about their physical, sexual, emotional, and spiritual health. "Alice!" answers questions about relationships, sexuality, sexual and emotional health, fitness, nutrition, alcohol, nicotine, and

other drugs, and general health. Although all the girls were introduced to the "goaskalice" website, only one of them, a fifteen-year-old, was initially fond of the site. However, because the cyber-girls were given opportunities to reflect on and share their experiences with each other on a daily basis, the other girls soon became fascinated by the site and began to ask questions too. One of the younger girls, however, felt she was too young for the information accessed on this website. As she writes: "I could have found it interesting, but the website was meant for older girls and not children like myself."

www.engenderhealth.org
This site is based on health issues. In addition to sections meant for girls, it has other sections, such as family planning and men's health. One of the younger girls immediately recognized that the site discusses the concerns of girls about their health as they grow up. The girls commented on various examples such as woman's health, maternal/child health, postpartum care, breast-feeding, HIV/AIDS, and so forth. An interesting development occurred when the girls began involving the research team, sending messages to us, as well as their peers, sharing what they were thinking and finding with us. Grace recalls that seeing what the girls were encountering was somewhat shocking at first. Describing her response to a daily "bigfatbaby" newsletter when the theme was "Ten reasons why sex is good for you," she notes:

> While the contents of the pages were quite helpful for me as an adult, I was imagining what effect it could have on the young girls in the study, who might not be considering sex in the nearest future. As a mother, I was particularly concerned about my 13 year old daughter who also participated in the study. This shows the part of the risks of the virtual world— exposure to uncontrolled environments and un-censored information. While girls in the study derived fun from the site, the younger participants might be embarrassed by the pages on "sex" earlier mentioned. This is evident in some comments by an 11 year old participant following her discovery in one of the subsequent websites. This implies a need for a customised website providing age-relevant information for girls, based on what they want and what is considered best for them. (Fieldnotes, Grace Sokoya)

What Girls Want

Data collected through focus groups, observations, cyber-girls' personal reflections and journal entries, as well as the interactive teaching and learning sessions revealed that the girls desire social connectedness with peers, friends, and relatives, through their activities of e-messaging (emails, e-cards, and chatting). More importantly, however, the girls are eager for education and information about their bodies, sexuality, and reproductive health. This finding was further confirmed during the second focus group and closing workshop, during which the girls had opportunities to share their experiences on the internet during the study period, and listen to a talk on female sexuality.

Case Two: Digital Hope (South Africa)

The second case takes place in rural KwaZulu-Natal and involves thirty-nine children in grades four, five, and six. Unlike the more intensive project in Nigeria, this study involves the participation of the children in a one-day event at a local internet café. The idea for the project came out of a "Theory and practice of media education" course at the University of KwaZulu-Natal where the children's teacher, Sipho, is studying. The focus of the course was on "digital hope," which involves the use of the internet and other forms of digital technology to examine issues related to social change. While the participating teachers tested out a variety of technologies, including digital storytelling, a particularly relevant aspect of their work was testing the viability of the various technologies in rural and disadvantaged settings. At the time, the UN Voices of Youth website www.unicef.org/voy/ was hosting a chat room on violence against children, an issue that is of global concern. It is a particularly critical issue in South Africa, where there are high incidences of gender violence and corporal punishment in and around schools (Bhana, 2006; Human Rights Watch Report, 2001), and also in homes and communities in the form of sexual abuse and neglect. While we were interested in what the children would have to say about these issues, we were equally curious to see what would happen in, what was for many, a first-time encounter with a computer and the internet.

The main activity of the day was organized around bussing the children to the local Spar Shop, which also has a small internet café made up of four terminals. By prior arrangement we had booked the terminals and also worked with a small support team from the university who could offer assistance to the children in logging in and so on. The team had made sure that email accounts were set up in advance so that the participants could immediately engage with the content of the chat room. Because of the large number of participants and the small number of terminals, children took turns on the computer and also worked in groups. They knew they would be expressing their views about violence against children so that in the time that they had to wait their turn they made notes on what they could write about. In some cases they also drew pictures of violence.

Technical Aspects of the Internet

We were interested in how they would approach the computers. As Caryn Barnes (2005), one of the team members and organizers of the day, observes:

> Considering the reality that these children have had little exposure to computers either in their homes or at school, it was interesting to see whether they found any part of the task difficult and if they did, how they dealt with their difficulties. There were five adults available to help with the variety of problems arising, including keyboard skills, spelling, translations and the fact that although the children had given some thought to the topic, no stories had been prepared. This was partially solved by allowing children who were waiting for access to a terminal to write down their stories so that they would be ready to enter them directly once they got access. In conversation with the children, I encountered only one who said she had a computer at home, but no internet access. Certainly, they all understood that their words could be put up on screen—what their understanding of the information superhighway was, I am not sure. Only a couple of the children had any trepidation in trying to type up their responses. Most were extremely eager to the extent that at each terminal where a group of three were working, there were sometimes as many as four hands trying to type simultaneously.

Access to computers

Interestingly, the school that the children attend actually has six computers, but they have never been installed. One of the reasons given by the school is that security is an issue. Schools are targets for vandalism in the area and unless there is some way to provide extra security by way of "burglar guarding" on the windows and perhaps a night-time security person, the computers could be stolen. The cost of this extra security on top of the initial cost of the computers is a critical issue. Additionally, very few primary schools have anyone trained to assist children with their computer learning. Indeed as Sipho, the classroom teacher who himself had only just learned to log on to the computer, expressed it: "I was ashamed to realize that I couldn't even help my grade five class. They have a right to more. As teachers we should be lobbying for more."

Language

Language, as Wasserman (2003) and others have written about in South Africa, is also a component of the digital divide where English and Afrikaans enjoy a much greater visibility. The children were all first language speakers of isiZulu, one of the eleven official languages in South Africa. Although they are receiving English instruction as well at school, clearly they were much more comfortable in isiZulu. The fact that they were commenting on a very sensitive and nuanced issue, violence against children, is, in and of itself a critical concern in terms of language. As Barnes (2005) further notes:

> The problem of English being the language of response in this exercise caused most of the difficulties. It is interesting that the child who was most involved in this exercise, and had to be dragged away from the terminal so that her classmates could have their turn was a very articulate little girl. Her story was more complex than her classmates and much less predictable. Her understanding of what was happening also seemed clearer than that of her classmates and she was quicker at entering her story. Her competence in English clearly aided her in the entire task.

About the Issue of Violence against Children

Like the project in Nigeria that had a dual focus—playing on the internet and looking closely at sexuality—the *Digital Hope* project was also meant to explore the ways in which the internet can be a critical tool for voice and agency. In this case, the issue was violence against children. Our young participants had a lot to say in their "pre-writings" and drawings. The difficulty of expressing these views online, however, cannot be understated. Clearly the issue of violence against children is sensitive and also very nuanced when it comes to violence in home and school environments, something we have found in our work elsewhere on children's experience of violence (Mitchell & Kanyangara, 2006). The stories and narratives that the children told would probably have been different if they could have been expressed in Zulu. As Caryn observed:

> The result was that the stories we got were quite formulaic and pre-dictable. The language dynamic means that the material has to be simplified, which results in a less rich dialogue. The ways I considered of dealing with this involve more teacher involvement, either as a stimulus to discussion or as a translator. Even if the children could have entered their stories in Zulu, if they wanted to be part of the worldwide dialogue they would

have had to be translated which would necessarily affect the tone and immediacy of the medium.

Nonetheless, the children did offer some of their views in a very forthright way. One participant, for example, called for the death penalty for all parents who sexually abuse their children. Another wrote about the unfairness of teachers hitting children in school. Several wrote about local examples of violence against children that had taken place recently. It was more difficult to get a sense of whether they had actually read any of the threads within the conversations that were already posted.

In retrospect, we realize that it would have been useful to have had more time for the play aspect first. In a similar session involving another group of rural learners who were bussed to a school that had internet access, we did incorporate time to simply play.

Discussion: Complicated Conversations in Studying Digital Divides

What we have seen in these two cases and in others that are part of the same study is that digital divide discussions are not just about gender or access to resources, though both of these are critical issues as Tapscott (1998), Walkerdine (1998), Luke (2000), and Reid-Walsh and Mitchell (2004) point out in their studies of children's uses of technology. The digital divide can also relate to language, although as Wasserman (2003) has pointed out, this could also be interpreted in the context of resources and availability of funds for translation and web-support. Sometimes, the issues are more about "control" in reference to who, in a school, home or community, wields the power. For example, we found that in one well-resourced urban school in KwaZulu-Natal, the computer lab was closed to anyone but the computer teachers and their classes. This meant that the media teacher with whom we were working had to ask the students to go to an internet café (at their own expense) to participate in the *Voices of Youth* chat room. In some cases the resources are there, but the sheer cost of connectivity as a result of state control of communications is the issue. The costs of internet access in a school or community, for example, are beyond the reach of most consumers (Hall, 2000). Digital divides can also be generational, though again, these are multifaceted and complex; children and young people in some cases may be far more computer savvy than their parents or teachers, something that exacerbates generation gaps. Sometimes the divides are about resourcefulness, creativity, and a "will" to make things happen, and we have been intrigued by the sense of activism that young people and their teachers have taken on. In one setting in rural South Africa, we saw first-hand how the internet could be a mechanism for breaking down racial and age divides when young people from a poorly resourced rural school were hosted by a more privileged school. In one instance, for example, a sixteen-year-old black boy sat alongside an eleven-year-old white girl. When we looked at the photographs of the day we saw that the eyes of both were glued to the screen, and although it was the girl's hands that were on the keyboard, they were both eagerly manipulating the "cyber-dress" site (Mitchell, Barnes, & Stuart, 2006).

We have also seen that some of the divides, particularly the have/have-not gaps (in terms of resources), still exist. What is new about this dynamic, however, is the growing awareness of the "have-nots" about what they do not have access to. This discrepancy is evident in the reaction of the brother of one of the cyber-girls. He comments on being left out of the discussions about sexuality, something that for him is further exacerbated by the focus on girls in the project. As he observes:

> Being left out from others is one of those things that are rampant among teenage boys. Excluded from teenage lectures, sensitization and empowerment programmes, boys often resort to forming groups in which they feel secure. We boys don't get the opportunity of someone sitting us down and really giving us a man-to-man talk on the dos and don'ts in teenage. For example talks about how to avoid HIV usually focus on girls. Since the commencement of the project, I have often asked myself whether it is only girls that are supposed to know about the internet. Are they the only ones supposed to have customized websites? Are they the only ones who desire to know about their body changes and health during puberty?

This idea of exclusion is something that we recorded in a focus group with teachers in rural KwaZulu-Natal. By the end of the discussions, they were both eager to push forward to find ways of securing access for their students. However, these teachers were also profoundly moved by the realization of what their students aren't getting and what they themselves have not been able to provide.

While social exclusion and access to technology has been taken up elsewhere in relation to discussion of digital divides (Holloway & Valentine, 2003), we think that there are many new "takes" on this exclusion as demonstrated by these two examples. A critical point of convergence between the two case studies is the sense of autonomy, agency, and "in the world-ness" that the children revealed either in follow-up interviews in the first case, or through follow-up interviews with the teacher in the second case. Notwithstanding the obvious issues of access, the children's responses point to the significance of some components of the apparent digital divide that are more imagined than real. The chapter also suggests ways in which internet exposure and new media can be reconfigured as central to "taking action" in social and geographic areas where the voices (and identities) of children and young people are critical to social change. Cell phone technology is a good example, since both South Africa and Nigeria are countries where the widespread use of cell phones offers fascinating new possibilities in terms of breaking down the digital divides, particularly in relation to taking action and social change. We have noted, for example, a case where students in a rural secondary school in South Africa imported their own music from their cell phones into a video documentary they were making on gender violence. While they had never even held a camera before, they clearly had a great deal of competence with their cell phones. Cell phones are now being used as part of health delivery programs in relation to HIV and AIDS in many parts of South Africa in that patients are being reminded to take their anti-retroviral medication. Such examples give way, we would argue, to hopeful digital futures.

Acknowledgments

We wish to thank all of the children and young people in Nigeria and South Africa who participated in this study. We would also like to acknowledge the contributions of Jean Stuart and the honors and masters students enrolled in Media and Classroom Practices at the University of KwaZulu-Natal, August–November 2005. Much of the success of Spar Shop internet café intervention is directly attributable to Caryn Barnes.

References

Barnes, C. (2005). Aspects of the digital divide in KwaZulu-Natal. Unpublished manuscript, School of Language, Literacies, Media and Drama Education, University of KwaZulu-Natal.

Bhana, D. (2006). "Doing power": Confronting violent masculinities in primary schools. In F. Leach and C. Mitchell (eds.), *Combating gender violence in and around schools*, pp. 171–179. London: Trentham.

Brown, L.M. & Gilligan, C. (1992). *Meeting at the crossroads: Women's psychology and girl's development.* Cambridge, MA: Harvard University Press.

Cherland, M.R. (1994). *Private practices: Girls reading fiction and constructing identity.* London: Taylor and Francis.

Christian-Smith, L. (1990). *Becoming a woman through romance.* New York: Routledge.

Hall, M. (2000). Digital S.A. In S. Nuttall and C. Michael (eds.), *Senses of culture*, pp. 460–475. Cape Town: Oxford University Press.

Holloway, S. & Valentine, G. (2003). *Cyberkids: Children in the information age.* London & New York: RoutledgeFalmer.

Human Rights Watch Report. (2001). *Scared at school: Sexual violence against girls in South African schools.* Retrieved September 16, 2003, from http://www.hrw.org/reports/pdfs/S/SAFRICA/SAFWOM1201.PDF.

Internetworld. (2004). *Internet usage in Nigeria.* Retrieved from http://www.internetworldstats.com/stats1.htm

Luke, C. (2000). Cyber-schooling and technological change: Multiliteracies for new times. In B. Cope and M. Kalantzis (eds.), *Multiliteracies: Literacy learning and the design of social futures*, pp. 69–91. London: Routledge.

Media Awareness Network. (2001). *Young Canadians in a wired world: The students' view.* Retrieved September 2, 2002, from www.media-awareness.com/engwebaware/netsurvey/pdf/natl_findings.pdf.

Mitchell, C., Barnes, C., & Stuart, J. (2006). *Digital hope and new media at Edgewood.* Retrieved from http://www.ukzn.ac.za/news/digitalhope.asp?navid=4.

Mitchell, C. & Kanyangara, P. (2006). Addressing violence in and around schools in Rwanda: Through the eyes of children and young people. UNICEF, Kigali.

Mitchell, C., Reid-Walsh, J., & Pithouse, K. (2004). "And what are you reading, Miss? Oh, it is only a website." Digital technology as a South African teen's guide to HIV/AIDS. *Convergence, 10*(1), 191–202.

Reid-Walsh, J. & Mitchell, C. (2004). Girls' web sites-a virtual room of one's own. In A. Harris (ed.), *All about the girl: Culture, power and identity*, pp. 173–182. New York & London: Routledge.

Tapscott, D. (1998). *Growing up digital: The rise of the net generation.* New York: McGraw-Hill.

Thas, A.M. (2003). Potential benefits of ICT and gender related barriers. Paper prepared for UNESCAP and presented at the Forum on Gender and ICTs, August 21, 2003, in Kuala Lumpur, Malaysia.

Walkerdine, V. (1998). Children in cyberspace: A new frontier. In K. Lesnik-Oberstein (ed.), *Children in culture: Approaches to childhood*, pp. 109–121. Houndsmills: Macmillan.

Wasserman, H. (2003). "Dial-up identity: South African languages in cyberspace." In. H. Wasserman and S. Jacobs (eds.), *Shifting selves: Post apartheid essays on mass media, culture and identity*, pp. 79–95. Cape Town: Kwela.

CHAPTER FOURTEEN

Contested Spaces: Protecting or Inhibiting Girls Online?

Leslie Regan Shade

Introduction: The DOPA Debates

While these sites were designed to allow their users to share virtual profiles of themselves to friends and like-minded users, the sites at most have become a haven for online sexual predators who have made these corners of the Web their own virtual hunting ground.

> —Republican Representative Michael Fitzpatrick, Pennsylvania, on U.S. House of Representatives debate on DOPA, July 26, 2006.
>
> URL: http://www.govtrack.us/congress/record.xpd? id=109-h20060726-41#sMonoElementm5m0m0m)

On 26 July 2006, the U.S. House of Representatives passed The Deleting Online Predators Act (DOPA) of 2006 by a vote of 410 to 15. However with the end of the Congressional session, DOPA died in the U.S. Senate and was never enacted. DOPA would have required that all public libraries and schools that received federal funding block access to social networking sites, chat sites and potentially (according to one interpretation of the Act) all blogs.[1] Proponents of the Act contended that it was designed to protect minors from online sexual predators and sexual exploitation, which the National Center for Missing & Exploited Children (NCMEC) estimated, had increased significantly: one in five youth received a sexual solicitation over the internet in 2005, with teen girls, the primary target, receiving two-thirds of the solicitations.[2]

Opponents of DOPA argued that threats are more pernicious for children accessing sites in their own homes without adequate parental supervision. Democratic Representative Bart Stupak of Michigan stated, "this legislation will actually drive children to go to unsupervised places, unsupervised sites to go online, where they will become more vulnerable to child predators." Alternatively, Democratic Representative Diane Watson of California argued:

> [I]t sends the wrong message to our children, our parents, teachers and librarians. The bill would curb Internet usage as a means to protect children, a counterproductive method to achieving such an important goal. Rather than restricting Internet usage, parents, teachers and librarians need to teach children how to use our ever-changing technology. The information age in which we live offers so much potential to our children, if they know how to use it.[3]

The furor around DOPA continued with the re-introduction of the Bill the following year, as *The Protecting Children in the 21st Century Act*, by Senator Ted Stevens (who infamously referred to the internet as a "series of tubes"). The Bill passed the Senate in 2008 but did not reach the House for a vote.[4] These pieces of U.S. legislation, which purport to protect children online, highlight the heated public debates that arise around the internet and youth. Opinions abound; not all of them based on research, facts, or rational thought. This chapter examines the way in which the emergence of new media has typically elicited disagreement, polarized responses, and panic regarding children and the protection of childhood, particularly insofar as girls are concerned.

Young people are avid users of social networking spaces such as MySpace, finding them to be a robust, innovative, and attractive method of communicating online to their friends and peers. Social networking spaces are webspaces where individuals can create their own online presence for uploading photos and profiles of themselves; within the larger web community users are encouraged to be interactive via posting lists of fellow users on their friends section, writing within the comments section, and letting other users link to their own spaces (Williams, 2006; "Teens hang out at MySpace," 2006). The "articulated social network of these systems" (Ellison et al., 2009, p. 6) makes networking with friends and creating new social relationships a pervasive component of young people's lives. Social networking spaces (SNS) create networked publics: "a space of relative autonomy for youth, a space where they can engage in learning and reputation building in contexts of peer-based reciprocity, largely outside of the purview of teachers, parents, and other adults who have authority over them" (Ito et al., 2008, n.p.). The Pew Internet & American Life Project estimates that 70% of teens use SNS (Rainie, 2009). The most popular spaces for youth include MySpace. com, Xanga.com, LiveJournal.com, and Facebook.com. Fuelled by the affordability and ubiquity of digital and cell phone cameras, these webspaces have also become lucrative. In July 2005, Rupert Murdoch's News Corporation purchased MySpace.com for 649 million USD, which in February 2006 boasted, according to some estimates, eighty-nine million users since its inception in late 2003. These figures have attracted diverse groups eager to tap into MySpace's youth demographic, including retailers, entertainment companies, cell phone companies, and youth-oriented brands.

By 2006, 150,000 new accounts were created every day, and the MySpace user population was equivalent to the 12th largest country in the world (Rosen 2006). Three years later, however, the site's popularity was eclipsed by *Facebook*'s (losing 5M unique visitors in two months in early 2009) and News Corp. was having difficulties meeting their ambitious revenue goals, with operating income declining from $47B to $7B. An ad deal with Google also expired, and it was not clear if this would be renewed (Stelter & Arango, 2009).

Larry Rosen's (2006) study of Los Angeles-area MySpace users revealed that "the typical MySpacer has about 200 'friends' with approximately 75 labeled as 'close friends', many of whom they have never met" (p. 2). MySpace clients use instant messaging (IM), e-mail, and post and read bulletins an average of two hours a day, five days a week. Combating pervasive negative media coverage of MySpace, Rosen asserts that MySpace offers positive benefits for teens: "more support from friends, more honest communication and less shyness both on and off MySpace," providing "a forum for teenagers to develop a sense of their personal identity" (pp. 5–6).[5]

Similarly, *Facebook* users cite its popularity and pervasiveness as a way to keep up with socialization and entertainment (Boesveld, 2008). *Facebook* surpassed MySpace in popularity and in 2009 boasted 300M users globally, with 50 per cent of active users logging on to *Facebook* on any given day (Stone, 2009). 2009 revenues were estimated to be $500M, with anticipated accrual up to "billions of dollars" in the next five years (Lawsky, 2009). Boyd (2009) argues that education, race, and class matter when it comes to which youth opt for *Facebook* over MySpace; with minority and lower-income groups using MySpace more than *Facebook*, social inequalities are replicated on SNS.

Critics of DOPA argued that the legislation would create an even more pervasive digital-divide amongst children and youth who have broadband access in their homes and those who can only access the internet through their schools, public libraries, or community centers. If these pieces of legislation to ban children from established networking sites were passed, it is unlikely that they would really succeed in preventing children from doing what they need and want to do—communicate and interact with their peers in a society (at least in North America) that is increasing reticent about the public mobility of children, especially girls, without adult supervision. As well as censoring constitutionally protected speech, DOPA and *The Protecting Children in the 21st Century Act* would also have exacerbated the "participation gap" amongst youth using and creating internet content, particularly for civic participation (American Library Association, 2006; Center for Democracy and Technology, 2006; Jenkins, 2006).

What to make of all this controversy? Using a case study of MySpace and DOPA, this chapter examines recent public discourses around childhood and the internet as it relates to girlhood, exploring the interplay between public discourse and policy objectives. Adopting Alison Adam's (2002) admonition that ethical debates about the social uses of information and communication technology (cyber-ethics) need to more proactively consider its gendered dimensions, this chapter also argues that internet policy on issues of sexual exploitation is inappropriately "gender-blind." For instance, although most victims of cyber-stalking, online child pornography, and pedophilia rings are females and most perpetrators male, Adam writes "almost nothing seems to be made of this fact by the policy makers who write such documents. Additionally, policy documents fail to address the issue that, in finding the cause of the problem and ways to counter it, the question of gender might be highly relevant" (p. 134). Gender is thus an important consideration in this discussion because of the active roles young girls are assuming as consumers and creators of internet content.

Burning Content

People have always greeted new communication technologies with both optimism and trepidation (Wartella & Jennings, 2000). Generations of adults have demonstrated particular concern regarding the influence of new mediums on young women's access to sexual knowledge and their ability to interact with the opposite sex. Carolyn Marvin (1990), for example, relates how the introduction of the telephone into the home disrupted courtship rituals, as all of a sudden the telephone could be used to facilitate un-chaperoned courting. The Payne Fund Studies of the 1930s examined the impact of the nascent film culture on American youth. Chapter seven of Blumer's study, "Emotional Possession: Love and Passion," related anecdotes from youth on the romantic influences of film:

> Female, 17: "When I see certain love scenes, I burn up and so does my boyfriend."

> Female, 16, white, high-school sophomore: "When I see a love picture or love scene, my heart beats faster, my stomach seems to roll, and I have a sensation of being deeply moved and thrilled. When I am with a boy and there is a passionate love scene, each of us can tell that the other is thrilled by it and unconsciously his arm goes up or his hand clasps mine. Seeing such scenes has made me receptive to love-making; before I didn't like it and thought it silly, but the movies have changed my ideas." (Blumer, 1933, p. 110)

The internet—variously characterized as an untamed frontier and a lawless and libertarian refuge—quickly became a lighting rod for policy makers and parents wishing to regulate content and protect children from illegal and offensive subject matter, particularly of a sexual nature. The mid-1990s witnessed rancorous debates over the Communications Decency Act of 1996, legislation designed to criminalize making available "indecent" and "obscene" speech or content for minors under the age of eighteen. In 1997 the Supreme Court of the United States, in *Reno v. American Civil Liberties Union*, struck down the online censorship provisions of the CDA, arguing that the indecency provisions violated the First Amendment guarantee of freedom of speech. Associate Justice John Paul Stevens wrote in his majority opinion that:

> Although the Government has an interest in protecting children from potentially harmful materials ... the CDA pursues that interest by suppressing a large amount of speech that adults have a constitutional right to send and receive. (*Reno vs. ACLU*, 1997)

Two other pieces of legislation designed to protect youth from internet content passed into law in 2000. The Children's Internet Protection Act (CIPIC) requires that any public school or library receiving federal funding for internet connectivity (under the government's "E-Rate" program) must ensure that appropriate internet safety policy and protection measures are implemented. This includes technological blocking mechanisms (software) that filter any internet content that is obscene, harmful to minors, or consists of child pornography.[6] The Children's Online Privacy Protection Act (COPPA) requires that all websites collecting personal information from their users must not collect any data from children under the age of thirteen except with explicit parental permission. COPPA also requires that websites provide appropriate privacy statements on their sites.[7]

We thus need to situate DOPA as merely the latest in a series of U.S. legislation that purports to protect minors from offensive, illegal, and sexual content and sexual exploitation. Certainly the debates over MySpace have been fuelled by a plethora of media reports emphasizing (as has been the tendency in the past when discussing new communication technologies and youth, tabloidization and titillation) sexualization and sensationalism (Shade, 2002). *Facebook* seems to have escaped some of the more sensationalistic coverage than that bestowed upon MySpace; more concerns have been expressed with *Facebook* over privacy issues rather then predators.

This is not to minimize the work of academics (Hughes, 2002), investigative journalists, and activist organizations (Hick & Halpin, 2001) in bringing public attention to the sordid world of child pornographers and international crime rings. Compelling accounts of young men performing sexual acts on webcams for gifts and money, and a proliferation of thinly disguised "model sites" that offer explicit sexualized images of young girls for pedophiles revealed by *New York Times* reporter Kurt Eichenwald (2005, 2006), point to the disturbing resiliency of the pedophilia subculture.[8]

Recent qualitative studies on children's use of the internet emphasize their intrepid use of the medium and report differences between what youth say they do online in contrast to how their parents think they utilize the internet (see chapters three and four in this volume). As one example, the Pew Internet & American Life Project reported that 62 percent of parents say they monitor their children's online content from home, whereas only 33 percent of teens reported that their parents monitor their use (Lenhart, 2005, p. 11).[9] Regarding children's exposure to online risks, Sonia Livingstone's *UK Children Go Online* study found that one-third of the surveyed nine–nineteen-year-olds who are daily and weekly users received unwanted sexual or nasty comments online or by text message (31 and 33 percent, respectively), while 46 percent have given out personal information to someone they met online (Livingstone, 2005). However, how parents react to these online risks—curtailing or monitoring their children's internet use—differs, depending on socio-demographics and familial–household dynamics (Valentine & Holloway, 2001).

MySpace in the Media

Supporters of DOPA and media accounts of MySpace escapades-gone-awry promote the view that all children's online activities will bring negative consequences. One could speculate that were it not for the persistent media coverage of MySpace within the last year, DOPA wouldn't have received the attention and support of the parents and legislators required to get it onto the legislative agenda as fast as it did. Media attention focusing on MySpace activity is also responsible for highlighting children's exposure to unsavory and illegal content, including terrorist subject matter (Osama bin Laden fan clubs, 2006), criminal activities, and sexual content and sexual predators. One newspaper article recounted the posting on MySpace of an alleged threat against a high school in San Antonio, Texas. Students, fearing the posted threats of a Columbine-like attack in their school, either did not show up or went home earlier from school. Said, a representative of the school district remarked, "the web site 'MySpace-dot-com' allowed several students to post threatening messages on its web site . . . This message said two boys were planning to show up at school with guns" (Online terror threat hits high school, 2005). This incident exemplifies how MySpace was used positively by teens in a local context (peer-monitoring) albeit with an ability to spread perhaps fallacious gossip, and also how adults negatively perceived the use of MySpace as a venue to display frightening and perhaps life-threatening comments.

Other media coverage that provoked fear in adults include CNN's report that a Michigan-area high school honors student flew to Jordan, Amman, to meet and marry a man who identified himself on MySpace as a twenty-five-year-old.[10] A Toronto resident was arrested for pretending to be a young gay man, and luring a thirteen-year-old teenage girl to perform sex acts on her webcam ("Police charge alleged sexual predator, 2006"). *Time Magazine* reported the arrest of a nineteen-year-old man for having sex with a minor he met on MySpace; her parents have filed a $30 million lawsuit in damages against MySpace, charging the company with failing to protect underage users from online predators. *People Magazine* reported the arrest of a man on rape charges after he streamed live sex-acts to a twelve-year-old girl on MySpace (Hewitt, 2006).

A series of articles have focused on the perils of posting online messages or photographs that can have repercussions for future professional ventures—job interviews, corporate recruiters, college admissions, and so on (Finder, 2006; Stone, 2006; What you say online, 2006). Other articles have focused on parents and school administrators learning to cope with MySpace ("Adults question . . . ," 2006; Duffy & Lissa, 2006; Dyrli, 2006; Hadju, 2006; Proudfoot, 2006; Zeller, 2005). Teen magazines have investigated debates about social networking software in schools; 91 percent of *ElleGirl's* "reader meter" agreed that "what students post on their own time is their own business" (Barth, 2006), while *Teen People* created a quiz to determine addiction to MySpace (DeSimone, 2006).

Paradoxically, the same media that promote stories warning about the potential dangers of MySpace also publish stories, sometimes even simultaneously, valorizing the creators of MySpace. Take, for example, the glowing accounts of the site's co-creators, Chris DeWolfe and Tom Anderson, which resurrect the heroic tale of two early 1990s dot.com guys who, with a good idea, some charisma, and the right social contacts, parlayed their vision into a million-dollar success (Verini, 2006). DeWolfe and Anderson's concept of a webspace which depended upon peer production of content and viral marketing was simple and elegant, allowing for a streamlined design that enabled easy uploading of content. Instead of hiring people to generate content, the idea was to encourage people who used the site to produce *their own content* and viral marketing, and give them a streamlined design that made it easy to upload content.

Linking to similarly attuned approaches, MySpacers created cultural capital and facilitated a robust and energetic space that grew exponentially. Use of MySpace by local and emerging music bands added to its usefulness and luster; not only did MySpace become the way to connect local communities virtually and physically, it expanded communities into wider spheres of taste cultures—whether it be music, fashion, colleges and universities, television shows, celebrity culture, or hobbies. Sensing the importance of capitalizing on youthful internet content, in July 2006, DeWolfe and Anderson's company was purchased by Rupert Murdoch, raising the News Corp. media holdings to an estimated worth of $23.8 billion.[11] Rather than being consumed by the media behemoth, MySpace memberships instead quadrupled in the first year, positioning it as a lifestyle brand (Reiss, 2006).

To counter negative media coverage of MySpace as a haven for sexual predators, MySpace increased staff that monitor content, made their "Safety Tips" section more explicit, and initiated a hotline to report suspected online bullies and cyber-stalkers (Yang, 2006; Rawe, 2006; Reiss, 2006). Business publications strive to dissect MySpace's "secret sauce," which depends heavily on youth participation:

> Content generation is the job of the teenagers, who spend an average of one hour and 40 minutes a month on the site, writing blogs, listening to

music, and viewing one another's photos. MySpace users are uploading photos at the rate of 1.7 million per day. Bigtime bands like REM and Nine Inch Nails—as well as about 500,000 not-so-big acts—use the site to premiere new music, allowing free listening ahead of an album release. (Lashinsky, 2005)

Dubbed by *Business Week* as "The MySpace Generation," or "Generation @," (Hempel et al., 2005), marketers see this demographic as an important target. Major brands, seeking the audience commodity of eighteen–twenty-four-year-olds, have been flocking to set up MySpace profiles: *Cingular, Dodge, Coke, Sony, Apple, Fox Movie Studios, H&R Block, Axe* deodorant, *Maybelline, Elexa* by Trojan (female condoms), and even the U.S. Marine Corps! (ForBiddeN fruit, 2006; Hempel et al., 2005; Morrissey, 2006).

Nielsen/NetRatings estimated that ad revenue in January 2006 was $40 million (Oser, 2005). Realizing that new techniques are needed to capture the fickle and lucrative youth market, some corporations are now emulating social networking to market their products and services to youth (Fass, 2006), in the hopes that youth-driven content will create a buzz and a branded impression. Of course, reliance on the "free labor" of youth-generated content in corporate spaces is yet another way online communities have become increasingly commodified.

Targeting Girls

Those people live among us. They prey on our youngest, our children, and they will do anything in their power to solicit those children.
—Republican Senator Ted Poe, Texas, on debates on DOPA

http://www.govtrack.us/congress/record.xpd?id=
109-h20060726-41#sMonoElementm5m0m0m

Returning again to Adam's concerns about the "gender blindness" of policy, we need only examine several recent educational campaigns about online sexual exploitation to realize that the main targets of white, male perpetrators are young girls. These campaigns do not feature young boys as the prey; rather, they all feature young teen girls. Are these campaigns realistically responding to statistics that indicate females are more coveted as targets of sexual exploitation than young men? Do we have reliable figures on the incidences of sexual exploitation of young men? Or, are these campaigns instead unnecessarily portraying young girls as more vulnerable and troubled than young men?

Beyond Borders, a Canadian-based NGO affiliated with EPCAT (the campaign to End Child Prostitution, Pornography and the Trafficking of Children for Sexual Purposes) reflects this assumed demographic in their latest campaign. Their home page features a poster of a middle-aged white man photographed from behind as he sits at a computer (he is balding and paunchy, attired in a sloppy plaid shirt) with the copy: "Meet Jenny13@email.com. Your child's new best friend."[12]

The Ad Council, a leading producer of Public Service Advertisements (PSAs), worked with The National Center for Missing & Exploited Children to produce a series of PSAs (Public Service Announcements) focusing on online sexual exploitation. Their goal was to target teen girls, warning them of the dangers of "blind" online relationships. The PSAs consisted of print, radio, and television ads, plus an interactive game. They targeted parents and teens, who were encouraged to visit the online site www.cybertipline.com for more factual information on online sexual exploitation and for information on protecting themselves from predators and dangerous situations.

Newspaper ads designed for parents highlighted the dangers of chat rooms. One ad displayed a set of fourteen users in a chat, with their "real" identities. Included were

Good2hug:	14, female, Daytona FL
Joey16:	16, male, Hackenstack NJ
robbieW:	38, male, Daytona FL
tu_tu:	16, female, Burlington, VT
QTPie:	30, male Chicago IL

This ad highlights how playful "handles" (online users' names) are frequently used to convey identities (whether truthful or wishful), and warns parents to be aware of potential adults (all men) lurking behind the innocuous online names.

Another public service ad declared:

Janine Marks, a 12-year old, was fairly normal. Janine spent a lot of time online. She felt more comfortable there. Janine met a new friend online, who liked the same bands as her, and who promised to keep her secrets. One day, they decided to meet at the mall, "only her friend wasn't in junior high, wasn't nice, and wasn't 14." The ads ended with "Every day, children are sexually solicited online."

"Places," a thirty-second televised PSA, featured shots of a playground, a park, a street with a locked bike, and a schoolyard. A voice-over reads, "To the list of places where you might find sexual predators, add this one," with a shot of a young girl typing at the computer. "Help delete online predators," the narrator says.

As still another example, PSA shows a computer monitor where an online chat is transpiring between chris98 and jenny79. chris98 asks jenny79 how the mall was and she responds that "mom wouldn't drive me." "Turned 16 . . . got MY license! i can take u anytime," writes chris98. "ok!," types jenny79. The view switches to an image of a middle-aged white bald man in an oxford-blue shirt typing at a computer. "Every day, online predators make their way into homes uninvited and unnoticed," says the female voice-over.[13]

The CyberTipline's "Don't Believe the Type!" campaign provides online educational and safety information for youth and their parents, also targeting young women and featuring photos of young females throughout the site. PSAs focus on the perils of online communication for young women and the threat of sexual exploitation. One television PSA shows a camera panning across a police crime scene in a bedroom where evidence is being photographed and a computer being taken away. The young female voice-over says, "Before you start an online relationship with a guy, think about how it could end."

The voice-over for another PSA is that of a young man. Over images of a young teen girl, the young man assures us that "Meeting a teen girl online is easy. They're so desperate for attention . . ." The voice-over then switches to the teen girl, who tells us that "Attention from older guys is flattering. They get me more than guys my own age." We then hear the voices of the young man and the teen girl intersperse:

He: "Age lets me play the supportive older guy and act interesting."
She: "It isn't the same thing. You get to know someone when you're chatting."
He: "Chatting seems unthreatening to them. Once I talk about how perfect we are for each other."
She: "Other people don't understand. If you trust someone what's wrong with . . ."
He: "Meeting them is the goal. That's when things get really interesting."

The PSA ends with another youthful female voice-over: "Online predators know what they're doing. Do you?" It is interesting to note that the narrator in these PSAs is female—a voice meant to evoke both authority and maternal concern.[14]

In an effort to increase online safety awareness "ID the Creep" (http://www.idthecreep.com/, The Girls Game), sponsored by the Ad Council and the National Council of Media Education of Canada, is an interactive game targeting girls, which allows them to keep score on who the "creeps" are in IM, email, or chat. The player can select from three characters: Alicia, a white thirteen-year-old who is just starting eighth grade and wants to make new friends, Kelly, an Asian sixteen-year-old who "loves to do all kinds of cool things" such as shopping and going to parties, and Shanna, an African American fifteen-year-old who likes all sorts of new things and uses IM to gossip. The premise of the game is to correctly identify, through simulation of online chats, who the "creeps"—depicted through their online handles—are. Should the player "lose" the game, the final score page displays a picture of a cartoon "creep"—a dark-haired white man with a grey streak on his temples, his arms crossed, eyebrows arched, and a deliberative, yet deceptive look on his face. The loser receives this reponse: "Unfortunately your choices indicate that creeps got too close to you and you may have been placed at risk. Remember the importance of not revealing personal information online to people you do not know."

And, finally, the National Center for Missing & Exploited Children's *Netsmart* site features "real life" video stories of teens who have been exploited; for example, in "Julie's Journey," she recounts her three weeks away from home with a convicted murderer she met online. Another video in the series, "Amy's Story," is about a teenage girl running away from home to meet up with an older man in the United Kingdom.[15]

How successful are these games, interactive sites, and video clips in educating parents and young girls about online safety? Are they counter-productive, fermenting more panic, and fear than is necessary? Consider the ethics of NBC Dateline's "To Catch a Predator" series[16] in which hidden cameras interview suspected child sex abusers entrapped in conversations with adult members of the online vigilante group, Perverted-Justice.com. While it is debatable whether these sting operations are legally sanctioned, such sensationalistic reporting, undoubtedly, rouses more concerns than are necessary.

Conclusion: Victims or Agents?

In an analysis of newspaper coverage of cyber-crimes and youth, Lynne Edwards (2005) notes how the majority of the articles framed teen girls as victims needing protection from cyber-predators. The problem is that adult protectors, such as police, further "substitute their voices and their experiences for those of girls, effectively making these girls, and the crimes committed against them, invisible to us" (Edwards, 2005, p. 27). Likewise, a large proportion of educational materials on sexual exploitation frame the exploited as young, white, and female, while the perpetrators are young to middle-aged white men. What is missing are portrayals of young girls as engaged, savvy, and "street aware" internet users. Rather than portraying girls as vulnerable victims who need constant adult supervision, we need to see more proactive images of young girls as users and producers of innovative online content.

Media coverage of MySpace is, as Roberto Hugh Potter and Lyndy A. Potter (2001) argued with respect to earlier discussions of cyberporn, a middle-class moral panic. Rosen (2006) concurs through his reportage that stalking incidences and sexual liaisons among MySpace users are extremely rare. He concludes: "MySpace is not a den of sexual stalkers nor is it a place where unknown people ask for sex. These episodes do happen but it appears that for nearly all adolescents, it is a momentary event that is quickly dismissed" (p. 6). danah boyd's (2005) study of MySpace teen users similarly emphasizes the dynamic ways that MySpace can be used to create a vibrant, necessary public space:

> Youth are not creating digital publics to scare parents—they are doing so because they need youth space, a place to gather and see and be seen by peers. Publics are critical to the coming-of-age narrative because they provide the framework for building cultural knowledge. Restricting youth to controlled spaces typically results in rebellion and the destruction of trust. (Boyd, 2005)

As boyd points out, many adults are exhibiting an increasing distrust and paranoia toward these public cyberspaces, a distrust that is probably not warranted by the relatively tame reality of most young people's online lives. For many teens, the "public–private spaces" of the internet are where they can experiment with identities, laugh, gossip, and reveal information they wouldn't ordinarily say in "real space." Subrahamanym, Greenfield, & Tynes 2004) argue that online venues such as chat rooms provide safe places to discuss "embarrassing topics in an anonymous social context" (p. 663). Discussion of sexuality and playing with identity (gender, sex, location) allows for more peer intimacy. "The medium is not doing something to adolescents," they write, but rather "they, instead, are doing something with the medium. Teen chat provides new affordances for old adolescent issues" (ibid).

The MacArthur Report confirmed the beneficial qualities of SNS sites for young people, and stated, with regard to concerns over risky behavior: "We saw almost no evidence that youth were engaging in risky behaviors online, and their online communication is conducted in a context of public scrutiny and structured by well-developed norms of social appropriateness, a sense of reciprocity, and collective ethics" (Ito et al., 2008; http://digitalyouth.ischool.berkeley.edu/book-conclusion).

An initiative arising from concerns over SNS and safety was The Internet Safety Technical Task Force, charged by the Multi-State Working Group on Social Networking, (comprising fifty state attorney generals, and MySpace/News Corporation), to investigate viable tools for combating online safety risks. While optimistic about technological fixes, the group's final report expressed caution against its over-reliance, emphasizing a need instead to consider parental intervention, online safety education, law enforcement strategies, and SNS and ISP policies, balanced with the privacy concerns of youth information (The Internet Safety Technical Task Force, 2009, pp. 6, 23).

Livingstone (2006, p. 225) advises that youth need to be given guidance on how to cope with online risks, rather than be issued blanket bans like those frequently made in online safety campaigns and public policy measures. It is important to give youth the opportunity to design their own safety programs, and integrate their voices and experiences into policy deliberations. As many scholars argue,[17] young people need to be addressed not as mere consumers of entertainment products and dynamic social spaces such as MySpace, but as citizens and active media producers.

The *DOPA* and *Protecting Children in the 21st Century Act* need to be situated within periodic attempts to censor internet content in the U.S. and framed within the conservative Republican "family values" ethos in which the legislation was conceived. The blogosphere has not been silent on DOPA; there have been trenchant critiques from internet civil liberties groups, political bloggers, and a public relations campaign from the Young Adult Library Services Association of the American Library Association on "30 Positive Uses of Social Networking"[18] for schools and libraries. Moreover, just as adult legislators are attempting to push forward their agenda, youth themselves are using the internet to mobilize against DOPA and promote social networking:

> I have friends whose lives have been saved because of these very websites. Suicidal youth who look out for help (and GET IT, through these sites), the kids who get beat up each day who need to find other kids to talk to who go through the same thing, many kids who do not even have a computer at home, or do not feel safe BEING at home. Over 69 million people use MySpace.com, and of those 69 million, 12 have been prosecuted for child abuse. That's hardly a measurable fraction. (Tevi Abrams-Slep from New York, NY)

This message is from the website of the SOS Campaign (Save Our Social Networks, http://www.mobilize.org/SOS), initiated by Mobilize. org, a youth-led political activism group using internet tools to notify and marshal their constituency in a letter-writing campaign against the legislation to Congress. Such political engagement belies the intent of DOPA, and illustrates how vital it is to consider youth voices in policy-making. Restricting access to social networking sites for youth under the guise of "protecting" them from sexual predators and adults with "devious intentions" denies youth their own autonomy and agency.

Notes

Thanks to the Social Sciences and Humanities Research Council of Canada for support of my work and to Sandra Weber, Shanly Dixon, and Maija Harju for their incisive reading and commentary on this chapter.

1. The Act may be found at the Library of Congress Thomas site at http://thomas.loc.gov/cgi-bin/query/D?c109:1:./temp/~c109As4HVd. At the time of this writing, DOPA has been referred to the Senate, read twice, and is scheduled to be voted on in the Senate during the fall session 2006.
2. The NCMEC is a U.S. national clearinghouse and resource center funded by the Office of Juvenile Justice and Delinquency Protection Program of the Department of Justice. The report citing these statistics is authored by Finkelhor, Mitchell, and Wolak, 2000.
3. See http://www.govtrack.us/congress/record.xpd?id=109-h20060726-41#s MonoElementm8m0m0m, last accessed August 28, 2006.
4. The Bill may be found at http://thomas.loc.gov/cgi-bin/query/z?c110: S.49), last accessed September 21, 2009.
5. Rosen's data was collected from 1,257 users of MySpace in the Los Angeles area, ranging in age from nine to sixty-seven. Only 3 percent of users in the sample were under fourteen. MySpace requires that users be fourteen and over, although this is hard to regulate.
6. For information on CIPIC, see http://www.fcc.gov/cgb/consumerfacts/cipa.html.
7. For information on COPPA, see http://www.coppa.org.
8. In her discussion of preteen modeling websites, Sophie Wertheimer points to her queasiness with girls' participation in them: "They remain located within a patriarchal framework, one whereby images of girls and women are commodified and sexualized. Additionally, these texts further reify the standards of ideal beauty dominant in North American society." Any semblance of empowerment and agency that the girls' might experience, she adds, is "problematic, limited, and certainly not ideal" (Wertheimer, 2005, p. 224).
9. See Shade, Porter, and Sanchez, 2005, for an overview of some of these studies.
10. See http://www.zoomcities.com/forum/showthread.php?tid=701, last accessed August 25, 2006.
11. News Corp. holdings include film (20th Century Fox, Fox Television, Fox Studios), cable (Fox News Channel, FX, Fox Movie Channel, Fox Sports),

TV (thirty-six U.S. stations in twenty-six markets, stations in Asia and Latin America), Satellite TV (SKY, DirecTV Group), newspapers (New York Post, UK's The Times), magazines (TV Guide, The Weekly Standard), books (HarperCollins), and other ventures such as MySpace, Sky Radio. See http://www.newscorp.com/index2.html.
12. See http://www.netsmartz.org/resources/reallife.htm#realamy.
13. See "Monitor" PSA from Ad Council: http://www.adcouncil.org/default. aspx?id=56, last accessed September 21, 2009.
14. See Don't Believe The Type. http://tcs.cybertipline.com/, last accessed September 21, 2009.
15. See http://www.netsmartz.org/resources/reallife.htm#realamy, last accessed September 21, 2009.
16. To Catch a Predator site is at http://www.msnbc.msn.com/id/10912603/.
17. Scholars addressing this issue are many: recent work includes Buckingham and Willett, 2006; Jenkins, 2006; Livingstone, Bober, and Helsper, 2005; and Seiter, 2005.
18. See YALSA blog at http://blogs.ala.org/yalsa.php?cat=27.

References

Adam, A. (2002). Cyberstalking and internet pornography: Gender and the gaze. *Ethics and Information Technology, 4*, 133–142.
Adults Question its Safety. (January 31, 2006). *USA Today*, 2d.
American Library Association. (2006). DOPA Information. Retrieved August 20, 2006, from http://www.ala.org/ala/washoff/WOissues/techinttele/dopa/ DOPA. htm
Barth, L. (May 2006). Too much information. *ElleGirl*, 110.
boyd, d. (February 19, 2005). Identity production in a networked culture: Why youth heart MySpace. Paper given at the American Association for the Advancement of Science. Retrieved August 20, 2006, from http://www. danah.org/papers/AAAS2006.html.
Blumer, H. (1933). *Movies and conduct*. New York: Macmillan and Company.
Buckingham, D. & Willett, R. (Eds.) (2006). *Digital generations: Children, young people and the new media*. New Jersey: Lawrence Erlbaum Assoc.
Center for Democracy and Technology. (August 11, 2006). CDT Analysis: Deleting Online Predators Act. Retrieved August 23, 2006, from http://www. cdt.org/headlines/925.
DeSimone, A. (Septermber 31, 2006). Are you addicted to MySpace? *Teen People*, 172.
Duffy, M. & Lissa, A. (March 27, 2006). A dad's encounter with the vortex of Facebook. *Time, 167*(13), 52.
Dyrli, O.E. (March 2006). Online social networking. *DistrictAdministration.com*, 99.

Edwards, L. (2005). Victims, villains, and vixens: Teen girls and internet crime. In S. Mazzarella (ed.), *Girlwideweb: Girls, the internet, and the negotiation of identity*, pp. 13–30. New York: Peter Lang.

Eichenwald, K. (December 19, 2005). Through his webcam, a boy joins a sordid online world. *The New York Times*. Retrieved August 20, 2006, at http://www.nytimes.com/2005/12/19/national/19kids.ready.html?pagewanted=1&ei=5090&en=aea51b3919b2361a&ex=1292648400.

———. (August 20, 2006). With child sex sites on the run, nearly nude pictures test laws. *The New York Times*, A1.

Fass, A. (May 8, 2006). TheirSpace.com. *Forbes, 177*(10), 122–124.

Finder, A. (June 11, 2006). For some, online persona undermines a résumé. *The New York Times*, A1.

Finkelhor, D.K., Mitchell, J., & Wolak, J. (June 2000). *Online victimization: A report on the nation's youth*. Washington D.C.: Crimes Against Children Research Centre, National Center for Missing & Exploited Children.

ForBiddeN fruit. (July 29, 2006). *Economist, 380*(8488), 60.

Hadju, D. (March 6, 2006). Instant gratification. *The New Republic*, 25–28.

Hempel, J. & Lehman, P. (December 12, 2005). The MySpace generation. *Business Week*, Issue 3963.

Hewitt, B. (June 5, 2006). MySpace nation: The controversy. *People, 65*(22), 113–121.

Hick, S. & Halpin, E. (March 2001). Children's rights and the internet. *The Annals of the American Academy of Political and Social Science, 574*, 56–70.

How to monitor the kids? Parents worry about the perils of social networking sites. (2006). *USA Today*.

Hughes, D. (Winter 2002). The use of new communications and information technologies for sexual exploitation of women and children. *Hastings Women's Law Journal, 13*(1), 129–148.

Jenkins, H. (August 2006). Four ways to kill MySpace [blog]. Retrieved August 25, 2006, from http://www.henryjenkins.org/2006/08/four_ways_to_kill_myspace.html.

———. (2006). *Convergence culture*. NewYork: NYU Press.

Lashinsky, A. (October 31, 2005). Look who's online now. *Fortune, 152*(9).

Lenhart, A. (March 17, 2005). *Protecting teens online*. Chicago: The Pew Internet and American Life Project. Retrieved November 3, 2006, from http://www.pewinternet.org/PPF/r/152/report_display.asp

Livingstone, S. (2005). *UK children go online: End of award report*. Retrieved August 27, 2006, from http://www.children-go-online.net.

———. (2006). Drawing conclusions from new media research: Reflections and puzzles regarding children's experience of the internet. *The Information Society, 22*, 219–230.

246 • Leslie Regan Shade

Livingstone, S., Bober, M., & Helsper, E.J. (September 2005). Active participation or just more information? Young people's take-up of opportunities to act and interact on the internet. *Information, Communication & Society, 8*(3), 287–314.

Marvin, C. (1990). *When old technologies were new: Thinking about electric communication in the late nineteenth century.* New York: Oxford University Press.

Morrissey, B. (February 2, 2006). Maybelline site MySpaces out. *Brandweek, 47*(6).

MySpace: Design anarchy that works. (January 3, 2006). *Business Week Online.*

Online terror threat hits high school. (2005). WOAI.com. Retrieved November 7, from, http://www.woai.com/news/local/story.aspx?content_id=569F4519-73E9-4810-B895-5C2336D6171C.

Osama bin Laden fan clubs. (March 9, 2006). Jihad recruiters build online communities: Internet brings together people of shared interests—including terrorism. *USA Today,* 4a.

Oser, C. (February 21, 2006). MySpace: Big audience, big risks. *Advertising Age.* Retrieved April 13, 2006, from http://adage.com/article?article_id=48592.

Police charge alleged sexual predator disguised on MySpace as gay. (July 12, 2006). *Canadian Press Newswire.*

Potter, R.H. & Potter, L.A. (2001). The internet, cyberporn, and sexual exploitation of children: Media moral panics and urban myths for middle-class parents? *Sexuality & Culture, 5*(3), 31–48.

Proudfoot, S. (May 11, 2006). Taking back MySpace. *The Ottawa Citizen,* E1–3.

Rawe, J. (July 3, 2006). How safe is MySpace? *Time, 168*(1), 34–36.

Reiss, S. (July 2006). His Space. *Wired, 164,* 142–147.

Reno vs. ACLU, No.96–511. (26, June1997). Majority opinion. Retrieved August 27, 2006, from http://www2.epic.org/cda/cda_decision.html#majority.

Rosen, L.D. (June 2006). Adolescents in MySpace: Identity formation, friendship, and sexual predators. Retrieved August 15, 2006, from http://www.csudh.edu/psych/lrosen.htm.

Rosen, L.S. (June 2006). Sexual predators on MySpace: A deeper look at teens being stalked or approached for sexual liaisons. Short report 2006–01. Retrieved August 15, 2006, from http://www.csudh.edu/psych/lrosen.htm.

Seiter, E. (2005). *The internet playground: Children's access, entertainment, and mis-education.* New York: Peter Lang.

Shade, L.R. (2002). Protecting the kids? Debates over internet content. In S.D. Ferguson & L.R. Shade (eds.), *Civic discourse and cultural politics in Canada: A cacophony of voices,* pp. 76–87. Greenport, CT: Ablex.

Shade, L.R., Porter, N., & Sanchez, W. (2005). "You can see anything on the internet, you can do anything on the internet!": Young Canadians talk about the Internet. *Canadian Journal of Communication, 30*(4), 503–526.

Stone, B. (December 26, 2005). The MySpace.com guys. *Newsweek, 146/147*(26/1).

———. (August 28, 2006). Web of risks. *Newsweek, 148*(8–9), 76–77.

Subrahamanym, K.P., Greenfield, M., & Tynes, B. (2004). Constructing sexuality and identity in an online teen chat room. *Applied Developmental Psychology, 25*, 651–666.

Teens hang out at MySpace (January 9, 2006). *USA Today,* 1d.

Valentine, G. & Holloway, S. (2001). On-line dangers? Geographies of parents' fears for children's safety in cyberspace. *Professional Geographer, 53*(1), 71–83.

Verini, J. (March 2006). Will success spoil MySpace? *Vanity Fair,* 238–249.

Wartella, E. & Jennings, N. (2000). Children and computers: New technology—old concerns. *The Future of Children: Children and Computer Technology, 10*(2), 31–43. Retrieved June 1, 2006, from http://www.futureofchildren.org.

Wertheimer, S. (2005). Pretty in panties: Moving beyond the innocent child paradigm in reading preteen modeling websites. In Y. Jiwani, C. Steenbergen, & C. Mitchell (eds.), *Girlhood: Redefining the limits,* pp. 208–226. Montreal: Black Rose Books.

What you say online could haunt you: Schools, employers scrutinize social websites such as MySpace and Facebook. (March 9, 2006). *USA Today,* 1a.

Williams, A. (August 28, 2005). Do you MySpace? *The New York Times,* style section, 1.

———. (February 19, 2006). Here I am taking my own picture. *The New York Times,* Style Section, 1.

Yang, J.L. (July 10, 2006). Can this man make MySpace safe for kids? *Fortune, 154*(1), 32.

Zeller, T. (November 3, 2005). For U.S. teenagers, life is an open web log. *International Herald Tribune.*

CHAPTER FIFTEEN

Reviewing Young Peoples' Engagement with Technology

Sandra Weber and Shanly Dixon

The online experiences described in this book vary considerably, not only in terms of the children's ages, but also in terms of context, location, media, access, and more. And yet, there are resonances and similarities across the chapters as well, commonalities that are especially significant because they are situated so differently. In this final chapter, we want to touch on the most salient points raised by the contributing authors and reflect both critically and speculatively on the important issues that emerged. Although we raise more questions than we answer, we hope that they are formulated in ways that point forward to further inquiry, and perhaps even to action and advocacy.

Media Participation and Agency

The young people we meet in most of the chapters are *active users and producers* of new media. In different locations and at both ends of the age and access spectrums, girls and boys exhibit a genuine interest and desire to participate in cyberculture. This will to use technology appears in a variety of ways and settings.

In Rebekah Willett's school workshops in England, girls engage in critical discussion of the "dress a doll" type websites they like to visit; in Diane Carr's video game club for girls, interviews and questionnaires focus on game preferences. The South African young people who had never even seen a video camera before Mitchell and Sokoya's study are eager to engage with new technologies and jump right in. The boys in Seth Giddings' chapter are playful and keen on adapting a video game for their off-line play. The girls and boys in Caroline Pelletier's chapter display a tacit grasp of many elements of game design, and have definite ideas about what they like.

In Susannah Stern's study, we see how important it can be for girls to use home pages as a mirror of sorts, a way to express and then reexamine one's own self while "half hoping" that known or unknown peers will drop in and participate. Similarly, Michele Polak's chapter demonstrates how marginalized girls use websites to express themselves through poetry, images, and writing that is often poignant, provocative, and revealing. The children in Shanly Dixon and Sandra Weber's chapter derive great pleasure in structuring their play around and through digital media. These are but a few examples of how young people are using digital technologies.

In online games and in social networking spaces such as *Facebook*, young people have growing online presence and power. As they adopt new technologies, converging in established spaces and creating many new ones for themselves, we wonder if they are in some sense colonizing online space, signaling an important shift in power sharing between children and adults. Indeed, as young people gain autonomy, we wonder if at some level the moral panics so prevalent around children's use of the internet might have a lot more to do with adult's unconscious fears of losing control than with the ostensible safety issues that dominates their discourse. Are we willing to trust young people and allow them more control over their own lives?

Consumers and Producers?

There are, however, other things to consider about young people's active participation—countertexts to the creative productivity described in many of the chapters. Paradoxically, young people are both constrained as well as empowered by the affordances of the technology—what the hardware and software does or does not allow them to create. Designed and produced by adults, the websites and games made for children may at times give them a sense of agency they do not in fact possess. Nonetheless, as we watch Giddings' sons play Lego in chapter two, we note that built-in restrictions can also be regarded by young people as opportunities or challenges to circumvent design hurdles or to deviate from official goals; a subversive reflex that, we suggest in a later section, is natural to children's play.

As Leslie Regan Shade describes in detail in her chapter, there are features of young people's online experience that many adults find worrisome, notably children's presumed vulnerability to online predators and easy online access to "adult content." She points out that although these concerns are usually overstated and seldom based on realistic assessments of actual risk or incidence, the ensuing public panics nonetheless influence government policy, which does not always keep up with research.

It is hard to reconcile this image of the internet as a very dangerous place with the experiences of the young people we meet in this book. Many of them seem fairly capable of judging for themselves what material is appropriate for them and they demonstrate at least some strategies for dealing with unwanted attention. They also show a willingness to ask adults for advice when they don't know what to do. A striking example occurs in Mitchell and Sokoya's chapter where a young first-time user of the internet in Nigeria declares that she does not feel ready to engage with a certain level or amount of information related to sexuality that was made available to her. She doesn't need adult censoring to know what material she feels comfortable engaging with. As a web-savvy Canadian girl on the other side of the globe puts it in Weber's chapter, "I'm not stupid." Across all that divides them, these girls demonstrate a remarkably similar sense of knowing what they can handle, which of course does *not* necessarily mean that they actually do know their limits. In some instances, their confidence may be unwarranted and their knowledge may not be as comprehensive as they think it is. The research reported in this book suggests that what is needed is not more regulation and control of children, but rather more in-depth digital literacy education (Buckingham, 2003). There is enough evidence in this book, however, to dispel any widespread notion of children as passive victims or the internet as a place from which they should be excluded.

In our view, we ought to focus not so much on the dramatic and statistically rare incidents that underlie public and media panics, but more on the subtle, subliminal influences of commercial interests. As Willett and Reid-Walsh caution in their chapters, young peoples' widespread online engagement makes them easily accessible markets for corporations who target them with a dazzling array of games and tween or youth-friendly sites. Problematically, corporate presence online is often so well concealed or integrated into the design of the space or the game that users may have trouble recognizing advertising when they encounter it (Schor, 2004; Seiter, 2004). The ensuing consumption and commodification of popular culture is often viewed as primarily negative (Dale, 2005; Schor, 2004). However, scholars such as Henry Jenkins (2006) and Mitzuko Ito (2008), as well as many of the authors in this book, caution against oversimplifying the complex interplay of consumption and production. They point out that the inevitable consumption of the images of popular culture is a more active, critical, and creative process than once believed; indeed, consumption is embedded in production. By this, we mean that consumption itself involves consumer interaction and acts of interpretation. Like most readers, young people of school age assess content rather than swallowing it whole; they choose certain popular images (while ignoring or discarding others) as "raw material," which they combine and use creatively for their own ends, changing the meaning in the process.

As children gain experience, they rapidly adopt skills to deal with online advertising, developing the ability to use the internet for their own goals such as playing the freebie games without buying the products. In Reid-Walsh's examination of Alice's websurfing, for example, we see how banner ads, pop-ups, and the like are shut down or tuned out. Very young children or less-experienced users, however, may be less critical and more likely to "buy" the advertiser's message (see Chang-Kredl, 2006). This changes as children grow in experience and years. The more skillfully they are able to create and contribute to online content, the better able they are to critique not only their own productions, but commercial ones as well. This is why we stress the need for media literacy education very early on. It is important for users of all ages to be able to recognize who is producing a website and to understand the broader scope of what they find online. It's not just about what they are being sold, but also about the reproduction of knowledge and social structures. Work by Buckingham and Sefton-Green (1994), among others, indicates that involving young people in forms of critical media production can be empowering for them, making them less vulnerable to manipulation by commercial interests.

Media Influence and Access to Technologies

What do the chapters about girls with virtually no access say about the chapters about girls who grow up digital (and vice versa)? Do comparisons raise important issues? When Mitchell, for example, introduced girls in South Africa who had little or no prior online experience to the "for girls only section" of our project's website, they spent a lot of time on the site and responded that they had enjoyed it. In contrast, Canadian girls who already had access and significant online exposure had quite a different reaction to the project site: They didn't much like it! They found it very basic in comparison to the commercially created spaces to which they were accustomed. What does this say about the construction of web tastes and web literacy? As the novelty of one model fades, is it the new "cool" being marketed that shapes their taste and expectations? The design and content of commercial sites frequented by young people does seem to influence their ideas of what websites should look like and how they should function, but as we pointed out earlier, this consumption of popular culture often becomes part of a more creative production process in which images are taken up and then rearranged or modified.

What emerges across the studies is a clear sense that, despite commercial interests that target young people online, and public anxieties about the suitability of content for children, digital media also afford opportunities: providing an outlet for young peoples' voices, a place to test out identities, a way to play and communicate with peers, obtain information and also provides multimodal means to actively produce and consume content. From gaming to instant messaging, from blogging and twittering to surfing the net, digital media proficiency translates into social networks and social inclusion (Seiter, 2004). Accordingly, perhaps the people we ought to be most concerned about are the young people who do *not* have access to the internet. It is important to research the implications of being excluded.

Developing Community

For some young people, the internet has created an opportunity for greater freedom and openness in regards to play, providing possibilities for participation in the public sphere. Online spaces such as social networking spaces, MMOGs, and blogs enable young people to engage in a public performative type of play, accessing a global community from which they were previously shut out. In Boudreau's chapter, *The Girls' Room*, preadolescent girls spend hours upon hours on their own, teaching themselves the skill-set required to build and maintain an online space where they can come together. When some of them are excluded from social groups or bullied both online and off-line, their webspace gives them a sense of both agency and comfort. Through participation, they learn the consequences of public posting and modify their behavior accordingly. Similarly, the girls in Polak's chapter who identify themselves as "pro ana" (eating disorder as lifestyle) devote themselves to building online communities, putting up new sites as soon as their old ones are forcibly shut down, thereby demonstrating a deeply felt need to be in touch with each other and share information. In Dixon and Weber's chapter, video games are very much about social interaction; they provide a context, pretext, and space for playing with friends. In other words, gameplay is not only about mastering or adapting or playing around the game; it's about shared experiences that create a bond or sense of community. Contrary to the popular myths of technology as separating and isolating children, the findings in this book demonstrate some of the ways in which technology brings them together, facilitating interaction and encouraging a sense of community.

Public is the New Private? Generational Tensions

As children and teenagers "go public" online, many adults watch in trepidation, trying to explain that anyone could access their personal online information. There seems to be an intergenerational tension between many adults and young people regarding the difference between "public" and "private," an adult resistance to the inevitable and evolving blurring of the boundaries between the two. As we saw with Julia in Weber's chapter, as well as the girls in Kelly Boudreau's chapter on the *Girls' Room*—at least some young people feel that there is what might be called a *private public space*, one that, yes, is out in open cyberspace, but that nonetheless is meant to be treated by adults as a closed private space. Kitzmann (2004) refers to this blended notion of a public sort of privacy as "*connected privacy*" (p. 91), a privacy that connects the small community for which a site is intended and establishes or confirms a group space with permeable boundaries that nonetheless afford an experience of relative privacy. It's a question of audience, really, a matter of negotiating and establishing the rules of engagement in terms of how and where to participate as both audience and producer.

Our research suggests that young people are developing their own sense of "*net-iquette*," one that adults might not share. Many young people do not want adults checking out their online sites. Such actions are regarded as an invasion of their right to privacy. As Julia suggested, they *know* that their private cyberspaces are potentially accessible, but the idea that a parent, teacher, or any adult they know would go searching out their home page or blog without asking first is almost akin to reading someone's diary, opening their mail, or eavesdropping on a telephone conversation. It's a question of social codes and audience. Not everything that we share with our peers is necessarily intended for all audiences. From some young people's perspectives, *we are the ones who don't show consideration for the* evolving meaning and norms of privacy. In writing about weblogs, Lois Ann Scheidt (2005) points out that for the most part, personal postings are not exactly like secret diaries; rather they

> blend personal narrative with performance characteristics, like stage settings, through the use of color and image and interaction with the audience

by way of reciprocal discussion in comments, posts, and via communication lines outside the weblog space using channels such as email and instant messaging. These channels are controlled by the author and limited only by the technology and the author's capability to use the technology. While these characteristics can be found in webpages as well, the frequent updating that defines weblogs provides for a higher level of performance and interactivity. (p. 3)

In other words, there is an awareness that others will access personal postings and this sense of potential audience shapes online genres encouraging a performative sort of intimacy within a connected group. The conflict emerges when those outside of the intended audience view the performance.

Although young people assume or at least hope that adults will not invade their spaces unless implicitly or explicitly invited, the rights to privacy and freedom of movement in cyberspace are contested and issues of control and power are being negotiated as digital discourse and technologies evolve. For many children and youth, the desire to have a place of their own in cyberspace appears to outweigh the risks inherent in revealing themselves online. As they move from space to space in reaction to adult incursion, young people are not likely to give up the right to cyberspace. Intergeneration dialogue, such as the kind of research reported in this book, is perhaps the only way that scholars will understand the nuances of young people's online experiences.

Play and Childhood Revisited

Because of play's significance to online activities and childhood experience, in this section, we reexamine conceptions of play and childhood in the light of the research presented throughout the book. We begin with play, and with the question, "where do children play?"

Extending Playspaces: Integrating the Virtual and the Actual

Young people spend significant time in spaces that are created through the use of new media and technology such as instant messaging, websites, video games, and so forth. Reactions by other scholars to this phenomenon tend to fall into two camps: spaces of childhood are viewed as increasingly technified, commodified, homogeneous, and global—a sort of "one size fits all"—or alternatively, as spaces that empower children, enabling increased possibilities for freedom, self-expression, political engagement, identity play, and possibilities for a wider range of social interactions. However, whether one views these evolving child-hood playspaces as hegemonic or empowering or both, the important questions, in our view, concern what young people are doing in those spaces and what meaning or significance those spaces hold for them.

As Giddings and Dixon & Weber illustrate in their chapters, the way young people play in virtual spaces is similar in many respects to their play in other spaces. Cyberspace in not a separate, discrete place during the play we observed. Rather, it becomes incorporated into a wider play-space that is simultaneously online and off-line, a space where children seem to blend the virtual and actual into their pretend play as needed, for example, giving objects such as toys a role in their video games, or integrating digital media in their off-line pretend play, as we see, for example, when Giddings' sons incorporated the computer keyboard and even the physics of a video game space into their play. Young people's imagination and play intentions thus shape their use of technologies, and as we discussed earlier, also affect the creation of playspaces.

Playmates and Possibilities

Digital technologies can alter not only where we play, but also who we play with. The internet offers young people the possibility of interacting with a wide range of people all over the world from the privacy of their own home; play can now extend way beyond the confines of one's neigh-borhood. These new opportunities are especially significant to those young people who, for a variety of reasons, have limited potential for interacting and playing with peers. These include children who are excluded on the basis of age, for example, they may be too old or too young to play with the people they want to play with, or exclusion can be on the basis of gender, for example, Fern Delamere's (2006) account of a group of woman power gamers who played in a world of tradition-ally male gaming culture. Disability can also be a basis for exclusion, as one mother we spoke to described how her daughter, who was isolated from peers due to a chronic illness, established a rich social life through her participation in online message boards created by a group of young people experiencing a similar illness. In other words, young people who were previously limited by their circumstances can now participate in larger social spheres if they have internet access.

It is interesting to note, however, that for the many young people who already have found the social interaction they seek within their local circle of friends, the internet is used not so much to go global, as it is to facil-itate and strengthen already existing local relationships (as demonstrated in so many chapters here). Some children seek new playmates, new experiences, or extended audiences while others do not; this can change over time and in different circumstances.

The Nature of Play Reconsidered

Johan Huizinga (1961), among other play theorists, describes the experience of play as being outside of the ordinary, theorizing the sphere of play as a separate and bounded space, a *magic circle* outside of the everyday. The player "travels" to the play sphere leaving behind the space of "real-life." Dixon and Simon (2005) challenge this notion of playspace as distinct and apart from other spaces, dismissing Huizinga's magic circle, which is often used to theorize video game play. Instead, they describe playspaces as fluid and unfixed, the virtual as being contiguous with the actual. Close observations and conversations with children at play suggest that the virtual spaces of digital play are simply a part or extension of physical playspaces. The theoretical divide between them is an imaginary one. Several authors in this book call for a blurring or even an erasing of the boundaries between physical and cyberspaces, between the imaginary, the virtual, and the actual. Their work suggests that children create playspaces for themselves that incorporate online and off-line spaces, experienced simultaneously. This needs to be taken up and examined more carefully.

Transgression and Power
Struggles in Playspaces

Part of the pleasure inherent to play can be found through transgressing accepted norms and social rules (this explains young children's delight in "bathroom" humor!). This is the sort of play that makes adults, who forget how much fun it is to be naughty within the safe context of play, so nervous. In Mikhail Bahktin's (1940) discussion of carnival play, he proposed that the temporary suspension of social hierarchies and order made possible by this type of play serves as a necessary, collective social release. Having opportunities to play incognito, to play outside of the typical boundaries imposed by race, class, or gender allows for the circumvention of prevailing hierarchies, regulations, and norms. Young people's play in spaces created by digital technology can serve to transgress boundaries safely, since transgression in playspaces is less dangerous, and holds less currency than those same transgressions would have in other contexts. For example, playing violent video games allows young people to behave in ways that they typically cannot (and most likely *would not*) in other spaces.

According to Brian Sutton-Smith (1997), children's play, especially boys' play, has historically had its own hidden character as children gathered in secret clubhouses, forts, fields, and back lots, hanging out, sometimes engaging in illicit behaviors and forming groups, attempting to negotiate and establish hierarchies within these social groupings. In the last fifty years adults have increasingly attempted to contain, control, and domesticate children through the introduction of playgrounds and playground equipment, enclosed school yards, organized sport activities, and so forth (p. 121). As a consequence, according to Sutton-Smith, children's autonomous play has had to go "underground," becoming more and more covert and hidden from adult eyes.

The rhetoric of progress suggests that children are supposed to be kept innocent, and therefore their illicit or resistant play, their rough, sexual, or politically incorrect play, must be kept hidden from adult eyes to preserve the illusion of childhood innocence.

> The adult public transcript is to make children progress, the adult private transcript is to deny their sexual and aggressive impulses; the child public transcript is to be successful as family members and school children, and their private or hidden transcript is their play life, in which they can express both their special identity and their resentment at being a captive population. (p. 123)

This tension between adult transcripts and children's transcripts is played out in the conflict inherent in the debates surrounding digital playspaces. As we mentioned earlier some of these debates focus on issues of access, ownership, safety, and privacy.

David Buckingham (2000) proposes that childhood is defined in opposition to adulthood. Being labeled "child" implies exclusion from adult practices. As we saw across the chapters, participation in online spaces such as blogs, games, websites, and message boards gives young people access to discussions and debates that were previously off limits to them, challenging traditional hierarchies and social orders. And it is that threat, Henry Giroux (2003) suggests, the idea that play will lead to demands for power, that really frightens adults and fuels the increasing regulation of their activities. Denying access to or controlling young people's play might constitute, in many circumstances, an over-regulation and disempowerment of young people. Moreover, these fears of a potential tyranny of youth are likely unfounded. Transferring power or taking power is more easily said than done. Much of the online content that young people engage with serves to reproduce or reinforce the same conventional social structures and norms that exist in off-line spaces.

Although access to play is power, considerable power also lies in the hands of those who construct and operate the playspaces, as well as the parents who call for increased surveillance of those spaces.

The field of play can thus be viewed, at times, as a power struggle between parents and children, as adults endeavor to control or organize the play of young people. Young people resist by seeking out autonomous playspaces like the ones described in this book. Sutton-Smith (1997) argues for the recognition of the importance of play, even illicit play, to our individual and collective well-being. During children's free, unsupervised play they can be autonomous in ways that they are unable to be elsewhere (Erikson in Sutton-Smith, p. 114). It is in the spaces of autonomous play, which include online spaces, that young people are free to negotiate their own hierarchies and try out different roles. Through digital play away from adult eyes, children engage in creative and sometimes transgressive play, experimenting with identity, pushing boundaries, trying things out, and learning about themselves and others. The research findings presented by different authors in this book illustrate the value of play and demonstrate how complex and significant this digital "playing on their own" can be.

Learning in the School outside of School

Despite our backgrounds in education and sociology, we deliberately decided not to focus primarily on the use of technology in schools; schools are not where most children engage spontaneously with digital technologies. As was the case with television and other older technologies, it is children's uses and engagement with new technologies on their own terms and on their own turf (in conjunction with other more traditional pastimes) that may provide the most valuable insight into their modes of sense-making and learning. Nonetheless, this book *does* address schooling in indirect but effective ways. What became interesting, for example, was how present school can be in children's lives outside of school, something Weber and Mitchell (1995) described as "the school outside of school." For example, both Boudreau's and Weber's chapters describe online activities that cement, disrupt, or facilitate school-based friendships. Instant messaging about homework, posting school-related photos and drawings, blogging that vents feelings about school-related people and topics—all of these and other such activities serve to give school a presence in young people's out of school lives.

Learning, which one hopes is at least partially what school is about, is at the heart of many digital play activities. We are referring here to a variety of learning modes: Julia's learning through careful watching in

Weber's chapter, as well as the peer coaching and learning by doing, which is evident in Boudreau's, Dixon and Weber's, and so many other authors' contributions to this book. This informal and self-motivated learning includes writing and design skills, internet protocols, web etiquette, aesthetics, game strategies, problem solving, information search techniques, cultural knowledge, scientific knowledge, and more. Most important is the *social learning* that occurs around digital culture as young people play with peers both on and offline—learning to get along in a group, negotiate, take turns and interact with peers away from adult supervision and control.

Multitasking and Learning

Chapter three draws a highly detailed portrait of Julia simultaneously using a combination of media to do a variety of tasks at once, some of them related, others not. A few of the activities are school-based, others are play-based, while still others focus on friendship and social interaction. This multitasking is evident in other chapters, too, and is typical of the ways that young people use digital technologies. We could even speculate that the ability of the internet and digital media to facilitate multitasking is the basis of much of its appeal to children, especially if it allows them to squeeze in a bit of pleasure or socializing while completing more obligatory tasks, such as homework. Children's digital multitasking has attracted the attention of parents, teachers, and scholars who question the efficacy of such behavior, especially since studies on adults suggest it is less effective than sequential single-tasking. Pilotta and Schultz (2005), however, point out that the research on adults has mainly consisted of measurements done in isolated environments, neglecting the patterns of everyday use. In their assessment, the emerging research on technologies-in-use tends to support children's spontaneous multimodal approaches to multitasking as both inevitable and beneficial.

McHale (2005) speculates that as a result of their digital environment and frequent engagement with new technologies, children of the Net generation think and process information in ways that are fundamentally different from those of the previous generation. As Prensky (2001) puts it, "These differences go far further and deeper than most educators suspect or realize. Different kinds of experiences lead to different brain structures." Although such pronouncements seem ahead of the evidence, if the children studied in this book are any indication, multimedia multitasking has become a characteristic mode of functioning and learning for many young people. The question is thus not "should young people multitask on line?" but rather "what are they producing, accomplishing, and experiencing through these kinds of activities?"

Extending Digital Spaces for Girls and Boys

As digital media were introduced over the last two decades, boys were quick to establish their claim on cyberspace, especially for gaming purposes. Girls' play took longer to migrate, remaining primarily in private off-line domestic spaces, usually more closely supervised than boys (Mitchell & Reid Walsh, 2002). In some ways this has not changed, girls still often play indoors, but their "bedrooms" or private spaces have greatly expanded; they too have gone digital. The internet has opened up new play possibilities for young women: they play in MMOGs equitably, and anonymously if they so choose, with players of varying ages, genders, and race; they blog, adding their voices to the public sphere (see Bell's chapter); they create their own webspaces as a resistance to the regulations imposed upon them (see chapters four, five, and eleven); they build their own communities. A noteworthy example of girls using the internet to circumvent social and cultural restrictions is provided in Mitchell and Sokoya's chapter where young girls use the internet to access important information regarding HIV/AIDS. Many online activities reproduce gender lines and stereotypes, but the ways young people can interact with avatars and use anonymous and sometimes gender-bending modes of self-representation points to an easily accessible and broader range or repertoire for identity processes. What the implications of this "new normal" will be for their adult lives remains to be seen. Perhaps the subsequent generations of scholars (the young people who we are now studying), socialized into a world of cell phones, text messaging, and networking spaces, will create new methodologies for examining digital experiences and will approach research questions from different vantage points, building on or deconstructing current theoretical work. It will be most interesting to see which findings and theories will stand the test of time.

References

Bakhtin, M. (1940, 1984). *Rabelais and his world.* (H. Iswolsky, trans.). Bloomington: Indiana University Press.

Buckingham, D. (2000). *After the death of childhood: Growing up in the age of electronic media.* Cambridge: Polity Press.

Buckingham, D. and Sefton-Green, J. (1994). *Cultural studies goes to school.* London: Taylor & Francis.

Chang-Kredl, S. (2006). Honey, I researched the kids. Presented at the *Trials & Tribulations: Negotiating research methods in cyberspace Conference*, November 10 &11, Concordia University, Montreal, Canada.

Dale, S. (2005). *Candy from strangers: Kids and consumer culture*. Vancouver: New Star Books.

Delamere, F. (2006). The politics of popular leisure: Giving voice to female gamers' experiences of violent videogame play. Presented at the *Trials & Tribulations: Negotiating research methods in cyberspace Conference*, November 10 &11, Concordia University, Montreal, Canada.

Dixon, S. & Simon, B. (2005). Boyhood spaces: Play and social navigation through videogames. Presented at the International DiGRA Conference: *Changing Views: Worlds at Play*, June 16–20, Simon Frasier University, Vancouver, BC, Canada.

Giroux, H. (2003). *The abandoned generation: Democracy beyond the culture of fear*. New York: Palgrave MacMillan.

Huizinga, J. (1967). *Homo ludens: A study of the play-element in culture*. (R.F.C. Hull, trans.). Boston: Beacon.

Ito, M. (Forthcoming). Mobilizing the imagination in everyday play: The case of Japanese media mixes. In S. Livingston and K. Drotner (eds.), *International handbook of children, media, and culture*.

Jenkins, H. (2006). *Convergence culture: Where old and new media collide*. New York & London: New York University Press.

Kitzmann, A. (2004). *Saved from oblivion: Documenting the daily from diaries to web cams*. New York: Peter Lang.

McHale, T. (2005). Portrait of a digital native: Are digital-age students fundamentally different from the rest of us? *Technology & Learning, 26*(2), 33.

Mitchell, C. & Reid-Walsh, J. (2002). *Researching children's popular culture: The cultural spaces of childhood*. London: Routledge.

Pilotta, J.J. & Schultz, D. (2005). Simultaneous media experience and synesthesia. *Journal of Advertising Research, 45*(1), 19–26.

Prensky, M. (2005). *Don't bother me, mom, I'm learning*. New York: Paragon.

Scheidt, L.A. (2005). *Adolescent diaries and the unseen audience*. E-server TC Library, http://tc.eserver.org,: University of Indiana.

Schor, J. (2004). *Born to buy*. New York: Scribner.

Seiter, E. (2004). *The internet playground: Children's access, entertainment and mis-education*. New York: Peter Lang.

Sutton-Smith, B. (1997). *The ambiguity of play*. Cambridge, MA: Harvard University Press.

Weber, S. & Mitchell, C. (1995). *That's funny, you don't look like a teacher: Interrogating images, identity and popular culture*. London: Falmer Press.

Index

Breinigsville, PA USA
15 April 2010
236173BV00002BA/1/P